Ethnic and Regional Foodways
in the United States

Ethnic and Regional
F O O D W A Y S
in the United States

The Performance of Group Identity

Linda Keller Brown *and*
Kay Mussell, *co-editors*

The University of Tennessee Press / *Knoxville*

Library of Congress Cataloging in Publication Data

Main entry under title:

Ethnic and regional foodways in the United States.

Bibliography: p.

Includes index.

Contents: Equal opportunity eating / Roger
Abrahams — Ethnic foodways in America / Susan
Kalčik — A framework for the analysis of continuity
and change in shared sociocultural rules for food use /
Judith Goode, Janet Theophano, and Karen Curtis — [etc.]

1. Food habits — United States — Addresses, essays,
lectures. 2. Ethnic folklore — United States — Addresses,
essays, lectures. 3. Food — Folklore — Addresses, essays,
lectures. I. Brown, Linda Keller. II. Mussell, Kay.
GT2853.U5E86 1984   394.1'2'0973   83-16715
ISBN 0-87049-418-X
ISBN 0-87049-419-8 (pbk.)

For my mother
  —K.M.

For Garrett and Victoria
  —L.K.B.

Contents

Illustrations

Ethnic and Regional Foodways
in the United States

Introduction

Linda Keller Brown and Kay Mussell

The elder religious leader of one of the groups discussed in this book was shown an early version of the essay exploring the foodways of his community. He read through the draft cursorily, handed it back to the author, and told this parable:

Once upon a time, there was a little boy who went with his mother for his very first train ride. He climbed on board and sat down. The conductor in his impressive trainman's uniform took the boy's ticket and punched a hole in it. As he did so, the train pulled out from the station. The little boy marveled that so small a thing as a punched ticket could cause so great a thing as a train to move with such power.

The leader added: "You must be careful with cause and meaning when you interpret from the part to the whole."

With that admonition in mind, the editors of this volume have sought to use foodways as a ticket to understand the power sustaining the continuity of ethnicity and region as matrices for the membership of individuals in groups. Our goal is to move beyond common surface perceptions of the relationship between food and group and to approach the problems of interpreting foodways with concepts that open new directions for future research. This book is unique in the range of disciplinary backgrounds the authors bring to their subject: folklore, anthropology, nutrition, popular culture, public health, American studies, and ethnography. It is also the product of considerable communication between the editors and authors from the initial conception of each essay through the final version. Each essay highlights a particular strategy within a larger, integrated framework of analysis, building upon the insights of previous research as well as public perceptions.

Mainstream Americans frequently use foodways as a factor in the identification of subcultural groups and find in the traditional dishes and ingredients of "others" who eat differently from themselves a set of convenient ways to categorize ethnic and regional character. Most

Americans, however, encounter ethnic and regional foodways in at-
tenuated situations, tinged with commercialism. Cookbooks and restaurants, for example, are sources of such commonsense knowledge,
but neither of these is the heart of ethnicity or regionalism in foodways. Cookbooks and restaurants convey relatively static concepts of
a subculture and reinforce stereotypical assumptions that are further
diluted by the imperatives of the marketplace.

As specialty restaurants proliferate in American communities,
changes inevitably occur in the foods themselves and, more significantly, in the meanings of the foods and their surrounding rituals for
the subcultural groups that produce and consume them. Except in
areas with high proportions of Mexican-American migrants, for example, Mexican foods in restaurants often exhibit a depressing mo-
notony and lack of imagination. Tacos, tamales, and enchiladas in
their ethnic/regional setting can be remarkably varied culinary delights. In a run-of-the-mill Mexican restaurant, they may be soggy,
fatty, and bland. Ethnic Americans (Mexicans or Chinese, for example) who consume highly spiced foods in their homes and communities may find it advisable to minimize the tang of foods served for
the public at large. In addition, the most exotic foods, or those with
ingredients that are unusual in American foods, may not appear on
menus for fear of offending customers. Some Chinese restaurants, for
example, have a separate section of the menu written in Chinese for
ethnic patrons, including specialties with those ingredients mainstream
Americans might define as exotic or "not food."

Ethnic cookbooks for a mainstream audience also simplify ingredients and methods of preparation, either because certain food items
are difficult to obtain or because cooks who use the books may not
be willing to invest the time or effort to prepare a dish in the traditional way. Exotic ingredients (certain species of mushrooms or vegetables used routinely in ethnic or regional recipes, for example) may
appear in the ingredients lists as optional. Only rarely do cookbooks
try to explain the cultural context of specific ethnic foods, either in
essays describing the circumstances under which certain dishes are
prepared and eaten or by suggesting menus for an authentic meal.
One notable exception is the Time-Life series "Foods of the World"
in which the recipes are printed in a separate booklet for use in the
kitchen. The main text of each volume includes extensive discussion
of foodways, and each is illustrated liberally to highlight the context
of traditional food items as prepared in the communities represented.
Although researchers may draw on popular sources and widely held
perceptions of group foodways, the issues faced by scholars are both

distinct from and more complex than the concerns of commercial purveyors of food information to the general public.

Issues Facing the Foodways Researcher

Scholars studying foodways face several key problems made particularly difficult by the complexity of the multi-cultural society of the
United States. In organizing research, the initial problem is an issue
common to all of the academic disciplines that study American culture: *how to determine the boundary definitions of the group to be examined.*
In defining regional or ethnic groups, the essays in this volume share
a methodological assumption: that groups, both ethnic and regional,
are most usefully defined *internally*, using the group's markers of self-
identification as key factors. This approach is significant because foodways in subcultural groups are rooted in tradition but express dynamic
aspects of in-group culture through a process that is highly charged
with meaning. Foodways bind individuals together, define the limits
of the group's outreach and identity, distinguish in-group from out-
group, serve as a medium of inter-group communication, celebrate
cultural cohesion, and provide a context for performance of group
rituals. Although this process may be easier to discern in ethnic groups
than in regional contexts, it is no less operative in the latter. Indeed,
region and ethnicity are often intertwined. As Don Yoder has pointed
out, "Viewed historically, each regional and national cuisine is a culinary hybrid, with an elaborate stratigraphy of diverse historical layers
combined into a usable and evidently satisfying structure."[1]

There is substantially more scholarly agreement on the markers
of ethnic identity than on regional configurations, although researchers have differed significantly in their use of such common factors as
race, place of origin, religion, language, migration patterns, politics,
and self-identification.[2] Susan Kalčik (Chapter 2) surveys the literature of ethnic identification and posits a *dynamic* view of ethnicity as
"performance of identity," a phrase that heightens our sense of both
the mutability of ethnicity and its metaphorical power. Defining group
identity as a *process* rather than as a series of relatively static markers
encourages researchers to go beyond such outdated issues as the "decline" of ethnicity and to focus instead upon the internal and external
meanings of symbolic group interaction.

Region, too, has been defined both statically and dynamically. As
Howard Wight Marshall explains in his essay on meat preservation
in Missouri's "Little Dixie:" "Like dialect and architecture, food traditions are a main component in the intricate and impulsive system that

joins culture and geography into regional character."[3] Marshall's insistence that regions embody "systems" becomes especially significant when we consider the many, and ultimately unsatisfying, ways in which regions are traditionally defined. Political boundaries—state and local—mark administrative distinctions rather than cultural continuities. Single-factor definitions based on economic or marketing groupings, religious affiliations, or migration patterns, may describe certain regional contexts but often oversimplify the whole. A more satisfactory scheme appeared recently in Joel Garreau's *The Nine Nations of North America,* a book that constructs an eclectic map based on a variety of factors: economic affiliations, historical development, ecological unity, or ethnic composition.[4]

Those papers in this volume that speak to regionalism, however, work in another direction. Beginning with the microcosm, geographically based, each essay explores regional group behavior from the inside—as the ethnographer seeks to understand the internal definitions of a cultural group. Geographical location alone does not define a regional group; as proximity encourages groups to coalesce into subcultures with a self-conscious sense of unity, the markers of group identity often interact with those of other affinity groups and are modified by ethnicity, by time, and by ecology. Like Suzi Jones in "Regionalization: A Rhetorical Strategy," these authors see regional identity as "a process with its own rhetoric."[5] We find, then, a striking similarity among these essays in the ways by which a subcultural affinity group is defined: from inside, from voluntary affiliation (based on inheritance or upon proximity), and bounded by the group's definition of itself.

Thus, each group described in this volume defines its own membership, at least partly through the shared foodways that distinguish in-group from out-group. Leslie Prosterman (Chapter 6) delineates strategies through which Jewish Americans have developed commercial contexts to maintain and accommodate their traditional foodways. Richard Raspa (Chapter 9) and C. Paige Gutierrez (Chapter 8) discuss the methods used by two ethnic groups to elevate their special food practices into a symbolic assertion of self against the mainstream culture dominant in their regions.

Raspa's essay, coupled with Brett Williams' (Chapter 5) discussion of Tejano (Chicano) migrants, demonstrates the *transportability of ethnicity* across region. Modifications in dietary practices inevitably occur as groups attempt to maintain ethnic traditions in new and often hostile contexts, but both the Italian-Americans of Utah (Chapter 9) and the Tejanos of the Illinois migrant camps (Chapter 5) manipulate their foodways as powerful symbols of group affinity, utilizing the homeliest and most mundane materials of daily life in a celebration of self with a highly significant metaphorical meaning for the group.

Region, whose markers are inextricably linked to ecology, is more difficult to transport. Regional groups that lack concrete ethnic components, such as the Pineys of New Jersey described by Angus Gillespie (Chapter 7), base their markers of identity on environmental factors — modes of survival that are appropriate for certain places but not transportable to another ecological context.

The many factors influencing the boundary definitions of ethnic and regional groups also contribute to a second and related problem for foodways researchers: *how to measure persistence and change* in group definition and in foodways practices. Region and ethnicity are both modified over time and through intra-group variation, not just because American foods are undergoing demonstrable change through increased processing and improved preservation and distribution, but also because individual preferences through generations continue to modify the daily diet. Foodways comprise a "code," to use Mary Douglas' felicitous term, with multiple meanings that lie in a "pattern of social relationships."[6] Foodways are interaction, encoding a highly ritualized, although taken-for-granted, set of behaviors. Foodways codes are also transmuted when social interactions between groups evolve and change. For example, when members of different groups come into contact in a multi-cultural society, the sharing of traditional food items may take on a variety of new meanings, depending upon the motivation of the giver and the response of the recipient. In the context of a festival, as Roger Abrahams (Chapter 1) and Susan Kalčik point out, members of ethnic or regional groups offer delicacies to an audience that comes prepared to appreciate it. Raspa, however, shows how the offering of food by the Italian-Americans of Utah to their Mormon neighbors may result in misunderstanding. In this case, the dominant culture defines as "not food" an item that to the minority is a delicacy; and the transaction results in a renewed sense of cultural separateness on both sides. Williams shows how a similar transaction, the offering of a tamale to a member of an out-group, is meant to obligate the recipient in matters of concern to the in-group. Each of these examples involves the same process but encodes a different social relationship inherent in the existing pattern between members of groups.

In a classic essay, Clifford Geertz asked researchers using the culture concept to engage in what he termed "thick description," an analysis of the meaning of social behavior that considers the context and shared significance of a wide range of cultural interactions.[7] For example, on one level of meaning the tamale is a time-consuming, labor-intensive food item, immersing the female preparer in what might seem to be oppressive household tasks. But Williams points out that, interpreted in the larger system of Tejano culture, the preparation of tamales signals not just a recognition of group preference in foodways but also a means of binding individuals into the group, metaphorically conveying to the recipient of tamales that the woman who prepares them is willing to engage in such a complicated task for the sake of interpersonal bonds.

Because foodways serve as such powerful metaphors of group identity, the problems of studying continuity and change are multi-faceted and require researchers to engage in Geertz's "thick description." Scholars have too often left the study of foodways to antiquarians and recipe collectors, although recently nutritional anthropologists and folklorists have begun to devise new strategies for addressing these issues. A researcher using a traditional strategy might address acculturation of immigrant groups by examining the use of ethnic recipes by cooks in subsequent generations. Because change has inevitably occurred over time, such a strategy almost inevitably results in a conclusion that ethnic character is declining.

If researchers assume that ethnic culture is dynamic, however, the issue of persistence and change may be addressed more fruitfully. This approach is especially productive if consideration is given to the conceptual problem of *defining the units of analysis*. In this volume, the essay by Goode, Theophano, and Curtis (Chapter 3) addresses both of these interrelated issues in examining the foodways of an Italian-American community in Philadelphia as a dynamic entity. Instead of merely seeking evidence of change in food items, recipes, or meal formats, this study considers a larger unit of measure — foodways seen as a cycle of meals, divided into the weekly sequence and the annual calendar of celebrations. From this perspective, the measure of acculturation is multi-faceted. While inevitable accommodations to the mainstream have occurred — especially in the lunches eaten outside the home — other factors reveal the persistence of ethnic patterns, especially in the structure of the meal cycle, which has altered less than an analysis of mere persistence of ethnic recipes might indicate.

After defining the group and choosing carefully the units of analysis to measure continuity and change, the foodways researcher is ready for the most meaningful problem: *how to decipher the metaphoric meaning* encoded in a group's patterned food system. The authors in this volume all find in group foodways the symbols and metaphors that underlie group solidarity. For the Cajuns of South Louisiana (Chapter 8), as for the watermen of the Chesapeake Bay, the abundance of a kind of shellfish — crawfish and crabs, respectively — becomes a powerful symbol of regional culture. These abundant local sources of food take on a metaphorical meaning as members of the out-group discover the item and try to consume it. Members of the regional group identify in these food items a special pride since they are the only ones who know how to prepare and eat them "correctly." In addition, however, the food may be prepared in a transformed or more complicated manner to appeal to members of the out-group — for example, in crab cakes or crawfish Newburg. The regional group members who live closest to the source know how to consume these items from the shell, and their shared knowledge becomes a strong element of regional cohesion and identity, separating the locals from the visitors. The Cajun sports a T-shirt reading "Crawfish Power," while Maryland abounds in bumper stickers reading "Maryland is for Crabs."

Material objects associated with foods and within foodways rituals may strengthen our understanding of the metaphorical significance of food in group identity. Special equipment is as important as unique ingredients or modes of preparation in allowing groups to continue eating their own foods. Although the wok, for example, has become a popular piece of food equipment in American homes — partly because its use allows a form of cooking that decreases the amount of fats in fried foods — it is not so necessary an item in the average American home as it is in the Chinese-American kitchen, where its absence would virtually eliminate an entire category of traditional foods.

As we see in Willard Moore's essay on the Russian Molokans of California (Chapter 4), however, material objects are not just useful in the preparation of foods. They also encode other group behaviors in analogous ways. Moore demonstrates how traditional dress defines status and function in an analogy to food traditions and rituals. Occasions on which the full panoply of food traditions are present are also those occasions on which the most formal dress requirements are encouraged.

In each case, the essays in this book address the issues from the *internal* perspective of the group itself, thickly describing the patterns and metaphors inherent in tradition and resulting in meaning. In addition, they demonstrate some of the more fruitful new directions in foodways research.

Directions for Future Foodways Research

The first new direction considered in these essays is *the nature and meaning of intra-group variation*. In studying foodways, researchers have drawn extensively from anthropology for their theories and field methodology. In so doing, they have absorbed the anthropologist's assumptions about intra-cultural homogeneity and the tendency to present cultural patterns in uniformist terms. Pertti J. Pelto and Gretel H. Pelto report that the predominant style in "anthropological reporting and theory-building continues to be made up of constructions reflecting fundamental assumptions of cognitive homogeneity and behavioral sharing."[8] The Peltos identify several factors contributing to this situation in the discipline of anthropology. These factors have similarly affected foodways research: ". . . the strong need to categorize and over-simplify typologically"; the tendency to pigeonhole "innumerable observations under broad labels"; the ethnographic research approach which relies on the interviewing of key informants and thus reduces the probability of directly observing heterogeneity; and researchers' reluctance to use quantitative analysis.[9]

When intra-group variations are carefully observed, as in the essays in this volume, the research orientation subtly shifts, converting uniformist concepts such as "Molokan traditions" into *variables* (for example, the degree of adherence to the traditions). In his essay on the Russian Molokans in the United States, Moore analyzes their complex society with a sensitivity to the wide disparity internally in the adherence of individuals to traditions in diet, costume, and other modes of expression. He delineates gradations of social and spiritual involvement, ranging from those individuals who casually observe dietary traditions to that segment of the community which is painstaking and legalistic in its observance of traditional foodways. In relating these gradations to community life as a whole, Moore finds that they also "reflect the extent to which individuals think of themselves as 'Molokan' as compared to other categories such as 'Christian' or 'American.'"

This theoretical reorientation also encourages careful attention to situational or structural factors that influence individual behavior. Goode, Theophano, and Curtis demonstrate how differences in diet between households in the community system are predictable, based on such factors as the composition of the household, generational cohort, activity patterns, and stage in the domestic cycle. From their consideration of intra-group variations, these essays proceed to identify the group's shared *sociocultural rules*. This new direction or emphasis in foodways research is especially significant because of its potential to revise linear acculturation models which imply that ethnic patterns weaken with each subsequent generation. In that view, differentiation in individual preferences is mistaken for an absence of a shared pattern and a breakdown of the old system. A consideration of intra-group variation and the structural factors that determine it can help to explain the cultural dynamic of persistence and change in ethnic communities.

A second new direction presented in this volume is *the expansion of the definition of affinity groups* — an extension of the basis for the construction of "groups." Most foodways research has assumed that ethnic or regional groups are the main locus of differentiated eating in the United States. This orientation was strengthened especially by the work done by the Committee on Food Habits of the National Research Council during World War II. The Committee assumed that ethnic groups were the locus of subgroup eating, and resulting anthropological work focused on ethnic groups as units of study. Other writers studied regional and rural/urban distinctions as major sources of differentiation.

Today foodways researchers need to explore *other socially bounded lifestyle groups* as well. The methods that illuminate the foodways of traditional ethnic and regional groups may also be used to understand the transactions of any socially bounded group whose social network includes the sharing of a food system. Thus, groups based on age, occupation, socio-economic status, neighborhood proximity, or any other basis of affinity can be analyzed as communities within food systems.

Such future research, while providing information on communities of affiliation, would also serve to enhance understanding of the parameters and the process of ethnic and regional influence on foodways. Goode, Theophano, and Curtis comment:

These status-based communities differ from ethnic groups in that there is usually discontinuity between the food pattern of the natal household of the homemaker and her current social group pattern. Ethnic groups thus still provide a unique opportunity to observe both inter-generational transmission and reinforcement as well as interhousehold processes. However, recognizing that many Americans share a community food system based on other social statuses leads to the recognition that the influences of childhood socialization are not rigid and absolute.

Eliot Singer's essay (Chapter 10) on the foodways of an American Hindu sect is an example of the rich possibilities of this expanded approach to the definition of group. While the enculturation of a child to a community pattern is a slow and methodical process, the conversion experience is a total and usually sudden restructuring of beliefs, what Anthony F.C. Wallace calls the "resynthesis of the mazeway."[10] Singer stresses that since, in conversion, the process of enculturation is "telescoped," the symbols employed must be "especially emotionally salient and intellectually potent." Food, because of its ability to evoke strong response, is a "symbolic vehicle of special significance in conversion." Singer details how *prasadam,* the foodstuff of the Krishna devotees, becomes a powerful symbol to restructure behavior and encode a system of shared meanings.

The chapter by Singer is also an example of the multiple levels on which many of the essays in this book may be read. Singer's structural analysis of the symbolic meaning of food in a Hindu sect presents an interpretation that goes beyond an individual community member's comprehension or ability to articulate. The members of the group would themselves not necessarily recognize these meanings and premises when stated explicitly, because enculturation is a coming-to-acceptance of shared subtle meanings, a taking-for-granted of the underlying existential criteria of a culture.

Singer categorizes the food of the sect by classificatory principles, binary oppositions (such as hot/sweet, raw/cooked), and syntactic rules that govern the combination of foods to create a "grammatical meal." This approach illustrates a third research direction presented in this book: *the use of structuralist insights to model eating as a cultural system.* Structuralism originated in the work of Ferdinand de Saussure and has been developed in the writings of symbolic anthropologists such as Mary Douglas, Clifford Geertz, Marshall Sahlins, Roland Barthes, and Claude Levi-Strauss.[11] In order to make explicit the covert meanings of a cultural system, structuralists seek to treat these systems as languages and to analyze them by methods and models borrowed from linguistics. Levi-Strauss explains, ". . . we can hope to discover for each specific case how the cooking of a society is a language in which it unconsciously translates its structure—or else resigns itself, still unconsciously, to revealing its contradictions."[12]

While an aspect of culture (for example, a food pattern) has a functional role, it also has a sign value which is juxtaposed to other signs to construct complex communication systems. Structuralists use structural linguistics to decode this belief system and discover the deep structure of meanings beneath surface communication. In focusing on foodways, Mary Douglas writes, "If food is to be treated as a code, the message it encodes will be found in the pattern of social relationships being expressed. The message is about different degrees of hierarchy, inclusion and exclusion, boundaries and transactions across boundaries."[13]

Kalčik deciphers all of these messages in the relationship between food and group. She explores the symbolic nature of food in establishing group identity, the symbolic manipulation of foodways to make statements about ethnic identity, the communication of the food code in across-group interactions, and the communicative messages of foodways in the performance of American ethnic identity. In this structuralist interpretation of the food code and the important messages of inclusion and exclusion, Kalčik demonstrates how shared foodways have a unifying ability so symbolically powerful that they can unite members of the group separated geographically—and even those separated by death. Social relationships are developed and maintained by symbols, and Kalčik shows that we tend to *see* groups through their symbols. Foodways can actually come to symbolize the group itself.

This power of identification is explored more fully in Abrahams' essay. By analyzing and interrelating the structure of food categorization and food grammar, Abrahams explains the development of food-related negative stereotypes about certain ethnic and regional groups. He also examines the intriguing question of the effect of the dynamic of enlarging food choices, of introducing ethnic pluralism into the process of choosing, cooking, and eating foods.

Structuralism offers a *trans*-disciplinary paradigm for explaining community food systems. A fourth direction with much promise for future research is *interdisciplinary interpretation,* what might be loosely termed *nexus studies.* Food is posited as a nexus for the convergence of traditional disciplinary methods and insights. This perspective is particularly valuable in framing public policy questions, because in the world of practical applications food-related issues defy disciplinary assignment. Several of the essays have such questions as a background to their discussion. Gutierrez demonstrates that the manipulation of the crawfish as a symbol of identity among the Cajuns of South Louisiana reflects the group's political aspirations as well as their sense of group cohesion. An important theme in Gillespie's discussion of the foodways of the Pinelands of New Jersey is the preservation of a regional way of life that is threatened by pressure from urban development.

The last two essays in this volume demonstrate this perspective in a specific case and in the broadest possible public policy question. These two essays by nutritionists confront public health issues by showing how scientific solutions to public problems can be enriched by an understanding of factors more commonly used by historians, folklorists, ethnologists, and political scientists. In so doing, these essays speak to the significance of cultural analysis in the formation of public policy.

Sandra K. Joos (Chapter 11) focuses on what initially appears to be a specific and limited public health problem: the increase in diabetes mellitus among the Florida Seminole Indians. Joos examines and interconnects the historical background of the alteration of the swamp environment, economic changes in the mode of subsistence, and the socio-cultural context of food consumption, including the conflicts between Indian medicine and "white" medicine. With this background to understanding the etiology of diabetes among the Seminoles, Joos can rethink the problem and the solutions and propose more promising approaches to treatment, particularly in the area of diet counselling.

The last essay in the book by Judy Perkin and Stephanie McCann (Chapter 12) considers the broadest possible public policy question—the role of the government in determining what Americans eat. In recent years, government groups have begun to examine the relationship of nutrition to health and disease prevention and to advocate patterns of food choices to the public. Government directives on diet and health do not include consideration of the research showing the viability of ethnic and regional foodways. Connecting ethnic food patterns, disease mortality, and the approaches of nutrition education, Perkin and McCann demonstrate how government guidelines could be translated into acceptable diets for various American ethnic groups.

This chapter elaborates a basic policy concern which links back to Abrahams' essay. Perkin and McCann ponder the failure of government dietary advice to address the needs and preferences of our various subcultures, and they probe, "Is this an oversight, or is there a conscious or unconscious effort to lessen ethnic identities by the promotion of one diet for the American people?" Abrahams comments on the willingness of ethnic populations to open their kitchens (for example, in folk festivals and fairs) "to highlight their stylistic distinctiveness and publicize their gustatory delights." However, Abrahams predicts:

In going public, a cultural contradiction reemerges, the one which has always resided at the hearth of American life: that in the celebration of many, a sense of oneness may emerge. Paradoxically, the very act of food preparation and cooking may simultaneously proclaim and undermine ethnicity. The means by which an individual maintains a sense of ethnic continuity and integrity in carrying on the food tradition becomes a way to articulate a social and cultural coming-together, as one kind of food takes its place alongside other ethnic and regional offerings in the festival setting.

Perkin and McCann would not argue against Abrahams' conclusion nor against the desirability of a voluntary and exploratory "coming-together." But they would stress that "Governmental dietary advice should reflect the cultural diversity of America and not, by design or default, attempt to turn the melting pot into a one-dish dinner."

June 1983

NOTES

1. Don Yoder, "Folk Cookery," *Folklore and Folklife*, ed. Richard M. Dorson (Chicago: Univ. of Chicago Press, 1972), 334.

2. For a fuller discussion of factors in ethnic definition, see William Petersen, "Concepts of Ethnicity," *Harvard Encyclopedia of American Ethnic Groups*, ed. Stephan Thernstrom (Cambridge, Mass.: Harvard Univ. Press, 1980), 234–42; Werner Sollors, "Theory of American Ethnicity," *American Quarterly* 33 (1981):257–83; and John Ibson, "Virgin Land or Virgin Mary?: Studying the Ethnicity of White Americans," *American Quarterly* 33 (1981):284–308.

3. Howard Wight Marshall, "Meat Preservation on the Farm in Missouri's 'Little Dixie,'" *Journal of American Folklore* 92 (1979):400.

4. Joel Garreau, *The Nine Nations of North America* (Boston: Houghton Mifflin, 1981).

5. Suzi Jones, "Regionalization: A Rhetorical Strategy," *Journal of the Folklore Institute* 13 (1976):118.

6. Mary Douglas, "Deciphering a Meal," *Myth, Symbol, and Culture*, ed. Clifford Geertz (New York: Norton, 1971), 61.

7. Clifford Geertz, "'Thick Description': Toward an Interpretive Theory of Culture," *The Interpretation of Cultures* (New York: Basic Books, 1973), 3–30.

8. Pertti J. Pelto and Gretel H. Pelto, "Intra-Cultural Diversity: Some Theoretical Issues," *American Ethnologist* 2 (Feb. 1975):6.

9. Ibid., 6–8.

10. Anthony F. C. Wallace, "Mazeway Resynthesis: A Bio-Cultural Theory of Religious Inspiration," *Transactions of the New York Academy of Sciences* 18 (1956):626–38.

11. For an overview of the literature of Structuralism, see John G. Blair, "Structuralism, American Studies and the Humanities," *American Quarterly* 30, no. 3 (1978): 261–81; David Pace, "Structuralism in History and the Social Sciences," *American Quarterly* 30, no. 3 (1978):282–97; and David Robey, ed., *Structuralism: An Introduction* (Oxford: Clarendon Press, 1973).

12. Claude Levi-Strauss, "The Culinary Triangle," *Partisan Review* 33 (1966):595.

13. Douglas, "Deciphering a Meal," 61.

PART I

*Food in the Performance
of Ethnic Identity:
Theoretical Considerations*

1

Equal Opportunity Eating: A Structural Excursus on Things of the Mouth

Roger Abrahams

In principle, we like to keep separate and discrete matters of talking, eating, engaging in sex. It is only human that we regard the major orifices, especially our mouths, as providing an access to our selves that must remain inviolate except in the most privileged moments, when openness is valued more highly than protection. But to mix up our modes of interaction on such privileged occasions is to invoke the worst kind of uncleanliness. In spite of this, we find ways of talking while we eat, and we even relate the two with sexual pleasures on occasion. When they are completed, we have those festive times-out-of-time of orgy, of bacchanal, of Carnival — but then we invent specially energetic ways to enter into the engagements of this upended sort, exchanges, through tongue-looseners — that is, by eating and drinking strange substances — to the point of "losing ourselves."

Any theory of culture must take such events into consideration, for these are the times when the orders and distinctions basic to a community's values will be self-consciously upended. Such festivities provide an occasion for an acting out of the exchange system of the group through selective abrogation of the rules. Being able to recognize the means of abrogation, and the rules and situations in which rules may be broken, is one of the basic steps in feeling as well as understanding the ways the group operates in the everyday.

But to comprehend what is being turned upside-down, one needs to know the ways in which the world is already invested with vigorous order and meaning, and the regular ways in which these meaningful orders are celebrated. This view of culture highlights the symbolic dimension of repeated actions, demanding of ethnographic observers that they discover the most important things one needs to know in order to get along in a society both during festivities and on everyday occasions. Such matters as etiquette attain an importance in cultural descriptions that was almost unknown in those cultural studies that were directed at explaining systems of governance, kinship, even religion.

Such microlevel cultural matters provide the fulcrum for this excursus on eating and ethnicity. In American popular culture we are engaged in a romance with ethnic foods of a great many sorts. Here I try to ask some questions not about why this is so but what effect the dynamic of enlarging food choice has on our basic notions of what culture is and how it operates. To get at how choosing, preparing, cooking, and eating foods enter into this popular dynamic, I will survey some of what can be said of similar cultural matters of foodways before ethnic choice was a possibility—that is, how such matters achieve meaning in the home country. To this end, I will survey the work of structural anthropologists that casts light on foods as one kind of symbolic universe among many. I will also refer to the work of social historians who have commented upon the impact of the expansion of food choices outside of any traditional world order—that is, what happened as popular culture developed through the so-called "civilizing process."

Cooking and eating enter into the achievement of individual ethnic or popular identification. A central feature of this process is the dynamic of making choices, especially as such decisions draw upon symbolically- rather than nutritionally-coded edibles. Here I refer not only to what foodstuffs are chosen and how they are prepared, but also how many distinct foods are served and in what combinations and quantity; under what conditions they are eaten, with whom, and on what occasion; and what is the received way of bringing the food to the mouth, the etiquette of eating under those circumstances. An analysis of Americans eating at this level would be concerned with, for instance, the distinction between "meal" and "snack," the number and size of "courses," "dishes" within each course, and "helpings" of those dishes.

Ethnic or regional identity can be acted out within the home by eating certain foods prepared in special ways. That this is an unconscious process, in the main, is clear, at least until the alternative foodways are introduced, at which point a choice is involved. Equally clearly, a different kind of identity-management is going on when the same foods are served at the same table but to people who are neither family nor friends, who come from elsewhere and who recognize the symbolic choices that have been made, whether consciously or unconsciously. Under such circumstances the most elaborate meals are served, using the best crockery or china, and ideally everyone is on his "best behavior." An even more radical difference is to be observed when the same foods are eaten in public at a church bazaar. "Table food" can be made into "finger food," even eaten while sitting on the ground, or while standing or moving: thus subverting the domestic character of the foods — uncivilizing them. In another kind of subversive move, the table-food can be made into a snack when it is a "left-over," thus altered from a meal to a between-meal consumable. By looking at such details, we can understand more fully how the poetics of food and food choice operates, and we are able to relate the food system to other kinds of exchange.

The language of what may be eaten and what may not is transferable to designate who may be eaten with and who may not. In a system in which eating lizards is forbidden, calling another group "lizard-eaters" is to place them in a symbolic category of non-humans. But this is an extreme case. We do place a very high value on eating with people who not only like to eat the same thing we do, but who don't like the same things we don't like, and — perhaps most important — who observe the same style of eating that we do. Thus, rules and styles of eating enter into the process of making social choices and establishing a system of social types.

Is there any question that the currencies of exchange of primary importance in culture are these three: food, sex, talk. Through the interaction of these three, we endow relationships with value and invest them with meaning through intercourse of several sorts. Each activity and each recurrent scene involves an etiquette, a repertoire of different foods and different ways of eating them, a decorum system that arises in the areas of talk and sex as well. As these scenes are learned, they invoke symbolic means, objects, and actions which are laminated with possible meanings to be achieved through interaction — meanings which carry the most profound, if everyday, cultural messages. Discerning with whom one may exchange sex, talk, or food is the central cultural lesson to be learned in growing up. I know of no culture that has not elaborated these access rules into symbolic as well as utilitarian processes, codes, and systems.

Thinking of someone as a pig-eater is hardly to banish him from your table (though referring to pig as 'pork' is still regarded as better table-talk); but thinking of someone as being a pig *does* affect whether or not we want to sit down with him at a table. Thus does eating enter the system by which we "type" people.

Such animal categories are hardly unique in the language of social intercourse. Indeed, they are merely one vocabulary of many which enter into the system of exchange within and between cultures, providing primary markers for subcultural or ethnic identity. The system will become more complex the greater the development of trade. For, as Marshall Sahlins has argued, though "the flow of goods is constrained by, [indeed] is part of, a status etiquette," when the relationship by those engaged in trade becomes distant, the rules of the etiquette are relaxed, and in the case of the total stranger, are dropped.[1] But this is commonsensical because we have already designated closeness or distance in terms of those with whom we trade and whether we eat or drink with them. We do not wince at bilking someone with whom we do not regularly sit down at the table; but once we invite them to our homes for a meal, the terms of exchange are altered. We are suspicious of what we eat at the market as well as what we buy, precisely because it is sold in the streets to people who are strangers.

Most of our discussions of food and foodways do not invoke these more exploitative—and sometimes antagonistic—relationships. But to fail to remind ourselves that we are involved often in an eat-or-be-eaten world would be to fall into Panglossian error. The very same codes by which we live within the family and community become resources for exclusiveness as we deal with those culturally different from ourselves, providing us with ample rationale for being wary of strangers and hateful of enemies. Even the language of eating, so deeply identified with hearth and home, is drawn upon as a privileged means of stereotyping and subordinating important "others."

At the deepest levels of our talk of others, our language provides us with attributions of their animal character which turns on their inability to "talk right," to "eat right," or to enter into approved sexual relations. This is what I call "the deep stereotype," because it refers to very general characteristics by which peoples throughout the world talk about strangers and enemies. The deep stereotype calls attention to a lack of civility through abnormal sexual proclivities, expressive disabilities and, of course, strange eating habits. The most condemned "unclean" food choices and eating styles are cannibalism, coprophagia, and carrion-eating. On a more superficial level, we see similar stereotyping mechanisms resulting in social distancing in the discussions of chittlin'-eating Blacks, tamale-eating Mexicans, potato-eating Irish, and most repulsive to some, the frog-eating Frenchman and the dog-eating Chinese.

Contrasting with the insularity of such stereotyping is the new spirit of culinary choice recently brought into play in America and elsewhere in the West. Not only do we see the introduction of ethnic pluralism entering into the process of choosing foods, cooking, and eating them, but we seem to want to be able to say of ourselves as eaters that we will try anything once. We become equal-opportunity eaters, especially in situations where we can sample unaccustomed foods while standing and walking around, as at a festival. This appears, in historical perspective, to be an extension of a capitalist-colonialist approach to life in which exploitation of subordinated peoples is not only expressed in terms of labor but also in appropriating their cultural styles, including their ways of cooking and eating.

Alternative culinary styles enter into our popular culture and become part of the civilizing process. But as with our adventuring in music, dance, and costume through the "trying on" and "trying out" process, we have learned some minimal lessons in cultural relativity, and have arrived at a point at which we can conceive of getting beyond the stereotyping of the strange eating habits of others. Just how sensitized we have become to the alternative cultural systems in which these styles have lived and developed is yet to be explored. What is certain is that we have hunger-habits for a wide range of foods, and that we look for public places where the cuisine is served with such authenticity that the 'ethnics' themselves eat there.

Perhaps even more significant is how this enlarged repertory of cooking and eating has entered into the dimension of the civilizing process—the dimension of talking through and about the most important distinctions of civility. Just as we have developed the ability to talk about ourselves pleasurably, in terms of our inner thoughts and our sexual proclivities, so we have expanded the discourse on cuisine, the pleasure of talking about eating. While stories about food gathering and about competition between man and nature for resources are legion in the world's storytelling traditions, one is overwhelmed by the sheer amount of discussion in Middle American culture of cooking, of different diets, of the new restaurants and specialty food stores that have opened, and of the great meals one has eaten.

Inevitably the question arises as to why there is such great discussion of food. The functionalist and utilitarian perspective would begin an answer by noting that culture itself is predicated on the development of technologically powerful devices for finding or producing food. The more that food is produced in surplus quantities, the more the power of its control and distribution will amplify. Moreover, as a way of flexing its muscles, this system will develop certain products which, while not needed for subsistence, are habituating; the control over such substances (whether pepper or cocaine) is all the more powerful precisely because these products *are* surplus and do not fill any dietary requirement.

In line with this pattern of physical dependency, all manufactured or refined devices become counters in the power-status 'game' as we see the development of the so-called "fetishization of commodities"— the worship of things for their own sake which grows in direct proportion to the distance between maker and user. Such a utilitarian theory rests ultimately on the notion that man in his simplest state ate only the things that were needed to subsist. To this, many anthropological theorists interested in understanding the symbolic and qualitative dimensions of culture have noted that dietary practices arise as much from the move to designate order of cleanliness and contamination— "good for you" and "bad for you"—as from the need to obtain a basic store of nurturing digestibles. The question of food choice is entailed in the larger symbolic ordering process by which humans endow the environment with meaning and feeling. By this we not only develop an understanding of what we may eat to survive but how we can place foods in larger categories that become part of the discourse on the universe. By this I mean we come together not only to break bread but also to talk about it: before, during, and after the act.

The sniggering suggestiveness of this way of talking about eating arises naturally in our discourse system. For, as I noted earlier, the languages of food and the languages of sex are always being conflated under the heading of instinctual appetites. Moreover, the observations which Michel Foucault makes concerning the modern tropism toward sexual confession (I nearly wrote confection!) are also apropos of foods. Noting the mutation of the ancient *ars erotica* mysterious tradition of sexual discourse to the more open and analytic *scientia sexualis,* Foucault notes that the "scientific model" of investigation takes on a life of its own as it generates distinctions:

It is often said that we have been incapable of imagining any new pleasures. We have at least invented a different kind of pleasure: pleasure in the truth of pleasure, the pleasure of knowing the Truth, of discovering and exposing it, the fascination of seeing it and telling it, of confiding it . . . of luring it out into the open—the specific pleasure of the true discourse on pleasure.[2]

Foucault, like so many of his *confrères,* is disgusted with our fascinations, fascinated with our disgusts. He is concerned primarily that the discourse system seems to arise out of delight in the working of the system. This delight leads to observation, and such surveillance enters into the fetishizing process, each ordered domain achieving a kind of life of its own, one in which 'pleasure' arises from observation, classification, confession, and comment—this being the latest development in becoming civil.

With the growth of the world market, we have become increasingly conscious of life alternatives, especially in the areas of stylistic differentiations. Freedom for the middle classes has come to mean the increasing availability of alternatives. Such options carry with them the need to submit the chosen objects to public surveillance "for our own protection." Nowhere is overseeing more open and dramatic than in the supervision of the franchising and advertising of food—franchises developed out of the emerging public consciousness of ethnic and regional foodstuffs and foodstyles. For what characterizes a franchise operation is the development of a special and visual, as well as culinary, style that is dictated from the national headquarters. Cleanliness and integrity are maintained by the use of "field representatives" who make sure that no deviation develops. One need only drive down the Plastic Alley of anyplace in the United States where there are purveyors of Southern-Fried, Mexican, Italian, German, English, and Chinese foods who make their products available on a drive-through, take-out basis. The whole process is carried out before our very eyes. Interspersed with these are sit-down, fast-food restaurants offering an even wider range of cuisines. And finally, no town of any distinction today does not offer a range of *haute cuisine* eateries, as well as the self-consciously retrogressive country kitchens serving up baked beans and scrod or pinto beans and barbecue. In foods, as with the arts, eclecticism has become the by-word in this post-modern world.

In line with this open eclecticism is our compulsion to reveal how it is done, to demystify the process of food transformation by making our private acts public. Culinary as well as sexual choice enters into our campaigns to manage our own identities by optimizing our stylistic choices constantly. (A food-rights movement in parallel with gay-rights and women's-rights?) One facet of this is the willingness of the various ethnic populations to open up their kitchens, and in the process to highlight their stylistic distinctiveness and publicize their gustatory delights. This is commonly accomplished by traditional means—that is, by making their in-group *festive* foodways more generally available to outsiders, especially in the competitive environments of folk festivals and fairs. These foods are commonly the ones which have always been sold to strangers at the marketplace. Surely we go to these events primarily to eat—to be caught with our mouths open in public. In going public, a cultural contradiction re-emerges, one which has always resided at the hearth of American life: that in the celebration of the many, a sense of oneness may emerge. Paradoxically, the very act of food preparation and cooking may simultaneously proclaim and undermine ethnicity. The means by which an individual maintains a sense of ethnic continuity and integrity in carrying on the food tradition becomes a way to articulate a social and cultural coming-together, as one kind of food takes its place alongside other ethnic and regional offerings in the festival setting. Intensifying the sense of paradox is that the foods being served up to the public are often the very ones focused on in the stereotype of the ethnic in the past ages. (For a Chicano to serve tamales in a multiethnic setting is like a Frenchman serving frogs, or a black selling watermelons advertised as fresh-stolen from the farmer's field.) The same motive operates with the bumper stickers calling for us to eat stereotypical—and despised—foods: *Eat More Menudo* (tripe), *Eat More Possum*, etc.

This focus on alternatives in cooking and eating parallels other changes arising out of what Norbert Elias calls "the civilizing process" —a development of the modern world in which we are overwhelmed by consciousness of the world's resources and alternative lifeways.[3] The state of multiple consciousness that arises when we are presented with the possibility of experiencing so many alternative cultural practices and products has led to a world in which everyone in the consumer class is potentially a connoisseur, an aficionado, a gourmand or a gourmet. Interest in ethnic foods or haute cuisine in such a view differs little from learning to discriminate types of cars, antiques, tools, or wines. The important feature of all involvements is that the adept must be able to make qualitative discriminations by learning the languages of his or her passion. Whether the talk is about "vintage years," "gear," "rig," or "moves," one must be able to discuss matters very deeply by knowing the right terms, the right distinctions, and especially the right adjectives of approval or derision.

Fernand Braudel argues the centrality of just such motives and just such abilities to make a set of systematic distinctions within the formation of the capitalist world view. Increased trade makes people more conscious of subtleties in home products and the range of similar things to be had from the rest of the "civilized" world. In his magisterial *Capitalism and Material Life: 1400–1800*, Braudel documents the cultural by-products of labor-intensive horticulture, the production of surplus crops, and the creation of merchant and leisured classes.[4] He documents this development in a number of domains in the domestic life of our ancestors during this period, with specific reference to the growing number of choices to be made in housing, clothing, and food and drink. Portraying each major addition as habituating, he documents the crucial importance of the serial introduction of spices, tea, coffee, tobacco, and most recently, mind-altering drugs. All of these are paralleled by the growing sophistication and differentiation of wines, beers, and heavier alcoholic beverages.

In a discourse on the relationship between the rich and the poor, Braudel brilliantly details the cultural independence of the ideal of luxury and the ways in which it comes to reside at the heart of the capitalist enterprise.

. . . . every luxury dates and goes out of fashion. But luxury is reborn from its own ashes and from its very defeats. It is really the reflection of a difference in social levels that nothing can change and that every movement recreates an eternal class struggle!

It applies not only to classes but to civilizations. Civilizations were incessantly eyeing each other, acting out the same drama as the rich played in relation to the poor. But this time it was reciprocal, and therefore created currents and led to accelerated changes, from near and far. In short, as Marcel Mauss wrote, "It is not in production that society found its impetus; luxury is the great stimulus . . ."[5]

To be sure, Braudel is castigating the *ancien régime,* in which extremely limited resources were deployed for the pleasure of the rich at the constant expense of the poor. But the implications of the argument for the understanding of the dynamics of food choice are patent: once a class-and-culture boundary is established, foodstuffs become counters in the exchange system, therefore foods must be endowed with some sense of power that makes them desirable. Ironically, the comestibles that ascend to this place of importance in this world market have been those stimulants that have little nutritional value. They are the product of refinement, a direct outgrowth of the new industrial way of organizing both productivity and social relationships.

Moreover, as Sidney Mintz notices of the foods chosen on the social occasions arising within industrial settings, the food items enter into the industrial process also by how they operate in the lives of the worker-consumers: "It is the special character of the substances consumed that, like sugar, they provide calories without nutrition; or like coffee and tea, neither nutrition nor calories, but stimulus to greater effort; or, like alcohol and tobacco, respite from reality."[6] It might be argued, of course, that all such symbolically encoded foods will provide such a respite, creating an alternative reality of their own, simply because they are employed at set-aside times and consumed in special places. Important in such analyses is precisely that such symbolic or non-utilitarian factors enter into the process of food choice, and that principles of prestige and exoticism created by their place in world trade underscore the symbolic character of these consumables.

Marshall Sahlins has noted that ours is a unique culture in regarding ourselves as descended from animals; all others, seemingly, see themselves as generated from (and by) the gods.[7] This notion of ancestry is certainly not fully shared by all. It is recognized as a unique perspective even by those who reject it in whole or in part. But it does point to the fact that as animals enter less and less into our lives, we have developed ever deeper collective and symbolic relationships with them; whether we see them as sharing our ancestry, or, as in the ecology movement, simply identify with their attempts to maintain themselves in their natural state. But in another dimension, by optimizing choices and intensifying the stylistic elaboration of foods we separate ourselves from the animality of our animal ancestors. This is not to argue that the practice of distinguishing humanity and the animals is absent from other cultures. Indeed as Levi-Strauss, among others, has demonstrated, one of the primary oppositions developed in symbolic terms in all cultures is how animals differ from humans with regard to what is to be eaten and how: thus, the much discussed nature: culture:: raw food: cooked (or transformed) food.

The focus on cooking and eating is, like primary incest rules, the beginning of what Mary Douglas calls "the purity rule," the minimal absolute statement of what may and what may not be done by members of a community or a culture. By endowing food choice, preparation, and eating with such a symbolic load, cultures invest heavily in themselves whenever they engage in eating. Although we forget such notions most of the time, eating rehearses some of the most basic ways in which the world is given significant order and value. Or, as Douglas nicely phrases it, "The common meal decoded, as much as any poem, summarizes a stern tragic religion" inasmuch as it reminds us of what is to be eaten, with what and in what order, and, by heavy contrast, what is not to be consumed lest it consume us.[8] We are reminded of these rules whenever bad manners are exhibited. We feel we must comment on such behavior, thus making open declaration of our separation from the animals. And the talk is usually couched in exactly these terms ("You eat like a pig!"; "You chew like a cow!"; "Don't wolf your food!")

Ironically, one food choice presented us is what might be called "the search for the perfect one-pot meal." This self-conscious dream of simplifying our lives, however, must be placed in the same niche in the museum-hall of our sentiments with the other depictions of the American version of pastoral. Picnicking, going to a barbecue, even camping out, all evoke self-consciously regressive, simplifying, and clarifying motives. They go "back to nature" in some dimension, by which we think we mean getting closer to the animals. "Dirt never hurt anyone" and other such "folk ideas" can come into meaning under such circumstances, but never at the dinner table. This weekend wildness and holiday hilarity represent our declaration of independence, our opting for the maintaining of choice.

What fictions we construct for ourselves, and how we do invest them with value! Another example: to the argument that animals eat raw food, humans cook it up, some wiseacre always replies, "Oh, I can eat anything." That response is seldom worth arguing against, because we do not want to test our own stomachs by asking him to eat carrion or feces. What is usually meant is that this person eats raw fish and meat. *Steak Tartare* is usually the example of the latter—those brave ones pursuing this (questionable) culinary treat forget in the fervor of the argument that although the meat is raw in the sense that it was not transformed in any way by heat, it is hardly raw in the sense of being natural. It is, after all, highly prepared, ground up, salted and peppered, served on silver plates and only in the most formal dining room setting, thus very cleaned up for human consumption. How many of those adventurers would eat the same meat straight off the hoof? About the same number as would eat fish straight out of the sea but nevertheless love *sushi* or *seviche.* These are matters which we like to forget so as to shore up our highly-ordered structure of sentiments (while we maintain our apparent independence from explicit cultural rules). Ultimately, the message we are delivering to ourselves is that civilized folks are allowed to play with food, but only under special circumstances, which in fact reaffirm the normal ways.

To relate eating and the order of things to notions of personal identification with regional ethnicity it is necessary to outline how foods enter into the dynamic of culture—a dynamic that involves motives of acceptance and avoidance, attraction and repulsion, celebration and rejection. Food choice and cuisine do not produce the only markings of such identification. But when a region such as the South or an ethnic group such as Afro-Americans is strongly identified with eating strange creatures like possum, squirrel, and raccoon, we are in the midst of a powerful symbolic dynamic, in which both a positive identifying factor is operating wherever such animals are hunted, cooked and eaten, and a negative stereotyping is involved, when a group is referred to as "coons" or "possum-eaters." To understand how such foods develop this power of identification, it is useful to survey the insights arising out of the structuralist approach.

Mary Douglas' book *Purity and Danger* encourages us to consider such notions in a systematic way; though it focuses on the food-choice rules of the Old Testament — the abominations of Leviticus — by extension it is concerned with food taboos in general. In the course of her discussion she rids us of the necessity to view dirt in terms of the presence of pathogenic organisms by redefining the concept of filth as "matter out of place." "Dirt," she argues, "is never a unique isolated event. Where there is dirt there is system. Dirt is the by-product of a systematic ordering and classification of matter, insofar as ordering involves rejecting inappropriate elements."[9]

This commonsensical approach draws upon all of our accumulated experience of things in and out of place. We have all been made uncomfortable or been revolted by having people put their feet or their hands where they ought not to be. Furthermore, it is abundantly clear that the more cherished the place, the greater the emotional involvement as the possibility of disruption arises. The more ceremonial the occasion, the more likely we are to react negatively to the presence of things out of place. We also know through past experience in intense situations that there are occasions in which not only can unclean things be done, but they are encouraged, and we can enjoy the experience; this is precisely what occurs at festivals and picnics and other kinds of free events. In such cases we are able to prepare ourselves, and to put that event in a frame so that we are reminded constantly that play is in process. Those very things which appear out of place regularly are susceptible to accumulating a kind of power — albeit the power of upsetting — which makes them effective. Things like feces or urine become potent cultural messengers when found in a practical joke, or as devices employed in an anecdote, or when used as part of an "act" in a stage play or Saturnalian performance.

Such symbols, then, have power and ambiguity, in their anomalous status within the system. There is an obvious sense of power in the operation of the classification system itself, that kind of dominion experienced whenever the orders and relational powers of the system are put on ceremonial display, as in a royal wedding, coronation, or state funeral. A different vocabulary is drawn upon for the display of anomalies and disorder in festivals, for here the objective is to invert social practices, often by dramatizing them subversively.

At least in one important dimension, culture is both the agreed-upon system and the conventional departures from those categories.

Anything unclean, or out of place, may be understood best in terms of canons of cleanliness and order; but the power residing therein exists because the anomaly is isolated and potentially capable of inducing contagion and chaos. Douglas has told us a good deal about the power which can be made to reside in in-between phenomena, a power generated by the system itself and not by the independent characteristics of any item within it. What she fails to recognize, strangely enough, is how such anomalies also tend to become organized into categories themselves. For instance, though we have endowed the snake with immense power, mostly because of its anomalous character (cold-blooded, scaly, amphibious animal without feet), it shares much of these undistributed, potentially confusing responsive energies with other "slimy creatures." Snakes also share in our accumulated responses to those wild creatures who invade the sphere of human habitation, a category largely populated by pests or vermin (indeed, in the American West, snakes are often included as "varmints"—i.e., pesky wild animals who intrude into the human domain).

In a study that parallels Douglas' in interesting ways, E.R. Leach discusses such creature categories, but he also ignores the grouping of in-between animals.[10] He argues that we make our basic distinctions in English between *pets, domesticated animals* (or *livestock, cattle*), *wild animals* and *game.* In his acknowledgedly sketchy excursus, he does not attempt to discern what the bases of the distinctions are, though he does consider in passing that the "folk" model he proposes depends on the availability of the animal as a food-resource for human consumption.

Closer observation indicates that in English we do, in fact, have a complex system of creature categories based on principles of cleanliness and contamination, in which we are not only concerned with whether a "thing" is edible, but also with whether it will consume us, or contend with us for our basic resources. There is an accompanying set of categories for plant life. Here we can designate the following categories along the parameter of "eat or be eaten by":

1) Our common food resources (*livestock, crops*), matter produced under human supervision which provides us with our basic food resources;
2) things also under our control but which "live with us" (*pets, houseplants,* and *flowers*) and which therefore we do not even consider eating, but which we also do not consider as contending with us for food resources;
3) things which, in fact, contend with us for our resources, and which, therefore, when they touch our food, contaminate it (*scavengers, vermin, germs, weeds*);
4) things which may kill and/or eat us (*wild animals* and *poisons*);

5) things which live in nature, but which we contend with and sometimes capture or gather for special eating purposes (*game, wild flowers, roots, herbs*), but in which case, we must prepare them by taking out features of taste too *strong, wild,* or *gamey* for us.

This system operates more or less by our sense of closeness or distance to the animal's domain, habits, or physiognomy. Pets and houseplants are members of the family, thus not to be exploited as resources; domesticated animals and plants are *cultivated,* under our control, the perfect coming together of nature and culture in an agricultural scheme, but must commonly be refined as well as prepared for consumption; wild things are beyond the pale, and dangerous as such, but available as special resources of natural energy when the human encampment runs out of resources from within. Finally, there are the weeds and the critters, nature's vagrants, who are both wild and yet always making incursions into our domestic spaces, bringing in forces of contagion and contamination. There are a number of other factors that enter, in interesting ways, into our attitudes about purity, power, contamination, and taboo. We ask questions such as: if we take milk from a creature, do we also eat it? We wonder, if meat is not connected to bone, is it edible? (If not, it is usually called *innards* and considered a questionable meat because of its "mushy" character.) In the case of game, we distinguish between the hooved and the pawed, the diurnal and the nocturnal — more properly hunted during the day or night — the tree-dwelling and the ground-dwelling, etc.

All of this is strongly coded in our vocabulary. The meanings of the categories are intensified, as Leach suggests, by our continuing use of animal designations as reference devices for individual humans in the dynamic of social typing. Thus, the imagery of pig and dog is maintained even though neither one is the between-category animal it once was. Both were the animals at the threshold in our more agrarian past — the ones who came to eat at our beck and call, and who ate the *left-overs* or *slops* from our tables. Now, of course, they have had their acts cleaned up: dogs are found either in the house or in the kennel, pigs in their clean feeding lots. But in our continued use of pig-references for humans, we maintain the old stereotype of a lazy, unmannered and unmannerly, dirty, ugly, brooding creature. And when we call humans "dogs," we usually mean the sexual rovings of *curs* ("you *dog,* you") or the snapping character of *bitches* (especially those in heat).

In the endeavor to come to a greater understanding of the relationship between food choice and ethnicity or regionalism it is interesting to begin to look at why the eating of certain foods are seized upon in the development of stereotypic notions. Having outlined the criteria by which we build creature categories, it is somewhat clearer why such animals as possum, coon, or squirrel might be regarded as strange ones to eat, and why those who eat them are regarded as cultural vagrants, or backward people. Coons, possums, and squirrels are *varmints,* animals who live in the wild state but who eat human food; worse, coons and possums raid our garbage. In fact, these two are exceptionally anomalous creatures, for not only are they pests, but they are also tree-dwelling critters. Moreover, they are nocturnal, forcing their hunters (and eaters) to pursue them at night, with specially trained dogs. They challenge a great number of our categories of edibility; for one to eat them, one must turn life around, sleep during the day and hunt at night in the trees. Of their closest categorical relatives — hunted varmints — fox and rabbit are diurnal ground-dwellers and squirrels are diurnal tree-dwellers. Clearly, those who hunt and eat varmints, then, are susceptible to being labelled as strange themselves.

Clearly, it is one thing for a group to engage in such hunting and eating practices, and another for others to categorize inhabitants of that region or set of ethnic groups as coons or as possum-eaters. This stereotyping, moreover, seems especially strange to anyone who has lived in the South, for not everyone there hunts such food animals or eats them when they have been cooked. Indeed, these are markers of low status to many Southerners, and the hunter eaters of such critters are regarded as strange (though one is seldom ostracized for this). In fact, the cultural conditions of these practices have not, to my experience, been investigated. There are the usual "folk-explanations" for who does it and why, explanations usually turning on attributions of ignorance, backwardness, or just plain poverty. But having discussed the matter with a few who hunt and eat these varmints the case is not so clear, for repeatedly they aver that, far from being a matter of simply holding off starvation, they do it because they enjoy it.

In fact, there has been very little systematic work done on Southern culinary practices, black or white, a subject that would reveal a great deal about the dynamics of life in which Africans, Europeans, and Native Americans came together explosively and developed a unique creole culture in a matter of a few generations. With regard to the foods that have been seized upon as symbolic of Southern cooking, the culinary pattern of the region seemingly is based more on African food choice, cooking and eating patterns than on any other. Yam, okra, and peanuts are examples of foods that are African in origin and preparation, as well as being the kind of cooking called "Southern Fried." But this is engaging in an impressionistic survey at the very point where controlled research is most required. I do so only to indicate the cultural questions that ought to be asked concerning the whys and hows of ethnically- or regionally-labelled foods — questions which are best addressed with reference to the structure of food categorization, whether animal or vegetable. It does not take imagination to recognize that the vegetable equivalent to coon and possum hunting is conjuring, doing "root-work." The special powers attached to these products of nature have to do with their identification with the night, the wild, and their anomalous relationships with the human community.

Categorization in one form or another is almost certainly a deep part of the cultural dynamic of any group. Membership within a society, and within the social units of a society, is often built around just such a category-system invoking animals (among other things), as students of totemism and of mascots remind us. More important, however, are the ways in which those names of creatures feared and rejected as a food resource are drawn upon as a symbolic resource as well, employed for stereotyping self and others. One need recall the ways in which such animal attributions have entered into the process of social exclusion in American history. Blacks have been legally designated as cattle during slavery, and consistently discussed as coons, mules, or monkeys. The Irish, too, have commonly been depicted as apes, and on and on. Surely, our extreme ambivalence about the simian sort is conditioned by our actual physical identification with them and our feeling that eating them would be close to cannibalism; on the other hand, from the perspective of popular evolution, designating others as apes is judging them to be like us, but representative of our animal character that we have only recently been able to transcend.

If there has been an eating revolution in America, surely it can only be comprehended in terms of our growing ability to get beyond such stereotyping. Because we have not allowed ourselves to study the problems of stereotyping and food choice within the context of a cultural dynamic, we have not been able to begin to ask how and why the revolution is being waged. It would be too easy to say that a culturally pluralistic and egalitarian ethic is taking over. To the contrary, eating other people's foods has often been a sign of their having been subjugated. But there is clearly a change in eating practices that is enlarging our range of tastes, one which is affecting our nation on every level of society. Though we have not yet learned to eat dog or monkey, we have developed sufficient flexibility and adventurousness of taste that we can eat the traditional foods of those we have called dogs and monkeys in the past.

Putting food into a central place in our discourse on pleasures means that we open our mouths to all manner of powerful but dangerous subjects. Surely this development reflects a process of cultural incorporation that is primarily concerned with motives of life enhancement. It would be reassuring to think that these are the only motives involved, but our history of taste and distaste does not encourage such a positive view. The process of consumption and exploitation are too deeply entwined. One way or another, we must carry on the discussion, knowing that breaking stereotypes — like breaking taboos — means playing around in the center of symbolic systems of thinking, acting, and judging.

ACKNOWLEDGMENTS

My thanks to the editors for helping me work out these ideas in relation to the theme of the book. Thanks also to: Susan Kalčik, Bess Lomax Hawes, John Szwed and Barre Toelken for long discussions on the subject of ethnic food in America, and to the cook and editor in my life, Janet Anderson Abrahams.

NOTES

1. "On the Sociology of Primitive Exchange," *Stone Age Economics* (Chicago: Aldine-Atherton, 1972), 186.

2. Michel Foucault, *The History of Sexuality:* Vol. I: *An Introduction,* trans. Robert Hurley (New York: Vintage, 1978), 71.

3. Norbert Elias, *The Civilizing Process,* trans. Edmund Jephcott (New York: Urizen Booke, 1978).

4. Fernand Braudel, *Capitalism and Material Life: 1400–1800,* trans. Miriam Kochan (New York: Harper, 1973).

5. Braudel, 123.

6. Sidney W. Mintz, "Time, Sugar, and Sweetness," *Marxist Perspectives* 2 (1978): 69.

7. Marshall Sahlins, *Culture and Practical Meaning* (Chicago: Univ. of Chicago Press, 1976).

8. Mary Douglas, *Implicit Meanings* (London: Routledge, Kegan Paul, 1975), 272.

9. Mary Douglas, *Purity and Danger: An Analysis of the Concepts of Pollution and Taboo* (London: Routledge, Kegan Paul, 1966).

10. E. R. Leach, "Animal Categories and Verbal Abuse," *New Directions in the Study of Language,* ed. E.H. Lenneberg (Cambridge: MIT Press, 1964), 23–63. As I demonstrate here, Leach's intuitions are more useful than his characterization of the relationships between these categories. As John Halverson argues in "Animal Cate-

gories and Terms of Abuse," *Man* 11 (1977): 278–300, Leach's etymologies and his parameters of comparison and contrast betray inconsistencies. Because both food choice and the social typing operation are both so complicated, one should not expect an exhaustive explanation of the process. These notes only indicate some of the more important features entering into the creation of an interlocking set of metaphors that affect the choice of who and how to enter into exchanges.

2

Ethnic Foodways in America: Symbol and the Performance of Identity

Susan Kalčik

When a sizeable number of Vietnamese refugees settled recently in a small Kentucky city, a rumor began circulating that people's cats and dogs were disappearing. The rumor suggested that the strange food habits of the Vietnamese were responsible for the vanishing pets. At the same time, in the Washington, D.C., area, which has approximately the third-largest settlement of Vietnamese in the United States, a large number of Vietnamese restaurants have opened and Vietnamese food is enjoying popularity in the press and at local festivals. These are examples of two very common processes involving food and groups of people. In the first a food stereotype is used as a weapon against an intruder: the formula operating appears to be "strange people equals strange food." In the second process the new group presents its food in acceptable, safe arenas where some Americans try it out and learn to like it and perhaps even learn to cook it themselves. The formula here seems to be: "not-so-strange food equals not-so-strange people," or perhaps, "strange people but they sure can cook."

The Vietnamese, as one of the most recent groups to migrate to America, illustrate other aspects of what happens to foodways in an acculturation or culture-contact situation. Traditional foods and ways of eating form a link with the past and help ease the shock of entering a new culture; thus many struggle to hold on to them despite pressures to change.[1] Immigrants open restaurants so that it is more convenient to get certain foods that take a long time to prepare; they open stores so that ingredients are available; they grow otherwise unavailable vegetables and herbs in their backyards. One Vietnamese couple in Maryland has started a small factory to manufacture a Vietnamese style of soy sauce that currently cannot be purchased anywhere else in the world; the first shipment went to large settlements of Vietnamese in Texas, California, and Paris.[2]

It is easy to predict that the Vietnamese will make some compromises between their desire and respect for the old foods and the food habits of their new country, because the groups that have come before them have done just that. John Bennett points out that people can feel ambivalent about food items "in areas where a conflict between an older behavior-pattern or attitude and a newer alternative . . . value has occurred."[3] But despite these compromises food remains one viable aspect of the folkways of American ethnic groups and a significant way of celebrating ethnicity and group identity.[4] At a conference on festivals held in Baltimore, representatives of various ethnic groups complained about what they saw as a stereotypical presentation of ethnicity at various festivals, a presentation that heavily emphasized food. Nonetheless, a typical program book on display at the same conference called Richmond, Virginia's *International Festival* "Richmond's Delicious Weekend"; the logo was a crossed fork and spoon; and of the twenty-two pages in the program book, ten were devoted to food. When interviewers talked with people visiting the Festival of American Folklife sponsored by the Smithsonian Institution in Washington, D.C., food was the most-mentioned marker of ethnic identity. Clearly, for old and new ethnic groups in America, foodways—the whole pattern of what is eaten, when, how, and what it means—are very closely tied to individual and group ethnic identity.

From early in our nation's history, people have observed and commented on the fact that different Americans eat different foods and that the differences involve more than class distinctions. In 1869 Benjamin Chase observed:

There were, however racial and regional variations in diet. The Dutch in New York, for example, prized the *oleykoek*. *Smearcase* pleased the Pennsylvania Germans. Scotch-Irish tenacity was reflected in porringers: "The Irish ate potatoes and the English did not. The Irish put barley into their pot liquor and made barley broth. The English put in beans and had bean porridge." Coastman, backwoodsman, northerner, southerner—each had his own food.

For example, cod and corn were typical of New England, white bread was eaten where wheat grew well, and sweet potatoes were eaten in the South.[5]

Despite fast food chains and processed food available in supermarkets, many people continue to prepare and prefer special regional and ethnic dishes.[6] Even in so basic a staple as bread, Margaret Arnott points to wide regional variations in preference. Southerners, for example, like softer bread, while people in New England and the North and East Central states prefer the firmest-textured bread of all Americans.[7] Ethnic groups try to use familiar types of bread whenever possible, despite the fact that economics and urbanization change bread-eating patterns.

The two factors that seem to operate to produce these differences in American tastes are varying food supply and varying ethnic group influences, depending on what groups settled an area of the country. Thus, regional and ethnic foodways are often intertwined. As with other aspects of ethnic tradition, there is often a drift from ethnic to regional identity: individuals without a strong sense of ethnicity may fill the need for a more specific identity than "American" with regional traditions, including cooking. Indeed, it is very difficult to deal with foodways as ethnically pure except in an idealized sense since, as Don Yoder points out, "Viewed historically, each regional and national cuisine is a culinary hybrid, with an elaborate stratigraphy of diverse historical layers combined into a usable and evidently satisfying structure."[8] Pennsylvania German culture and food, for example, is an acculturated system with aspects from British, Scotch-Irish, and German cultures.[9]

Factors Affecting Changes in the Foodways of an Ethnic Group

The acculturation and hybridization processes begin again when new ethnic groups or individuals arrive in the United States and experience the push-pull of cross inclinations about maintaining their traditional foodways. Some try to find and eat foods as similar to those in the old country as possible. Others give in to pressures from within and without the group to change their food habits. Both processes operate as ways of easing adjustment to life in the new country: one provides a continuation of the old lifestyle and makes the break less abrupt; the other process speeds acculturation. In his study of factors that retard or accelerate the acculturation of recent Hungarian refugees, S. A. Weinstock found those who cooked Hungarian food exclusively to be in the lowest acculturation group.[10] Although the tendencies to maintain and to let go of traditions affect many aspects of the culture of new immigrant populations, observers have noted that foodways seem particularly resistant to change.[11] It has been suggested that this is because the earliest-formed layers of culture, such as foodways, are the last to erode.[12]

Several key factors are involved in affecting changes in the food-ways of an ethnic group. One is generation. Generally the immigrant generation, especially those who were older when they migrated, hang on to their foodways longer than the second generation, and children are often observed to adapt first to American foodways and to intro-duce adults to American foods.[13] Gregory Gizelis qualifies this pat-tern by pointing out that the second-generation Greeks he studied al-tered foodways by simplifying food preparation, but they continued to make Greek food.[14] Margaret Arnott points out that the third gen-eration may take up the cooking and serving of ethnic foods skipped over by the second generation.[15]

Frederick Fliegel finds that in addition to age, the occupation of the breadwinner, the education of the cook, and the state of the fam-ily (for example, if there are young children) all influence the kinds of foods people eat.[16] Other researchers have shown how economics (whether foods are affordable), convenience (easy purchase and prep-aration), commercialization, and urbanization affect the retention or loss of ethnic foodways.[17] Gizelis suggests that changes he observed in Greek-American foodways in Philadelphia were not the result of Americanization but of urbanization. Although city life resulted in the dropping of some difficult foods and the adoption of easier prepara-tion methods, it also included the addition of ethnic dishes to the fam-ily's repertoire because of more convenient technology and because stores made certain foods available all year which formerly had been available seasonally or only in some parts of Greece.[18]

Status is another factor in changing foodways. Many individuals choose to drop ethnic foodways because they are signs of low status.[19] In some cases, only certain foods are perceived to be of low status (such as the blood sausage which Illinois Germans found was offen-sive to their American neighbors), and these are dropped.[20] Women seem particularly resistant to change in foodways and can be signifi-cant in maintaining foodways if they are in charge of the family meals.[21] Among the Japanese immigrants in Hawaii, for example, the older-generation females remained at home to cook, and although there were changes in the food items, the methods of preparation remained much the same.[22]

All immigrants and their succeeding generations find their tradi-tional foodways altered to some degree. All have to make compro-mises which they pass on. Sometimes traditional foodways are rele-gated to a particular meal, usually dinner, since breakfast, snacks, and lunch seem more responsive to acculturation pressures.[23] Herbert Pas-sin and John Bennett describe our food habits as comprised of a core diet, secondary core, and peripheral foods. They found the greatest emotional resistance to changes in the core diet; hence, these foods might continue to be served with others dropping away and new ones added on.[24] For example, the Japanese kept rice in their diet but added rice substitutes such as crackers.[25] For most immigrants and ethnics, ethnic foods are often still served on special occasions.[26]

The struggles of the immigrant generation to keep, adapt, and shed their traditional foodways affect the repertoire of foodways that suc-ceeding generations can call upon to use in symbolic displays of eth-nic identity. In many cases the struggle to keep or give up ethnic food habits continues into the succeeding generations as they struggle to adjust their sense of ethnic identity and their relationship to the larger unit of American society. One influence on that struggle, for both immigrant and ethnic, was how the rest of American society, the non-ethnic part, felt about ethnicity in general and ethnic foodways in particular. Our history includes periods of toleration for ethnics and periods of antipathy toward them. The prevailing attitude affects dis-cussions of ethnic food habits in a given period.

Richard Cummings tells us that cooking classes were introduced in public schools in the East in the 1880s, and efforts were made to teach the poor to shop wisely and eat nutritiously. Some of these classes and efforts affected the immigrants who were beginning to pour into America, as did the struggle to regulate food processing and sales that characterized the period between 1911 and 1916.[27] After World War I, social workers increased their efforts to teach nutrition to Blacks and immigrants. As Cummings puts it, ". . . though the negro who failed to use sufficient protective foods was coming in large numbers to the northern cities, education was facilitated by the fact that the horde of foreign born whose dietary habits were frequently malad-justed to American life had been cut by immigration restriction."[28]

Cummings wrote in 1940 but he clearly reflects, and probably even minimizes, the fear and antipathy Americans felt toward the second and third waves of immigrants, a fear that extended to their foodways.[29] The period of greatest immigration was paralleled by attempts to "Americanize" the immigrants and their children in the schools, in settlement houses, and other institutions of social workers. American-ization included attempts, varying in degree of compassion, to change "maladjusted" diets. Velma Phillips and Laura Howell present the results of a survey done by students of Teachers College, Columbia University in 1917–18 of food habits of "Italians, Hebrews, and Ne-groes," intending to help nutrition workers, home economics teach-ers, and those doing school lunch programs to understand more about the actual eating habits of some of the people they were trying to serve. Although the survey found nutrition problems such as rickets, the authors warned that the foreign women were not being reached by current methods, such as nutrition lectures.[30] Phyllis Williams' remarkable study of South Italian folkways in the New Haven, Connecticut, area was based on eleven years of firsthand experience (approximately 1927–38) and was aimed at an audience of social workers, visiting nurses, teachers, physicians, and others who dealt with the south Italian community, and it treated Italians honestly and with respect.[31] A chapter was devoted to their foodways in Italy and America, describing problems in nourishment and health caused by immigration to America. The Depression brought new attempts to understand the food habits of ethnic groups so that relief efforts would be as economical and efficient as possible, and nutritional education of the poorer ethnics continued.[32]

As America's entry into World War II became imminent, concern with our nation's nutrition in general was renewed. There was concern about poorly nourished men who did not qualify for the armed services and about the high percentage of the population that was undernourished, affecting the nation's defense efforts. Slogans such as "Eat the Right Food, U.S. Needs US Strong" reflected these concerns. (Germany, meanwhile, was training its people to change their priorities and accept food substitutes with slogans like "Guns Instead of Butter.")[33] With our entry into the war other problems, including rationing and food aid to the rest of the world, became significant. A group of anthropologists working through the National Research Council, the Committee on Food Habits with Margaret Mead as its head, shared results of its various research projects with seventeen government agencies concerned with national nutrition during the war. The Committee's major concerns were to define a good diet and determine how to get people to accept it.[34] The second problem provided new impetus for studying the foodways of ethnic groups in America, because the Committee found it imperative to understand *why* certain groups ate what they did before efforts could be made to change food habits.[35] The Committee produced a handbook for the study of foodways, a bulletin on the issues of changing food habits, and a number of studies of specific ethnic and regional groups, their foodways, and how these might be capitalized upon or modified to aid nutrition efforts.[36]

Another war-related effort was the Common Council for American Unity's attempts to teach nutrition to various ethnic groups by means of food tasting and workshop programs.[37] The Council stressed the meeting of different groups over the subject of food and the fact that ethnics and Americans had much to learn from each other. These and other war-time efforts were characterized by a tone of acceptance and respect for the traditions of the different ethnic and racial groups in America; this tone is understandable since the period called for a strong sense of unity despite differences. This attitude is reflected in the following statement from Mark Graubard's work of the period: "Scientific nutrition can be a practical testing ground for tolerance. There are different roads that lead to a common goal and in the course of the common search for it, much is learned about other people and groups. Different national groups working together in a community will learn to know each other by cooperation, will learn new dishes and recipes, learn tolerance and true democratic unity."[38]

In the 1960s Margaret Mead mentioned poorer ethnic groups as one of the undernourished groups in America, but by this time the focus of food problems had shifted in such a way that ethnic foodways no longer posed the kind of threat that they did during the heavy immigration period or the war.[39] New problems had been added to that of undernourishment; many Americans struggled with the problems of over-nourishment, for example, and all were affected by a growing list of food contaminants. Food problems were viewed in a world-wide context as well, so that Americans turned their attention to balancing the world inequity between nations with plenty and those that were starving.

Although some attempts are still being made to adapt ethnic diets to one standard, in general the period from the end of World War II to the present has been characterized by a live-and-let-eat mood.[40] At one level Americans are said to be much alike, in food habits as well as other areas of culture, and official food is "American" food. College and high school classes, for example, focus on the foods of WASPs.[41] Fast foods, growing food chains, the processing of foods, and the rise in eating out mean that many kinds of food are shared by Americans. Regional distinctions exist, but they too foster the sense that in certain areas of the country, at least, Americans eat the same kinds of food. In R.M. Pangborn and C.M. Bruhn's 1971 study of how three groups of Americans view the foods of other ethnic groups, some informants insisted that all Americans eat the same kinds of food. The authors suggest that one reason for such a response is "an attitude prevalent among several young people that to dwell upon the differences among the cultures of the various groups which constitute our country suggests racial bigotry or an unpatriotic viewpoint."[42]

In relatively private spheres of life, people who wish to do so continue to eat ethnic and regional foods that do not fit into this harmonious picture. Here, again, the domains of family, ethnic, and religious group are significant as places where differing food habits are acceptable. Festivals and other public and private celebrations are also acceptable places to display food distinctiveness. Women's magazines, particularly around holiday times, exploit the rich repertoire of ethnic and nationality foods in their glossy pages. Nationality restaurants provide another public setting in which tasting foods of others is acceptable, and food fads such as French cooking or the Chinese wok craze encourage people to incorporate the food of other nations into their own repertoires.[43]

The new acceptance and visibility of ethnicity in the late 1960s and 1970s give some public sanction to what people have been doing all along—eating what they are comfortable eating. But encountering the foods of new groups such as the Vietnamese, or moving to a new area and finding new foods and not finding old foods, remind us that eating is a highly emotionally charged activity. We are led again to the questions of why people eat ethnic foods, and why these traditions may be maintained over many generations or given up by some immigrants and ethnics. In other words, we are led to examine the meaning of food, its symbolic nature, and the communication and performance aspects of food choices.

The Symbolic Nature of Food in Establishing Group Identity

Foodways can be charged with emotion and significance for both old and new Americans because food is potentially a symbol of ethnic identity. Recent scholarship on ethnicity has helped to refocus the conceptualization of the ethnic group from the idea of "thingness" to the idea of "process." We are now not so much concerned with defining ethnicity as a category whose characteristics and traits we want to list, but as a social process in which the relationship of individuals and groups and the communication of identity are significant.[44]

Frederik Barth sees ethnic groups as a form of social organization for which the significant characteristic is self-ascription or ascription by others of membership in the group: "A categorical ascription is an ethnic ascription when it classifies a person in terms of his basic, most general identity, presumptively determined by his origin and background. To the extent that actors use ethnic identities to categorize themselves and others for purposes of interaction, they form ethnic groups in this organizational sense."[45]

He urges taking into account what the actors see as significant, since "some cultural features are used by the actors as signals and emblems of differences; others are ignored." Barth sees the cultural content of ethnic dichotomies as being of two kinds: 1) "overt signals or signs—the diacritical features that people look for and exhibit to show identity, often such features as dress, language, house-form, or general style of life"; and 2) "basic value orientations: the standards of morality and excellence by which performance is judged."[46]

Barth argues that the nature of the continuity of ethnic groups depends on the maintenance of boundaries between groups. The cultural features used as signals of these boundaries may change form and content, just as the personnel of the groups can change, without damaging boundary maintenance. But in order for ethnic groups to perpetuate themselves when in contact with other groups, they not only need "signals for identification, but also a structuring of interaction which allows the persistence of cultural differences." This structuring Barth calls the rules that govern inter-ethnic relations. His work helps us focus on the processes of ethnic group identification and on the communication of that identity through the manipulation of symbols in certain settings and by following rules of group interaction—in other words, through performance.[47]

Another anthropologist, Abner Cohen, who defines the central theoretical problem of cultural anthropology as the dialectical relations between symbolic action and power relationships, offers us further insights into the processes of ethnicity and performance.[48] He defines the kinds of symbols he is discussing as: "objects, acts, concepts, or linguistic formations that stand *ambiguously* for a multiplicity of disparate meanings, evoke sentiments and emotions, and impel men to action. They usually occur in stylized patterns of activities like ceremonial, ritual, gift exchange, prescribed forms of joking, taking an oath, eating and drinking together."[49]

Such symbols operate to help the individual develop a sense of selfhood and to confront human problems such as life and death, and thus are both expressive and instrumental. The symbol system is flexible in that symbols can be replaced, different symbols can perform the same function, and the same symbol can change its function. What looks like continuity of symbols may upon close analysis reveal old forms being used to meet new needs.[50]

One of the most important functions for such symbols is the "objectification" of relationships between individuals and groups. Social relationships are developed and maintained by symbols, and thus we tend to *see* groups through their symbols and to identify ourselves through symbols. To Cohen, "all social behavior is couched in symbolic forms," and "symbolic behavior is dramatic behavior."[51] Cohen seconds Barth's injunction that we must examine the symbol system and its performance to understand the symbolic strategies of group organization. Informal groups in particular, of which ethnic groups are one type, use symbolic forms to define their identity and distinctiveness. Cohen outlines five types of symbolic forms informal groups use: mythologies of descent, alliance under female symbolism, ritual beliefs and practices, moral exclusiveness, and style of life.[52] These symbolic forms are not merely strategies of distinctiveness, however; they are also strategies for communication.

For example, in the ethnic group parts of traditional culture will be exploited "to articulate informal organizational functions that are used in the struggle of these groups for power within the framework of formal organization" since ethnic groups are part of a larger population competing within the framework of the nation.[53] Cultural identity is the major symbol of the ethnic group's distinctiveness, but it also operates as a channel for communication. It helps

in articulating an authority structure by mobilizing kinship, friendship and religious obligations in support of an informal authority agency. Similarly, the hierarchies within religious congregations and organs for welfare and mutual help can become vehicles for the routinization of decision-making procedures. The symbols providing these organizational mechanisms are ideologically integrated within such mottoes as "our customs are different," "the sacredness of our traditions," and so on. The ideology is further elaborated to cover a narrative "historical" account of the origin, the goings and comings of the group. Finally, through the continual observance of the customs and ceremonies peculiar to the group, the members are continually socialized in the culture of the group.[54]

Cohen sees the preservation of such traditions as part of a healthy social process. They are not a matter of conservatism versus modernism, but dynamic organizational mechanisms.[55]

Studies of ethnicity such as Barth's and Cohen's urge us to examine the symbolic use of traditional culture for a greater understanding of the processes by which ethnic groups form, reform, and maintain themselves and how group and individual ethnic identity is communicated to in-group and out-group members by means of symbol and performance. Foodways are one of many aspects of ethnic traditional culture which can be studied as a communicative or semiotic system much as language is studied. The term *semiotics* refers to the study of signs and symbols including linguistic and para-linguistic communication, what Margaret Mead calls the study of "patterned communications in all modalities."[56]

It is within this framework that Mary Douglas tells us that "if food is treated as a code, the message it encodes will be found in the pattern of social relations being expressed. The message is about different degrees of hierarchy, inclusion and exclusion, boundaries and transactions across the boundaries. . . . Food categories therefore encode social events."[57] This is true because of the relationship between a system such as foodways and other ordered systems associated with it in the culture. Douglas argues that a system such as food habits and taboos may operate symbolically or analogously to communicate or reflect the "boundaries between categories of people."[58] Hortense Powdermaker suggests similar ideas about the relationship between food and group: "The communal eating of food and customs concerning it may be said to have a double social function: (1) to maintain the cohesion of the society and of groups within it; (2) to determine, in part, the relation of the individual to the society and to the smaller groups within it."[59]

As we work towards an understanding of how foodways come actually to symbolize a group, we can begin with the idea suggested by Douglas and Powdermaker that food is related to social boundaries. We see this quite clearly when presented with the foods of strangers. Generally, we humans accept food most readily from our friends and allies and fear the food of strangers.[60] In his discussion of prejudice, Gordon Allport points out that familiarity gives humans the sense of goodness, and strangeness evokes a sense of wrongness or evil. Habituation lessens the fear of the strange in a short time, but humans still have an initial hesitant reaction to strangeness. It seems logical to us that visible differences imply real differences. Such differences as skin color, language, religious practices, and food habits give people visibility and identifiability, and hence a group may seek to hide such signs or to maintain them depending on its desire to remain visible or invisible.[61] The Tibetans of the Kansu-Tibetan border, who connect foodways with religious affiliation, ask of strangers, "Is their mouth the same as ours or is it like the mouth of the Moslems, or do they have some other mouth?"[62] A group's eating habits is one clue to which side of the boundary the strangers should be placed. Strange "food habits set the group apart from the community as a whole," for although we accept minor modifications of the community's eating patterns as an expression of individuality, major diversions from the norm are seen as an attack on the community and its sense of unity.[63] The use or avoidance of certain foods becomes identified with a group and symbolic of it. Such symbolic foodways may strengthen the group's internal ties or indicate out-group status. In other words, foodways help mark existing social boundaries and, depending upon one's viewpoint and focus, inclusion within or exclusion from a group. Any part of the pattern of eating may operate in this manner. For example, as Mary Douglas points out: "Drinks are for strangers, acquaintances, workmen and family. Meals are for family, close friends, honored guests. The grand operator of the system is the line between intimacy and distance."[64]

The sense of inclusion is described by scholars in different ways. Kurt Lewin and Miriam Lowenberg say that food and eating create a feeling of group *belongingness*.[65] Hortense Powdermaker refers to the *cohesion* that eating together creates for group and family, and J.C. McKenzie uses the terms *"community integration"* and *"social well-being."*[66] Margaret Cussler and Mary de Give suggest eating together implies *"a kind of kinship."*[67] Whatever we call it, this sense of unity with family or other group members is so important in many cultures that people will suffer some hardship and discomfort to attain it. Efforts to supply Greeks during World War II with a daily hot meal failed when it was discovered that they preferred to eat their soup cold but with their families at home rather than eat it hot in an institutional setting. Similarly, many Americans expend considerable effort to share a symbolic meal with family on Thanksgiving, Easter, or Christmas.[68] Barre Toelken describes how the celebration of Thanksgiving binds one American family to each other and to their rural past.[69] The sense of unity created by sharing food is so significant and recognizable that it figures centrally in many rites of inclusion. For example, the American bride and groom symbolically feed each other pieces of the wedding cake before sharing the cake with their guests.[70] Food can even be used to link distant family members, as when food packages are sent to children at college or to family members in the armed services. The sending of food is so common at Christmastime in the U.S. that recipes for Christmas cookies often include information on how well they travel and keep.

So strong is the unifying ability of shared food and foodways that it can operate not only between members of the group that are separated geographically but even between those separated by death. It is the practice in some countries to leave food for the dead who are thought to return on All Souls Day.[71] Some Mexicans leave a burning candle, sweets, and toys for the soul of the dead child. Altars or *ofrendas* to adult departed will also be set up with candles, flowers, incense, and fruits and foods of all kinds, especially those the person was fond of during his or her life.[72] The Vietnamese also cook favorite foods of the departed on the anniversary of their deaths and leave them on the altar to the ancestors in the home. Phyllis Williams tells us of another time that food is left for the dead. In Italy some people thought that the soul of the departed person did not vacate the home immediately and the survivors left a loaf of bread and a candle near an open door for three days after the death, when the soul was believed to settle. Some funeral practices involve providing food to sustain the dead person. Williams describes an Italian-American family filling a child's coffin with Jordan almonds as food for the next life.[73] In each of these examples, food is still thought of as necessary for the dead, and the living feel a responsibility to fill that need. Thus, the dead are still included in the group. It is also a common practice in many funeral ceremonies to provide food for the bereaved family and for guests who come to the funeral or to the family's home to express condolences. This eating ties the living together. The living eat "to keep up their strength," perhaps as a celebration of their living status. The group plays a part in making sure the living go on supporting life. Eating at such a time is a celebration of life in the face of death.

This kind of celebration of life occurs at All Souls Day in some countries. The English eat "soul cakes"; the Italians eat a pastry called *fave dei morti* (beans of the dead); and the Mexicans eat *panes de muertos* (bread of the dead), as well as sweets in the shape of coffins, skeletons, and such during the celebration of this holiday. They are symbolically consuming death, thus celebrating the fact that they are living. But they are also symbolically expressing an acceptance of death and union with dead friends and family.[74]

The functions of inclusion and exclusion are two sides of the same coin: to include only certain members in a group is necessarily to exclude all others. Mark Graubard quotes a Canadian farmer who classified all food into two groups: "'Fit to eat,' and 'the Injuns ate that.'"[75] Cultural groups and subgroups make a basic distinction between what they eat and what others eat, and the distinction may be used as a symbolic expression of the exclusion of other groups. The group may refuse to eat food associated with the other group even when it is not forbidden. These distinctions may become formalized by religion or custom.[76]

Besides indicating inclusion or exclusion from a group, the food code can also be used to express rank or hierarchy within groups and between them. Eating together or eating similar foods in similar ways is an expression of equality, which is why integrating restaurants was so important in the early Civil Rights movement in the United States.[77] Reserving certain special foods for a favored group as the Nazis did when they kept foods like citrus fruit out of the hands of such lower-status groups as Poles and Jews[78] would clearly indicate a lack of equality. Frederick Simoons suggests that reserving some foods for a favored few may be the origin of many food taboos.[79] In any event, we do not need to look far to see that certain foods and kinds of food preparation and service are associated with different castes and classes of people, with the rich or the poor.[80] Food differences may also express the differing rank of the sexes (with women usually ranked below men), of different ages (with children ranked below adults), and different locations (with rural foods usually, but not always, ranked below urban).[81]

A change in eating habits could thus be used to signal a change in status, usually from a less to a more desirable group.[82] Children adopt adult foods to signal their leaving childhood behind; people adopt the foods of sophisticated groups to appear more worldly.[83] In the second half of the nineteenth century in the United States, the poor and working classes often imitated the food habits of the wealthy even at the expense of adequate nutrition.[84] Non-Western people adopt Western foods and food prejudices to indicate that they are progressive and civilized, and immigrants adopt the foods of their new land to indicate a shift in status.[85] Kurt Lewin points out that status was an important value in food selection during World War II and that Americans were coerced into eating kidneys, a nutritious but unappealing food to them, by enhancing its status with descriptions of its preparation and consumption in England, considered a high-status country by many Americans.[86]

Foods also change status as the people and groups associated with them change. Jitsuichi Masuoka describes how Japanese immigrants in Hawaii were able to afford many of the Japanese high-status foods because of greater wealth, but as these same foods began to be associated with the old country they lost status. The money was spent instead on American foods that had become more desirable in rank.[87] Miriam Lowenberg and others suggest that once one has attained high status or a strong sense of identity and satisfaction with present status, one can afford to eat low-status foods.[88]

The Communication of the Food Code in Across-Group Interactions

Another aspect of the communication of the food code is across-group interactions. At a symbolic level, eating foods across groups suggests crossing or even breaking down social boundaries. David Gottlieb reports that a study of armed service personnel aboard ship showed that they demanded foods similar to those of the countries and ports where they were taking shore leave, but did not want these foods at other times. They wanted teriyaki and sukiyaki when in Japan, but in South Carolina they requested hush puppies and black-eyed peas.[89] Army personnel also tend to adopt the food of the land in which they are stationed.[90]

In a wartime report on the Common Council for American Unity's plan to introduce the foods of different ethnic groups to Americans and spread the nutrition gospel, the following description is given of what happens at a food lecture tasting party:

> But toward the end of the meeting there was a noticeable stir. The audience milled around a table laden with samples of food — strange food, but tempting. It was being offered as the simplest way of explaining some of the concrete contributions the foreign-born housewife can make to the solution of the problems of the general American housewife in wartime.
>
> The exciting thing that was happening, however, was not just the food itself, but the sudden warmth of atmosphere that had been created among the most unlikely fraternalists. A Polish-American club woman and a thirteenth-generation member of American society tasted with interest a Russian dish now known as the stand-by of the Soviet Armies as well as of Russia's civilian population. An Italian-American welfare worker compared notes with the maker of a Czech lentil soup that could feed a family of six for sixteen cents. Food apparently was food and knew no political distinctions. Thus was born what was to develop into the pattern for a down-to-earth program to promote understanding among the varied peoples that compose New York City.[91]

We can all probably think of circumstances when reaching across social boundaries was desirable and was symbolized by eating the foods of another group. Festivals that celebrate American cultural pluralism are often characterized by the availability of a variety of ethnic foods.

The opposite is also true. Richard Dorson tells of a Black informant who had tasted Mexican food and liked it but stopped eating it when friends told her that tacos were made with meat from dead cats.[92] Clearly in her community this was a line she should not cross. Food, then, may be used to express tensions across cultural boundaries. Margaret Cussler and Mary de Give found "among White attitudes towards Negroes the prevalent belief that Negroes do not need as much to eat or to live on as the Whites, and are less discriminating in their choice of food." One of the informants claimed: "Some niggers never think about anything but corn bread half-cooked, and syrup. Up there where we used to live, the niggers eat kidneys — Daddy said the niggers saved everything about a hog but the squeal. They eat fat-back three times a day and this ole poke salat. Sometimes we cook it in a big pot and feed it to the pig. They just don't have milk and butter. Them niggers don't have stuff like that."[93]

Misinformation and stereotypes about other groups' foods is one symbol of cross-group tension; real or purported lack of knowledge is another. When R. M. Pangborn and C. M. Bruhn tested three groups (adults in food services, college students, Anglo- and Mexican-American migrant workers) on their knowledge and concepts of the food habits of other ethnic groups, they found that socio-economic and cultural backgrounds influence people's knowledge of foods eaten by others. Although older, more-travelled, better-educated Americans tended to have more knowledge of food habits across cultural lines, these criteria by no means assured such knowledge and, in general, the findings showed "only casual awareness of foods eaten by people of other cultures." The food lines paralleled cultural barrier lines as revealed in the following comments of Anglo migrant workers who were questioned on their knowledge of Negro foods, to which they had been exposed while working in southern states: "Their relative unfamiliarity with Negro eating patterns probably derived from mutual distrust; when asked about Negro foods, some Anglos said, 'That's a sore subject,' or 'We don't associate with them.'"[94]

Using folk recipes as a way of measuring intercultural penetration in a small Kansas town with three major ethnic groups, Marjorie Sackett also found little knowledge of the groups' foodways changing hands, except in the cases of intermarriage and not always then. Her conclusion is that "each ethnic group in Concordia maintains fairly rigid lines of demarcation."[95] McKenzie suggests that such lines are likely to remain rigid in the case of immigrants because people hesitate to visit or entertain immigrants since they are afraid of what will be served to eat in the immigrant's home or confused about what to serve if the immigrant visits their home.[96]

Margaret Mead suggests that the fear of the strange foodways of the various ethnic groups in our plural society may explain the uniformly tasteless foods we find in American public eating places:

Culturally standardized objections to complex food dishes in which the constituents cannot be identified may also be referred to the situation in which people with very widely different food habits have found themselves in close association with each other, dependent upon alien cooking, alien serving, alien ownership and management of food distributing agencies. An investigation conducted by the Committee [on Changing Food Habits] into ways in which emergency feeding could make maximum allowance for cultural differences in food habits showed that the most practical way of avoiding giving offense to anyone in a mixed group is to cook single foods with a minimum of seasoning and serve all condiments separately. Contemporary cafeteria procedures in America and the large development of self-selected types of meals are an example of a social institution which is adapted to a variety of mutually incompatible food habits. It is probable that many other characteristic American attitudes toward foods, including taboos on all subjects which may arouse disgust during eating, may be referred to the experience of different mutually unacceptable food patterns.[97]

A Washington, D.C., restaurant specializing in smoked meats and fish which serves the meat plain with a choice of four sauces (Southern and Texas-style barbecue sauces of various degrees of hotness) is an example of the sort of compromise made in the public arena to which Mead refers. It may be that Roy Rogers' hamburger "fixings" bar is symbolic of our society's attempts to deal with its multi-cultural situation.

Because foodways encode so much about social events and interactions and the groups involved in them, specific foodways often come to be associated closely with the groups that practice them. To insiders and to outsiders, foodways may symbolize both a group and attitudes toward that group. Jerry Della Femina, in describing cooking in his neighborhood, gives a clear picture of how ethnic group membership is communicated by foodways:

We ate either at our house, or Cousin Ronnie's, or Uncle Dom's or wherever. My grandmother would start making her meat sauce at seven in the morning on Sunday and within five or six hours that smell would be all through the house, covering everything — clothing, furniture, appliances — and then it would go out the front door and into the streets, to mix with the aroma of neighboring meat sauces. Except that, for some reason, we didn't call them "sauces"; we called them "gravies" rather than "sauces." I could enter the neighborhood at one end and sample the air quality of the gravy, and the odds were that it would be about the same at the other end of the neighborhood, with the exception of the Sicilians, who were strange in just about every other department, too. They were much more violent than the Neapolitans and as far as their dialect went, we couldn't understand a word they were saying. They ate weird things; at least we Neapolitans thought so. They ate macaroni with pumpkin, and who the hell would do something like that?[98]

Arthur Berger argues that certain kinds of drinks can be associated with cultural, national, or geographical groups. For example, Mediterraneans drink wine and coffee, and Atlantic peoples drink beer and coffee, except for the British who drink beer and tea. Coca-Cola, however, represents America, and drinking it involves making a statement about being American, or like Americans, and thus progressive.[99]

The association of a group with a particular food is a common process which can have positive or negative value depending on the situation and the person or persons passing judgment. Often foods associated with particular groups are negatively valued and thus condemned as part of a stereotype. During the First World War, British, French, and Germans were stereotyped as "Limeys," "Frogs," and "Krauts."[100] Mark Graubard tells us that during the Nazi regime in Germany, garlic was associated with the Jewish people: "Buttons with a picture of the garlic plant or its name [were] worn by many Hitlerites to prove their ardent hatred of the people garlic [was] meant to symbolize. The mere mention of garlic by a Nazi orator [caused] the crowd to howl with fury and hatred."[101]

Symbolic Manipulation of Foodways to Make Statements About Identity

Since foodways operate at a symbolic level to communicate information about group membership, status, boundaries, and so on, they would be an obvious choice for symbolic manipulation by individuals and groups who wished, consciously or unconsciously, to make a statement about identity. As Molly Schuchat says of ethnic groups in the United States, "it can be seen that food style is not based on geography and/or economics alone, but becomes a means of self-identity as well as a group-membership card. In other words, people tend to eat as they would like to be perceived, so that it is as much a matter of 'you eat what you wish to be' as of 'you are what you eat.'"[102] Foodways provide a whole area of performance in which statements of identity can be made — in preparing, eating, serving, forbidding, and talking about food.

Miriam Lowenberg suggests that the adoption of certain eating patterns can make a political statement. For example, the eating of organic foods by some groups in the United States has operated as a protest against mainstream culture and a political and economic system that, by relying on chemical fertilizers and preservatives, puts profit and convenience ahead of ecology and people.[103] John Leo makes a similar point when he suggests that the adoption of vegetarianism by American youth is an example of using food to act out the generational battle.[104] Black Muslims reject certain foods that they associate with negative aspects of Black history in America. If foodways communicate about people, then people may use foodways to communicate about themselves.

Foodways are an especially significant symbol in the communication of statements about ethnic identity in the United States—about links with ethnicity and denial of it. We have already seen how foodways operate in general as symbols or signals of group and individual identity to in- and out-group members and how foodways are an especially potent symbol for making identity statements. Two other aspects of the foodways-ethnicity relationship make it one of the most commonly used semiotic systems for communications about ethnic identity: it is relatively safe, and it is relatively easy to use.

As in the case of the Vietnamese, ethnic food peculiarities are not always sanctioned by other groups in America, but our history is generally one of adopting and adapting ethnic foodways. The plurality of our cooking has been celebrated as itself symbolic of "Americanism." In times of security, diversity in foodways is accepted and even encouraged. Food seems of little consequence when measured against religious, political, or racial differences. In times of insecurity, of course, the power of this symbol is reflected in our hostile attitude, e.g. towards German and Japanese foods during the Second World War.

Waverly Root and Richard de Rochemont point to an important aspect of America's culinary pluralism when they argue that ethnic foods did not "melt" into mainstream "American" cooking, which remains basically Anglo. Only Dutch and German cooking truly integrated with the Anglo tradition. Their comment on the rich ethnic food traditions of New York is that "each of the foreign cuisines available in New York remains isolated in its own context. They do not borrow from one another; they do not merge their separate styles into a common amalgam." Despite some examples of such mergers as in Tex-Mex and Creole cooking, this generalization applies to all American food.[105] The plurality of American food, then, is such that we may cook and eat a variety of ethnic foods, if we so choose, because ethnic food traditions remain strong and viable in their isolation. Their very separateness from each other and mainstream American food is one reason for their usefulness as symbols.

Many ethnic foodways are practiced in the private domain, among family members or in-group members, in the home, the neighborhood, the church hall, or at special in-group functions. This makes them safe symbols of identity for kin and group members to manipulate. Certain public arenas and times have also developed in our history as safe for the public display of ethnic foodways differences, e.g. holidays, restaurants, and festivals.

For a number of reasons, ethnic foodways are accessible to almost anyone who is interested in ethnic identity. Beliefs about food, reci-

pes, and food customs are easily transported across geographical boundaries. Foodways are adaptive to new food sources and technology.[106]
Even if recipes or customs have been forgotten, the bearers of the tradition are hardly small in number. The third- or fourth-generation
ethnic whose parents may have — or claim to have — forgotten how to
make a special food, has a wide range of resources, both living and
printed, from which to get the needed information. As Molly Schuchat points out, no great talents are needed for cooking and certainly
not for eating. This is not to say that there are not especially talented
cooks recognized and respected by their communities, but "learning
to cook in specialized fashion is far easier than learning to embroider
intricate patterns. And casseroles and cakes are more quickly made
than pottery. So the preparation and presentation of food becomes
among the most accessible of crafts."[107] The authenticity of recipes
and other foodways is not as important as the fact of making what
is a recognizably ethnic dish. "Practitioners of ethnic cookery have
developed substitutes, or significant modifications, which are acceptable because the use of the food so presented is symbolic. Therefore
one does not have to be authentic to be ethnic."[108]

Liking ethnic food or actually eating it is not necessary to make
a statement about ethnic identity. Among the Swedes in America a
tradition of stories, complaints, and tall tales has grown up around
certain ethnic dishes which are considered inedible by many in-group
members. *Lefse,* a kind of potato pancake, is said to be so tasteless
that many mistakenly eat the paper doily under a stack and do not
know the difference. *Lutefisk* (lye fish) is another food for which many
comic recipes are given, none of which really renders it edible. By
knowing and telling the joking traditions surrounding these foods, individuals can make ethnic identity statements even if the food is not
appealing to them.

Communicative Messages of Foodways in the Performance of Identity

The performance of ethnic identity in America can be divided
into three types, or three communicative messages. First, immigrants
may wish to express the adoption of "Americanism" and the partial
or total rejection of their ethnic immigrant identity. Second, immigrants or ethnics may wish to communicate maintenance or the adoption of ethnicity. Third, immigrants, ethnics, or non-ethnics may wish
to communicate acceptance of the pluralistic aspect of American identity and underline intergroup harmony in the United States. Each

of these types of ethnic statements may be made with varying degrees of self-consciousness. Each may be made in the private or public domain, as a communication to the self or in-group, or as a communication to the out-group.

An example of the first communicative message is revealed in the symbolic weight of foodways to immigrants in Jitsuichi Masuoka's thorough study of the changes in foodways of Japanese living in Hawaii for thirty to forty years. One change he focuses upon is the adoption of American foods and eating habits, which he sees as encouraged by the public school education of the Nisei (the first generation born in America), an education that results in the wider participation of this generation in the American way of life. In the following comments taken from a personal document and translated into English, a member of the Issei (the generation born in Japan) comments on the Americanization of the younger generation in such a way as to link American identity and American foodways:

I don't say much to my children. I know that they know and understand about America better than I. My children tell their mother what foods are good for our health. They say that we must eat more vegetables and fruits and less rice. They learn this in school—American school, I mean. I believe that their teachers are better informed along this line so I do not interfere nor ignore their suggestions. I believe firmly that the children should obey their teachers.
Judging from what my children tell me, nearly all the ideas that the *Issei* have are greatly different from what they learn in the school. It is impossible for us, *Issei,* to become Americanized and act and talk like *haoles* (white people in Hawaii are called *haoles*). We have "old heads" or set minds. Even though we know that we should be Americanized, since we intend to stay here for good, we cannot. But, we know that our children could because they know how to talk *haole* language and associate with them more freely. When we pass away, we are sure that they become Americanized.[109]

For most Americans who have made a conscious or not-so-conscious choice to be ethnic, or adopt or accept the ethnic role as one of their identity markers, ethnic food has a second communicative message; it is a symbol that can convey their choice of an ethnic role to in- and out-group members. Ethnic foods may be cooked in the home every day or for special days such as holidays and family get-togethers. Ethnic food may be made outside the home in restaurants or businesses to earn a living; or it can be prepared in church halls and other places for special events, such as a church function or festival. Ethnic food may be eaten in public or private whether one makes it oneself or buys it. Modern technology has made it easy for people to get and eat ethnic foods that are difficult or time-consuming to make. Depending on where one lives, *pierogi,* spring rolls, or blintzes may be in the freezer case of the local grocery store.

Like members of other ethnic groups that have migrated to the United States and groups facing maintenance of identity in a world shaped by Western technology, the Vietnamese refugees have had to make adjustments in their food habits. Many foods are difficult or time-consuming to prepare in the home, and working mothers and the busy schedule of jobs and schooling make it impossible to serve them every day. A Vietnamese restaurant owner says that a large percentage of her customers are other Vietnamese who find this the most convenient way to get familiar foods. On Saturday mornings, especially, her place is crowded with Vietnamese who want a traditional breakfast of soup and other delicacies. Several businesses have grown up in the Washington, D.C., area to provide prepared foods such as *cha gio* (spring rolls) and *chalua* (a meat paté). These are sold in local Vietnamese groceries. The owner of another business told a gathering at a demonstration of some of her products that in Vietnam her family had made shrimp chips in a form that could be fried at home. The Vietnamese liked the taste of the home-fried chips. But in the United States this product did not sell very well because no one had time for the elaborate preparation, so the company now markets the chips already fried. Community groups and religious groups can also supply special foods that individuals do not have time or talent to make. The Vietnamese, for example, sell or provide appropriate holiday foods at Tet (New Year) and at the Mid-Autumn Festival, wherever the community gathers to celebrate these holidays. Another way to solve the food problem is for particular members of a family who have the time or skill to provide food items for the rest of the family. In one Vietnamese home, two family members made the special Tet rice cake, *Banh Chung,* and a niece of the family made the crystalized fruit flowers that are also traditional at this time of the year. The rest of the family could share the food without having to make it themselves.

In front of a church in Youngstown, Ohio, a sign appears on alternate weeks that announces simply "Pierogi This Friday" (on the other week the sign reads "Pray for Peace"). Very early on that Friday morning a group of Slovak women gathers to make and sell freshly made *pierogi.* All over the country similar church and secular organizations produce special ethnic foods for other members of their communities. In a sense they are specialists, perhaps even *ritual specialists,* in this aspect of their traditional culture. As Elizabeth Goldstein and Gail Green point out about a similar group in New York state, such women are expressing their cultural identity through this activity: "These foods carry cultural and ethnic associations. Likewise the work itself is an act of symbolic as well as culinary significance for the ladies. Through their labor they express and affirm the values which have shaped their lives." The women of St. Mary's parish, by making *pierogi* and *babka,* are communicating their own "cultural stance" and thus acting as examples, or "surrogate grandmothers" to a community of customers to whom they give not only food but a sense of their own values. "The women of St. Mary's make available to customers, young and old, participation in an ethnic tradition through the ordinary yet unique work of cooking."[110]

· In her discussion of Greek Americans, Janet Theophano points out that foodways create a bond among community members who are far apart. Food links people across space and time, so that it helps create a bond with past members of the group as well as between living ones.[111] Festival and holiday foods are especially important in this way since not all members of the ethnic group will eat Greek foods every day, but most will on these special occasions.

The fasts and feasts of the church calendar mark a departure from secular time and a merger with the myths and the sacred. They are also social events which constitute and order the community. The choice of Greek cuisine and foodstuffs to mark these occasions is not without significance. At once an expression of religious piety and shared identity and community, the sumptuous and elaborate display of food in America is imbued with new meaning. That meaning involves the bond of a shared past and importantly a shared present.[112]

Foodways help the Greek community "underline its communal and historical unity" during ritual and festive events and thus are an important symbol of that unity.

A recent national television news program describing the celebration of the fourth of July by Vietnamese refugees now living in Georgia commented that the family's picnic was typical of the American holiday—with the exception that they were eating noodles instead of potato salad and roast chicken instead of hot dogs. The commentator reflects Americans' attitudes toward the new refugees, a sense that in some ways they have not yet learned to be part of us. In time, the Vietnamese may learn to eat potato salad and hot dogs, on July 4th at least. However, it is just as likely that their fellow Americans will try Vietnamese noodles and roast chicken, for the third important use of ethnic foodways is to make a statement about the acceptance and acceptability of the idea of American pluralism.

The idea that America can and does accept food from its many different groups is a common notion, reflected in the conceit that the real American "melting pot" is actually a stewpot. Articles on ethnic foods in popular magazines and eclectic cookbooks are places where this notion might typically be expressed. The following quotation from Walter Oleksy's *The Old Country Cookbook* expresses the idea in an international framework: "I like to think that there is another Common Market at work in the world, not only in Europe. It is the marketplace of the breadbasket; the *dining* table at which men of all national origins can sit in brotherhood and share the land's bounty." [113]

Waverly Root and Richard de Rochemont point out that many of our so-called ethnic foods were actually invented in America, but such foods as cioppino, chili con carne, Swiss steak, Russian dressing, chow mein, and vichyssoise give the American food vocabulary an international flavor. [114]

Another way that food is used to underline the plurality and simultaneous unity of Americans is to point out that "American" food is ethnically derived. Thus, we are likely to run into a popular media reminder that the all-American hot dog, pizza, taco or what-have-you has ethnic origins. [115] The very processes of Americanizing ethnic foods and ethnicizing American foods parallel what happens to the immigrant groups that come to this country. For example, Marc Tull's discussion of Kosher brownies shows us how a popular American dessert has been incorporated into the special diet of Jewish Passover. [116]

Americans seem to take comfort from these notions, as they do from the idea that although ethnic foods may seem strange at first, one can actually find many similarities between them and more familiar foods or among various ethnic foods. Bread is a common example selected; the staff of life may take many forms, but there is some essential "breadness" that links them all. [117] Or the similarities between foods such as *pierogi, wanto,* and *kreplach,* all dough wrapped around filling of some sort and boiled, might be pointed out. This "strange but similar" image parallels our "plural but unified" sense of American culture. The fact that the foods may not be all that different reassures us that we can remain one people despite superficial differences.

The idea that even the differences in foods are paralleled by a level of similarities is a comfort too, in that it suggests foodways as a channel for communication that is available when others may not be. Americans set aside certain times and places for tasting food across cultural boundaries and thus experiment with crossing those boundaries in a very safe manner. Restaurants and festivals offer two such arenas. Many people who attend festivals delight in experimenting with the various types of food offered and even mixing them on one plate. At one multi-ethnic festival, the Polish and Black food booths were next to each other. One Black man was heard to tell a customer he was serving to be sure and try his "Polish" hot sauce on the chittlins. This was his way of acknowledging his Polish neighbors and expressing a sense of unity with them. Politicians who have themselves photographed at festivals and ethnic celebrations eating various foods are manipulating the clear message that eating across ethnic boundaries communicates.

Although stories of the strange food habits of the Vietnamese and other new immigrants to our country express our fears of these new strangers, our acceptance of them is also being signalled by the fact that we are learning to eat their foods in restaurants and in our homes. Americans must eat the foods of all their ethnic groups, Americanizing them in some ways, because by this act we perform the sense of our national ethnic identity. By ingesting the foods of each new group, we symbolize the acceptance of each group and its culture.

NOTES

1. J.C. McKenzie, "Social and Economic Implications of Minority Food Habits," *Proceedings of the Nutrition Society* 26 (1967):200.

2. Joan Nathan, "The Venerable Soy Sauce from Vietnam," *The Washington Post*, 4 Oct. 1979; Abby Rayman, "Vietnamese Participant in Festival Grows Special Vegetables," Smithsonian Institution, Office of Public Affairs, Press Release, 13 Sept. 1979.

3. John W. Bennett, "Food and Social Status in a Rural Society," *American Sociological Review* 8 (1943):564.

4. Barre Toelken, *The Dynamics of Folklore* (Boston: Houghton Mifflin, 1979), 73.

5. Richard Osborn Cummings, *The American and His Food: A History of Food Habits in the United States* (Chicago: Univ. of Chicago Press, 1940), 11–12.

6. Waverly Root and Richard de Rochemont, *Eating in America, A History* (New York: Morrow, 1976), 276–312.

7. Margaret L. Arnott, "The Breads of Philadelphia: A Survey," *Ethnologia Europaea* 5 (1971):143, 147.

8. Don Yoder, "Folk Cookery," *Folklore and Folklife*, ed. Richard M. Dorson (Chicago: Univ. of Chicago Press, 1972), 334.

9. Don Yoder, "Historical Sources for American Foodways Research and Plans for an American Foodways Archives," *Ethnologia Scandinavica* 5 (1971):41–44.

10. S.A. Weinstock, "Some Factors that Retard or Accelerate the Rate of Acculturation with Specific Reference to Hungarian Immigrants," *Human Relations* 17 (1964):335.

11. Alberta B. Childs, "Some Dietary Studies of Poles, Mexicans, Italians, and Negroes," *Child Health Bulletin* 9 (1933):85; Magnus Pyke, *Man and Food* (New York: McGraw-Hill, 1970), 160; Frederick J. Simoons, *Eat Not This Flesh: Food Avoidance in the Old World* (Madison: Univ. of Wisconsin Press, 1963), 123–24.

12. Melford E. Spiro, "The Acculturation of American Ethnic Groups," *American Anthropologist* 57 (1955):1249–50.

13. N.D. Humphrey, "Some Dietary and Health Practices of Detroit Mexicans," *Journal of American Folklore* 58 (1945):255–56; Gregory Gizelis, "Foodways Acculturation in the Greek Community of Philadelphia," *Pennsylvania Folklife* (Winter 1970–1971):10; Jitsuichi Masuoka, "Changing Food Habits: The Japanese in Hawaii," *American Sociological Review* 10 (1945):765; Herbert Passin and John W. Bennett, "Social Process and Dietary Change," in *The Problem of Changing Food Habits*, National Research Council Bulletin No. 108 (Washington, D.C., Oct. 1943), 122; E.G. Stern, *My Mother and I* (New York: Macmillan, 1917), 79–80.

14. Gizelis, 12.

15. Arnott, 144.

16. Frederick C. Fliegel, *Food Habits and National Background*, Pennsylvania State University Agricultural Experimental Station Bulletin No. 684 (Univ. Park, Oct. 1961), 3–7.

17. Arnott, 147; Humphrey, 256; McKenzie, 200; Passin and Bennett, 122.

18. Gizelis, 12–13.

19. Simoons, 121.

20. Passin and Bennett, 122.

21. Simoons, 123–24.

22. Masuoka, 764. Also see Larry Danielson, "Swedish-American Mothers: Conservators of the Tradition" (paper delivered at the 1977 American Folklore Society Annual Meeting), and Dorothy Lee, "Folklore of the Greeks in America," *Folk-Lore* 47 (1936):294–310, for examples of women as conservators of traditional culture.

23. Masuoka, 763–64; McKenzie, 200.

24. Passin and Bennett, 113.

25. Masuoka, 763.

26. Humphrey, 256.

27. Cummings, 81–82, 91–110.

28. Ibid., 164.

29. Peter Roberts, *The New Immigration; A Study of the Industrial and Social Life of Southeastern Europeans in America* (New York: Macmillan, 1912), 96–98, 151.

30. Velma Phillips and Laura Howell, "Racial and Other Differences in Dietary Customs," *Journal of Home Economics* 41 (1920):396–411.

31. Phyllis Williams, *South Italian Folkways in Europe and America* (New Haven: Yale Univ. Press, 1938):51–66.

32. Childs; Dorothy L. Bovee and Jean Downes, "The Influence of Nutritional Education in Families of the Mulberry Area of New York City," *Milbank Memorial Fund Quarterly* 19 (1941):121–46.

33. Mark Graubard, *Man's Food, Its Rhyme and Reason* (New York: Macmillan, 1943), 7, 190.

34. Carl E. Guthe, "History of the Committee on Food Habits," in *The Problem of Changing Food Habits*, National Research Council Bulletin No. 108 (Washington, D.C., Oct. 1943), 9–19.

35. Margaret Mead, "The Problem of Changing Food Habits," in *The Problem of Changing Food Habits*, 21–25.

36. Committee on Food Habits, *The Problem of Changing Food Habits*, National Research Council Bulletin No. 108 (Washington, D.C., Oct. 1943); Committee on Food Habits, *Manual for the Study of Food Habits*, National Research Council Bulletin No. 111 (Washington, D.C., 1945); S. M. Benet and Natalie F. Joffe, *Some Central European Food Patterns and Their Relationship to Wartime Problems of Food and Nutrition* (Washington, D.C.: National Research Council Committee on Food Habits, 1943); Mary L.

de Give and Margaret T. Cussler, *Bibliography and Notes on German Food Patterns* (Washington, D.C.: National Research Council Committee on Food Habits, 1944); Natalie F. Joffe, "Food Habits of Selected Subcultures in the United States," in *The Problem of Changing Food Habits;* G. Gizzardini and Natalie F. Joffe, *Italian Food Patterns and Their Relationship to Wartime Problems of Food and Nutrition* (Washington, D.C.: National Research Council Committee on Food Habits, Aug. 1942); Svatava Pirkova-Jakobson and Natalie F. Joffe, *Some Central European Food Patterns and Their Relationship to Wartime Problems of Food and Nutrition: Czech and Slovak Food Patterns* (Washington, D.C.: National Research Council Committee on Food Habits, 1943); Natalie F. Joffe and T. T. Walker, *Some Food Patterns of Negroes in the United States of America and Their Relationship to Wartime Problems of Food and Nutrition* (Washington, D.C.: National Research Council Committee on Food Habits, 1944).

37. Common Council for American Unity, *What's Cooking in Your Neighbor's Pot* (New York: Common Council for American Unity, 1944).

38. Graubard, 194.

39. Margaret Mead, *Food Habits Research: Problems of the 1960s,* National Research Council Publication 1225 (Washington, D.C.: 1964); Margaret Mead, "The Changing Significance of Food," *American Science* 58 (1970):176–81.

40. For attempts at a single standard, see discussion in this book's essay by Judy Perkin and Stephanie F. McCann, "Food for Ethnic Americans: Is the Government Trying to Turn the Melting Pot into a One-Dish Dinner?"

41. Rose Marie Pangborn and Christine M. Bruhn, "Concepts of Food Habits of Other Ethnic Groups," *Journal of Nutrition Education* 2 (1971):106–10.

42. Pangborn and Bruhn, 106.

43. Yoder, "Folk Cookery," 335–36. Note the distinction between nationality foods—foods of other countries—and ethnic foods—foods related in some way to one's family's ethnic identity.

44. Wsevolod W. Isajiw, "Definition of Ethnicity," *Ethnicity* 1 (1974):111–24.

45. Frederik Barth, *Ethnic Groups and Boundaries* (Boston: Little, Brown, 1969), 13–14.

46. Ibid., 14.

47. Ibid., 16.

48. Abner Cohen, *Two-Dimensional Man: An Essay on the Anthropology of Power and Symbolism in Complex Society* (Berkeley: Univ. of California Press, 1944), 13–14.

49. Ibid., preface.

50. Ibid., preface, 29, 39.

51. Ibid., 30–34, 52.

52. Ibid., 69–75.

53. Ibid., 91–92.

54. Ibid., 98.

55. Ibid., 15.

56. Thomas A. Sebeok, Alfred S. Hayes, and Mary Catherine Bateson, eds., *Approaches to Semiotics,* Transactions of the Indiana University Conference on Paralinguistics and Kinesics (The Hague: Mouton, 1964), 5; Margaret Mead, "Vicissitudes of the Study of the Total Communication Process," in *Approaches to Semiotics,* 279.

57. Mary Douglas, "Deciphering a Meal," in *Myth, Symbol, and Culture,* ed. Clifford Geertz (New York: Norton, 1971), 61.

58. Douglas, "Deciphering a Meal," 80, 68.

59. Hortense Powdermaker, "Feasts in New Ireland: The Social Functions of Eating," *American Anthropologist* 34 (1932):236.

60. Harriet Bruce Moore, "The Meaning of Food," *American Journal of Clinical Nutrition* 5 (1957):78.

61. Gordon Allport, *The Nature of Prejudice* (Reading, Mass.: Addison-Wesley, 1954; rpt. Garden City, N.Y.: Doubleday Anchor Books, 1954): 128-30.

62. Simoons, 41.

63. McKenzie, 201.

64. Douglas, "Deciphering a Meal," 66.

65. Kurt Lewin, "Forces Behind Food Habits and Methods of Change," in *The Problem of Changing Food Habits,* National Research Council Bulletin No. 108 (Washington, D.C., Oct. 1943), 44; Miriam E. Lowenberg et al., *Food and Man* (2nd ed., New York: John Wiley, 1974), 150.

66. Powdermaker, 246-47; McKenzie, 209.

67. Margaret Cussler and Mary L. de Give, *Twixt the Cup and the Lip: Psychological and Sociocultural Factors Affecting Food Habits* (New York: Twayne, 1952), 32.

68. Dorothy Lee, "Cultural Factors in Dietary Choice," *American Journal of Clinical Nutrition* 5 (1957):166.

69. Toelken, 131-36. For further discussion of food and kinship see Audrey I. Richards, *Hunger and Work in a Savage Tribe; A Functional Study of Nutrition among the Southern Bantu* (Glencoe, Ill.: Free Press, 1948), 131-36; and James H. S. Bossard, "Family Table-Talk—An Area for Sociological Study," *American Sociological Review* (1943):295.

70. Lowenberg et al., 135.

71. Robert Jerome Smith, "Festivals and Celebrations," in *Folklore and Folklife, An Introduction,* ed. Richard M. Dorson (Chicago: Univ. of Chicago Press, 1972), 163.

72. Dorothy Gladys Spicer, *Feast-Day Cakes from Many Lands* (New York: Holt, Rinehart, and Winston, 1960), 105-107.

73. Williams, 201, 209.

74. Spicer, 99-107. For a discussion of "Sin-eating" and related practices which offer other examples of how, through food, a relationship between the living and dead members of the group is expressed see Sidney E. Hartland, "Sin-Eating," in *The Encyclopedia of Religion and Ethnics,* Vol. 9 (1908-1927 ed.), 272-76.

75. Graubard, 5.

76. Simoons, 41.

77. Lowenberg et al., 146.

78. Graubard, 15, 179, 191.

79. Simoons, 109-10, 115.

80. Lowenberg et al., 59, 974; Graubard, 11-12; Cussler and de Give, 63, 65, 70-72; Douglas, *Purity and Danger,* 151-52; Claude Levi-Strauss, "The Culinary Triangle," *Partisan Review* 33 (1966):590. For fuller discussion of the social strata of various communities, see Bennett, Passin and Bennett, and Cussler and de Give.

81. Powdermaker, 247; Cussler and de Give, 37; Simoons, 110; Cora DuBois, "Attitudes toward Food and Hunger in Alor," *Language, Culture and Personality,* ed. Leslie Spier et al. (Menasha, Wisc.: Sapir Memorial Publication Fund, 1941), 277; Moore, 82.

82. Simoons, 121.

83. Moore, 82.

84. Cummings, 80-81.

85. Simoons, 3-4.

86. Lewin, 44, 64.

87. Masuoka, 762-63.

88. Lowenberg et al., 118.

89. David Gottlieb, *A Bibliography and Bibliographic Review of Food and Food Habits Research* (Washington, D.C.: Quartermaster Food and Container Institute for the Armed Forces, 1958), 26–27.

90. Lowenberg et al., 144.

91. Common Council for American Unity, 1.

92. Richard M. Dorson, "Is There a Folk in the City?" *Journal of American Folklore* 83 (1970):212–213.

93. Cussler and de Give, 71.

94. Pangborn and Bruhn, 108.

95. Marjorie Sackett, "Folk Recipes as a Measure of Intercultural Penetration," *Journal of American Folklore* 85 (1972):80.

96. McKenzie, 202–203.

97. Mead, "Problems of Changing Food Habits," 23.

98. Jerry Della Femina and Charles Sopkin, *An Italian Grows in Brooklyn* (Boston: Little, Brown, 1978), 23.

99. Arthur A. Berger, "Soft Drinks and Hard Icons," in *Icons of Popular Culture*, ed. Marshall Fishwick and Ray B. Browne (Bowling Green, Ohio: Bowling Green Univ. Popular Press, 1970), 29, 32.

100. Simoons, 41.

101. Graubard, 142.

102. Molly Geiger Schuchat, *Hungarian Refugees in America and Their Counterparts in Hungary: The Interactions between Cosmopolitanism and Ethnicity* (Ph.D. diss., Catholic Univ. of America, 1971), 90.

103. Lowenberg et al., 146–47.

104. John Leo, "How to Beat the Beef Against Meat," *Time*, 5 Nov. 1979, 112.

105. Root and de Rochemont, 276–312.

106. See Gizelis on the adaptation of Greek foodways in America.

107. Schuchat, 102.

108. Ibid., 147; see also 123–24, 146.

109. Masuoka, 765.

110. Elizabeth Goldstein and Gail Green, "Pierogi- and Babka-Making at St. Mary's," *New York Folklore* 4, Nos. 1–4 (1978):71, 78.

111. Janet Theophano, "Feast, Fast, and Time," *Pennsylvania Folklife* (Spring 1978):25.

112. Ibid., 29.

113. Walter Oleksy, *The Old Country Cookbook* (Chicago: Nelson-Hall, 1974), xiv.

114. Root and de Rochemont, 276–78.

115. Ibid., 306.

116. Marc Tull, "Kosher Brownies for Passover," *New York Folklore* 4, Nos. 1–4 (1978):81–88.

117. Joan Nathan, "Festival of Breads," *The Washington Post*, 23 March 1980.

3

A Framework for the Analysis of Continuity and Change in Shared Sociocultural Rules for Food Use: The Italian-American Pattern

Judith Goode, Janet Theophano, and Karen Curtis

A systematic study of food systems promises to help us understand not only *what* people eat, but *why.* Several conceptual problems must be confronted in order to develop a common framework for description and analysis of the group-shared rules which govern food systems, to compare them and to observe changes within them. One conceptual problem centers on the process of identifying bounded (or relatively bounded) sociocultural units within which to study a food system. This is especially difficult in a complex, highly mobile society like America where groups based on class, age, region, and cultural origin are hard to delineate and where individuals move frequently among such groups. A second problem is separating, at least analytically, the group-shared, internally coherent, socially transmitted *cultural* patterns of food use from both the food usages which respond easily to external situational pressures (such as household income and activity patterns) and those which respond to idiosyncratic individual preferences. A third problem is defining the significant units and levels of analysis within a food system in order to describe and compare such systems.

After several years of studying the food systems of one American ethnic group, the Italian-Americans in Philadelphia, we have developed a framework for the analysis of a group-shared food system and its elements of continuity and change over time. We chose an ethnic group as the unit of analysis because one could expect to find elements of historical continuity in the food pattern within a group based on common cultural origin. We could thus have a base line for studying adaptive changes in the system. The project involved a comparison of two separate enclaves of Italian-Americans in the Philadelphia area. It also incorporated several different, complementary kinds of data.

The two enclaves differed in several ways, such as the nature of initial migration from Southern Italy, the nature of the host or receiving population in each area, and the type of occupational and political experience of the Italian-Americans in each context. The comparison enabled us to better understand the process of ethnic group formation and boundary maintenance over time. We could identify differences in the processes of boundary strengthening (social closure) and boundary permeability (open to outside influence), especially in relation to rules for food use. In this paper we are focusing on what was *shared* in both enclaves: the basic Italian-American pattern.[1]

Several techniques of data collection were used in this research. Formal interviews were used to identify the *ideal* shared food pattern among Italian-Americans. A clearly recognizable pattern emerged from these two-hour interviews in more than 200 households. Realizing a need to collect data on actual meals led us to use the technique of having informants keep diaries for a weekly period and for special feasts. We were also able to collect data based on long-term participant observation for at least one month in several households. Thus, we were able to observe the decision-making process involved in shopping and menu planning. This intensive data allowed us to develop an understanding of the process of *menu negotiation* in which the ideal group-shared system of rules interacts with external constraints (time, money, personal sensory preference) in order to produce actual meals.

Interviews are biased toward the past and misleading about actual behavior, but they did inform us of community consensus about appropriate food events. Meal diary data lead to the perception of widespread, idiosyncratic household variation and a lack of shared patterns. However, the use of both of these techniques in concert with direct observation of the process of menu negotiation provided a comprehensive view of the food system.

Before discussing our findings it is necessary to examine some frequently made assumptions about the relationship between food and ethnicity. It has long been assumed that ethnic or regional groups are the main locus of differentiated eating in the United States. The anthropological work done on food patterns during World War II assumed that ethnic groups were the logical locus of subgroup eating in America and thus focused on them as units of analysis.[2] This work was done when the kitchens of many households in the northeast United States were still headed by immigrant women, and the persistence of ethnicity as the primary basis of food habit differentiation was more appropriate than it is today. Other studies at that time, such as the work of Bennett and Cussler and DeGive, focused on regional and rural/urban distinctions as major sources of differentiation.[3]

Earlier research assumed that ethnic or regional food habits are very conservative. The argument is made that food habits are learned early, internalized strongly in intensive social and affective situations, and thus are persistent. Spiro goes so far as to say that food patterns are the last aspect of ethnicity to change.[4]

A contrary view states that ethnicity today may not play as significant a role in food patterning as in the past. While the common wisdom, often promulgated in the newspaper food section, still emphasizes ethnic differences, some recent studies have called attention to the decreasing significance of ethnicity. Jerome, for example, found that household ethnic identity was not significant in differentiating food habits (as measured by food frequencies) in Kansas City.[5] It is also frequently assumed that ethnic foods are now maintained only for special ritual occasions. The contradictory views of the decreasing significance of ethnicity to food choice on the one hand and the myth of ethnic persistence on the other can be ascribed to two basic views of contemporary American eating habits. Both are variations on a theme of acculturation and homogenization. First, American food systems can be seen as increasingly uniform and homogenized versions of a national pattern disseminated by a national system of food production, distribution, and media-generated demand. Uniformity of food availability is a concomitant of mass supermarket shopping and model meals and dietary preferences presented in magazines and on television.

However, in presenting mass-produced articles of "authentic" ethnic origin, the message is transmitted that there *are* vast differences in the cuisines of America. But each and every cuisine is available to all Americans in an almost literal melting pot. Restaurants purvey "authentic" cuisines (although in fact, the ethnic restaurant is far from a mirror of the typical food of a group). Mass producers of "Italian" sauces try to convince us that their products are genuine articles identical with the ethnic standard, when in fact there is no single taste, texture, or color uniformity in the sauces real Italian-Americans eat.

Birds-Eye "international" vegetables are advertised as so authentic that ethnic wives can deceive their husbands with them. The message is clear: all Americans can and should be sharing in the vast array of easily available ethnic foods. Demand is generated in a mass audience. In this view, the myth of closed ethnic eating communities is maintained only to extend mass products to all Americans.

In social science, the typical linear acculturation models imply that an ethnic food pattern weakens in a linear fashion with each generation. Moreover, the mass system is viewed as a complex mixture of many different ethnic cuisines, increasing variety of newly created foodstuffs, and the proliferation of health food and weight-loss movements. The individual is viewed as picking and choosing from this plethora of alternatives without any social group mediation. The passage of time and the availability of alternatives are the major forces seen as affecting the otherwise expected replication of an ethnic diet, a pattern learned early and preferred strongly.

Our research findings have led us to frame the relationship between food and ethnicity differently. Ethnic food systems are not simply conservative and tenacious, nor are they disappearing over time. Eating patterns are socially mediated, transmitted, and reinforced. If an ethnic group remains relatively closed, exhibiting little movement away from group through out-marriage, out-migration, or occupational class movement, then the structure of the food system continues to be transmitted and reinforced through social interactions and social sanction.

Moreover, ethnic or regional groups are *not* the only locus of differentiated eating patterns in America. Other non-ethnic socially bounded lifestyle groups can also be studied as differentiated food systems. Any population in which significant interaction and social network ties are contained within a relatively bounded group will tend to have a shared food system which differentiates them from other groups. The existence of individual household networks of kin and friends which tend to overlap within a community leads to a relatively bounded set of households who tend to share meals, special food events, and food exchange, and thus generate a community-shared food system. Thus, communities based on occupation (both territorial and dispersed), age, or any other basis can be studied as a group with a food system. An example of such a non-ethnic food system is that which occurs on American military bases and is shared throughout the system as a result of the constant movement of families between bases.[6]

These status-based communities differ from ethnic groups in that there is usually discontinuity between the food pattern of the natal household of the homemaker and her current social group pattern. Ethnic groups thus still provide a unique opportunity to observe both intergenerational transmission and reinforcement as well as interhousehold processes. However, recognizing that many Americans share a community food system based on other social statuses leads to the recognition that the influences of childhood socialization are not rigid and absolute.

Community-Shared Rules

We began with a focus on the household within relatively closed ethnic communities as the major unit in which food choices are made. The significant question was: to what degree did the household participate in a communitywide (ethnic) set of rules governing eating events and food selection? How was this pattern transmitted and reinforced within and between household units by gossip, statements of value judgment, and other social sanctions? The communities consisted of stable networks of kin and friends lasting from childhood to adulthood. These social networks were very important in maintaining the food system. How were these community-wide patterns transmitted to children? How did competing patterns brought in from schoolmates, workmates, or national media interact with the community pattern? How did such constraints as income and activity schedules affect the pattern? How had the community pattern changed over time?

Eating events can be singularly private events. Household food choices and meal patterns can develop strictly as a result of the influences of the homemaker's experience in her own natal family and that of her husband. This process is indeed very significant, but by itself it leads to each household perceiving as "ethnic" those features recalled from their childhood with no collective interpretation of rules at the community level. Much of what is done in the name of ethnicity would be idiosyncratic and incorrectly remembered. This is only a partial view of actual social transmission. Major eating events occur in much larger social contexts for weekly meals, holidays, and life-cycle feasts. These occur within the relatively closed network of kin and friends. Shopping, food preparation, and other food-related activities are also shared or observed. A significant network of other households is thus the meaningful social context in which community-wide norms are reinforced and maintained.

Other weekly eating events—particularly lunch in school or the workplace—occur under the evaluative influence of peers from outside the household and community. Finally restaurant eating, an increasing factor in American life, exerts still another set of normative pressures. Thus, the meal models of a household and its choices are heavily influenced by several different sets of norms and mechanisms for reinforcement: first, the intergenerationally transmitted norms of the natal families of household adults; second, the shared norms of those extended kin and friends who form the social network in which the household is embedded (friends who come to dinner or are hosts for dinner or for holiday meals, parties, and life-cycle events like showers and weddings); third, the set of co-workers and schoolmates with whom some members of the household eat some meals (these rules are limited in the extent to which they are brought into the household pattern); fourth, the influence of restaurant menus and the acquaintance with new dishes in restaurants; and fifth, indirect experience with meal models and recipes through the media.

In this scheme there are two ways in which ethnic food patterns can persist. One is through the linear intergenerational transmission from natal households, which will largely be idiosyncratic in selecting which rules to maintain and which to drop. The other is through the existence of a relatively bounded ethnic community in which household networks of kin and friends tend to be ethnically homogeneous. In such circumstances, an ethnic community is relatively bounded socially and will tend to use food as a social and cultural boundary marker.

Components and Levels of a Food System

Selecting a social or population unit to study requires the focus on who shares a food pattern. This definition of unit is based on the ways in which a food system is socially transmitted and how norms are reinforced from household to household. Another major issue in developing a framework for studying food systems is determining what are the components of the food system itself which are to be analyzed. Food choice within a system takes place on many levels. Some available food *items* are used frequently and others are not used at all. Some combinations (*recipes*) occur in some groups and others not at all. Some types of meals occur in some groups while others never occur. Previous studies of ethnic food systems provide us with several examples of the use of different components.

In some analyses, the critical markers of an ethnic food system are assumed to be certain foods and the frequency of their use. Bennett in his work in midwestern rural systems and Jerome in her work on urban populations both use *food-item* frequencies as indicators of different food systems.[7] Thus, pasta, tomato-based sauces, greens, and certain cheeses would be viewed as the hallmarks of Italian cuisine. However, as we shall see, it is not the frequency of use of such items which marks Italian cuisine. In fact, it is likely that many Americans eat as much pasta or use tomato-based sauces as frequently as many members of the ethnic community.

Another marker used by researchers is the style of food preparation. This is a different level of complexity, for we are dealing with the *recipe* rather than a single food item. Here, the markers would be such attributes of the recipe as flavors or spices, fats and stocks for cooking, methods of heat application, and patterns of cleaning and cutting foods. Thus, Gans (who never directly studied Italian food) assumed that the people he studied in Boston "italianized" foods by using Italian spices and methods of cooking.[8] Fratto describes the essence of the Italian food system in terms of recipes.[9] Rozin assumes that flavors are the markers of distinctive cuisines.[10] Chang and Anderson and Anderson locate the diagnostic characteristics of Chinese cooking more in methods of preparation than in the food items themselves.[11] If such a level of analysis were applied to Italian cuisine, the significant features would be the use of garlic, parsley, and other spices, particular cuts of meat, methods of breading and frying, or simmering one-pot dishes. However, as we will see, many of these components are unstressed in or are missing from homes which are still very much participating in a shared Italian-American pattern.

Recipes are more complex than food items because they emphasize form and structure rather than content. Recipes incorporate rules for relating items: segregating them, combining them, and opposing them. Such rules are more complex than the presence, absence, or frequency of items. What we shall find is that these rules governing form and structure persist over time while items can and do change easily.

Meal formats (menus) are still another level of complexity. Meal formats are model structures for arranging dishes in course sequences or in synchronic presentation within a meal. Courses can consist of single dishes or multiple dishes. Certain dishes must go together, others must be separated. Some dishes must follow others. Often, proportions of different dishes are mandated so as to distinguish between stressed foods and their accompaniments.

The most complex level of analysis is the *meal cycle*. This refers to the patterning of the use of different meal formats over time (the week, weekend, annual holiday cycle, and life cycle.)[12] It is at this level that we found great persistence in the ethnic pattern. It was in the system of meals rather than simply the food-item frequencies or recipes in which we found a pattern which was shared within both our Italian-American enclaves and which was socially transmitted from generation to generation and from household to household across community networks. There was much less uniformity between households in terms of food-item frequency and even in the persistence and transmission of many recipes. Households varied in the way they cooked meatballs or defined the desirable thickness of tomato gravy as well as the kinds of tomatoes which were used and the degree to which garlic or olive oil were used, if at all, as flavoring. However, there was great uniformity in the structure of meals and cycle of meals for different times of the week, year, and life. While items and recipes were somewhat more important in the immigrant generation, there were always household differences in style. Recipes, flavors, and style of preparation were not as persistent as the cyclical patterning of meals which still occurs in the third generation.

What was once pictured in the literature as a remarkably uniform food pattern among Italian-Americans in the northeast United States has now been transformed.[13] All four levels of the food pattern have been significantly modified by external forces including changes in food availability, food processing, the use of mass communications to create mass demand, the nature of work and leisure activity cycles, and the entrance of women into the labor force. However, by looking at the food system as a whole and paying particular attention to major choice points in the food system (shopping and menu planning), one finds considerable group-patterned behavior. Change has occurred at all levels: items, recipes, meal formats, and meal cycles. However, one of the most significant types of change is the addition of new formats. New dishes and items are introduced through new formats. It is through this process that the range of choice in formats broadens. All of this serves to mask the persistence of old formats and their continuous patterned periodicity.

For this discussion we will limit ourselves to a consideration of the food system as *a set of shared rules* for making menu decisions, e.g. what type of meal (*format*) to serve for a particular time or social event and what *content* to select for the meal. We would like to emphasize the importance of looking at the food system holistically and continuously in order not to miss the cyclical structural patterns. The patterns which emerged in our study would have been missed if we had only sampled meals, days, or even weeks. Such short temporal units of observation are typical in the study of food (e.g. 24-hour recall) and preclude the observation of very important patterns.

Meal Cycle

We approached our data by locating meal events within larger spatio-temporal units. These units were generated by both the data and the community members' conceptualizations of their time frames. The week, the weekend, the season, and the year (punctuated as it is by regularly occurring feasts) became the units of organization by which we began our analysis. These larger units enabled us to discern the complexities of continuity and change which may be misrepresented by other units. As the day's progression is punctuated by meals, so too the week comprises a series of meal events which mark the week's activity cycle. This culminates in a weekend pattern which is an inversion of the mundane week. These redundant cycles are in turn marked by feasts celebrating life-cycle and calendrical events. In combination, the daily and the festive reveal the structure of the food system which underlies decisions about particular meals.

Preliminary interviewing revealed a weekly pattern of alternation between two types of meals on a daily basis. The week's end is marked by a "fasting" or "fish" meal on Friday evenings. The weekend activity pattern is highlighted at its conclusion by the Sunday evening meal. This cyclical repetition strongly resembles an historically based structure which has continued with modifications until today. The structure is found in many descriptions of early Italian-American immigrant enclaves as well as in the informants' recollections of their own childhoods. Had we looked only at meal content or individual meals we would have missed the structure which informs decisions about meal format and content. The structure is shared at a community-wide level and is found in both Italian-American communities studied. There is consensus as to the appropriateness of particular meal events for particular occasions. By comparing and contrasting daily and festive meal events across households during a yearly cycle, a pattern emerged revealing consistencies and criteria for appropriate choices.

The Week

Each day's round of activities culminates in an evening meal which takes one of two generic forms:

1) gravy (one pot)   (Italian)
2) platter   (American)

Gravy dishes are one-pot mixtures of spicy tomato- and meat-based sauces served over pasta with cheese added. Everyday forms are simmered while more festive forms are baked (lasagne, raviolis). Platters are simultaneous and segregated presentations of meat, starch, and vegetables. The content for these meals is largely American in item and style.

The systematic alternation of these forms on a daily basis has altered over time as has the content, but the structure of the dual system persists and can be culled from the manner in which these foods are presented during the week. Most households today still have at least one gravy meal during weekdays. (For many this occurs on Thursday, others Wednesday, etc.) If we had randomly picked one or two evenings' meals for observation, rather than the week in its entirety, we might have overlooked this systematic pattern which reveals the persistence of a shared community pattern.

An interesting parallel to this meal *repertoire* consisting of two basic types occurs in Jerome's recent description of the two basic dinner-meal types among Black migrants to a northern city. She refers to the distinction between "boiling" nights (one-pot, starch, vegetable, and legume dishes) and "frying" nights (meals focused on fried meat).[14]

In the weekly pattern there is structural continuity from the past, but the structure has been modified. The daily pattern found in immigrant communities throughout the northeastern United States consisted of two meal formats: breakfast, and a major and minor main meal. The major main meal at noon differed from the minor meal in the evening both in scale and format. Evening meals were smaller in scale and composed of the opposite format of the midday meal. The repertoire of formats for the main meals was larger than today's. Rather than the simple opposition of gravy and platter, there were several conceptually distinct one-pot formats. There also existed a platter-like format focusing on Italian, not American, items and usually featuring vegetable- or egg-based dishes as opposed to meat. However, the same principle of alternation existed then. We find one-pot meals alternating with meals consisting of synchronically presented, segregated components throughout both the day and week as we find them today alternating throughout the week.

Today the week's end is signaled by a Friday night meal which symbolically reiterates the church's former ban on meat. It is a "fasting" night. In many cases, this avoidance pattern is only partially adhered to. In some cases, meat is served but fish is also present. The range of variation includes both meat and fish dishes, fish alone, or non-meat, non-fish dishes alone. In any case, in most households some attention is paid to this tradition. However, if only one Friday night had been observed, this pattern would have been missed, because the community recognizes a series of circumstances which permit the over-riding of the Friday fasting rule. During Lent more rigid restrictions are enforced concerning "fast" days.

New formats recently added to the weekly repertoire include two types of "short-cut" meals. These new formats tend to be found clustered near the weekend break in routine activities but are also used when unusual circumstances force expedience during the week. These formats include "expedient" eating out (fast food or diners) and the hot sandwich meal.

The Weekend

Sleeping and eating patterns change in response to different activities scheduled for the weekend. No longer constrained by work schedules, shopping and leisure-time activities dominate the scene, loosening the fixed intervals of time between meals. Following the Friday night fast or quick meal, evening leisure-time activity culminates for some families in an early breakfast outside the home at dawn on Saturday mornings. A larger breakfast is served later on Saturday morning in which an extended family and friends can participate. As with many weekend patterns, the Saturday breakfast is not historically persistent but is a response to the patterning of American activities. Lunch is often neglected and dinner can be either a quick and informal meal or a celebratory occasion. The weekend meal activity is generally highlighted or culminated in an extended family Sunday dinner. The Sunday dinner, an elaborate gravy meal, acts as a paradigmatic meal from which all other eating events are drawn. The dinner itself can be condensed or expanded to suit an occasion, and elements of the meal can be drawn out for expansion into various feast (special occasion) formats. The Sunday dinner is historically continuous and can be found as a major feature in the base-line food system.

Feasts

We looked at the yearly cycle of food events and ranked special occasions (life-cycle and calendrical events) hierarchically according to criteria generated by the community. Both the highest-level feasts (weddings, Christmas, Easter) and the lowest (Sunday dinners, women's club, and Tupperware parties) have restricted and invariant formats, while the middle-range feasts generate variability in format and content. As the middle feasts allow for the widest latitude in interpretation of significance of the event, so too the meal-format choices and food-content selections accompanying the events vary widely. Analogies made to other events allow a multiplicity of interpretations.

There are five possible format choices shared by community members which in turn can be elaborated or condensed to suit the definition of the occasion, the size of the attendance list, and the resources of the family. These are the possible formats from which community members can choose to celebrate an occasion. Most of these formats are constructed from elements in the weekly meal cycle arranged in new relationships. The five formats are: 1) elaborated Sunday dinner (additional courses added); 2) buffet-style; 3) buffet; 4) simple party; and 5) sit-down catered.

In addition to these five formats, the ritual cycle of the year consists of events at which very specific items must be present. These items are never eaten on other occasions. Sometimes specifically seasonal foods or prepared baked goods are associated with a holiday season and made available for the whole span of the feast. Specific cookies are characteristic of Christmas. Ricotta pies and other baked goods are characteristic of Easter. Here, the simple presence or absence of specific items *is* what is significant since no meal format rules are involved.

Two other specific holiday practices are extensions of the Friday abstinence rule. One of these is a specific format, reserved for Christmas Eve. An odd number of meatless, fish, and vegetable dishes is served sequentially in this format. The number of such dishes can range from three to thirteen in different households. The typical number seems to have diminished through time. The Lenten season is another extension of the Friday fast rule and affects all meals throughout the season.

The five formats in the regular feast repertoire are mixtures of old and new Italian and American structures, dishes, and items. The traditional feast formats were probably limited to the elaborated Sunday dinner and buffet-style patterns. The *elaborated Sunday dinner* contains many more courses than the paradigmatic Sunday dinner. One or more antipasto courses, a soup course, whole roast course, multi-dish dessert course, and an ultimate course of nuts and fruit can be expected. The meal is served to a seated group.

The *buffet-style* format is an extension of the elaborated dinner, which was probably developed as a response to enlarged lists of guests. It is also a format which enables several households to contribute dishes to the meal thus enhancing its potential for social linkage through food exchange. The size of the meal is expanded by the addition of more dishes rather than increasing the quantity of each dish. Another distinction between this meal format and Sunday dinner is that the buffet-style meal contains elements of several different meals. Both platter and one-pot components are mixed and the meal is really a combination of elements which could compose several individual meals. The foods are all presented simultaneously on a buffet table as individuals serve themselves and then sit together at a common table. It is likely that this format was used in the past with largely Italian content. Today such a format permits both dishes of Italian and American origin, although Italian items dominate. A typical menu would include several chicken dishes, starch foods, vegetables, gravy dishes, and salads, i.e. components of both platter and gravy meals. This is an open format in that content depends very much on the household and network likes and dislikes. Network members' specialty dishes are usually included. Buffet-style components are actual dishes from typical weekly meal formats.

The *buffet* format is a more uniform, rule-bound structure. It seems to have emerged in the development of the grocery-delicatessen catering pattern in the period after World War II. The components of the buffet are not drawn from daily menus and the content is not as open to choice. The meal is presented at a large table. Guests sit individually or in small groups after selecting their food. This format is used for very large groups. Whereas the buffet-style format tends to be Italian in content, the buffet format is always a mixture of Italian and American items. Gravy meats (meatballs, sausage, veal) served in tomato gravy are presented to be used for sandwiches in Italian rolls along with some Italian accompaniments (e.g. salads, roasted peppers). In addition, American meats (roast beef in brown gravy, ham, and turkey) are also presented along with cole slaw and potato salad. This format is almost uniform in content whenever it is used.

The *simple party* format is totally American in origin. It consists of two components: hors d'oeuvres and cold beverages. An extended version includes a second course of dessert and coffee. In spite of its non-indigenous structure and content, this format is frequently used for intimate network occasions strictly within the ethnic enclave. Several life-cycle events may use this format, and most women's group activities use this format.

The *catered dinner* is like the elaborated Sunday dinner in the complexity of its course structure. However, it is prepared by professionals and is usually served outside the home. Moreover, this format contains almost no Italian content. The appetizer, soup, meat, and dessert courses largely reflect the fads and fashions in the catering industry.[15] Yet this format is often used for the wedding, the highest-level feast.

There is no simple relationship between the choice of traditional formats and the degree of ethnic identity or adherence to the traditional
food system in everyday life.

The formats, once selected, are structures within which specific
content decisions are made. Family size, including the size of the extended family and close friendship network, dictates the attendance
list and limits the feasible formats. Similarly, economic circumstances
limit both choice of format and choice of items. Taste preferences are
much less significant than household structural features in these choices,
although individual household specialties can be expected to appear
especially in the buffet-style format. For middle-level feasts, the meaning
and significance of the occasion is ambiguous. Different families define and evaluate the occasion differently and do so without sanction.
Thus, variability and latitude in events are encouraged and acceptable
while still within the normative frame of the community's shared pattern. So it is that two graduation parties could be celebrated differently: one with a simple party and the other with a buffet. The variability is the result of differences in evaluation of the occasion and the
nature and size of the household social network. Both celebrations
were considered appropriate by the participants and the community.

We selected more comprehensive units of organization for our
analysis because through them pattern and structure can be perceived.
Without them, misperceptions are more likely to occur. In this case,
even where content has been changed (specific food items), a basic
structure persists. This structure would not be apparent in any random series or number of events. Each event has significance and it
is this meaning which is spoken about or amplified by the choice of
format and content. The meaning is usually revealed not at the level
of content, but at the level of structure, a structure which is shared
and consensually validated and which informs the particular choices
and lays bare the meanings of occasions. The presence or absence of
items only rarely symbolizes an occasion. The units of weekly temporal organization and the number of different festive meal formats
differ from one American subgroup to another. However, a focus on
such a total comprehensive inventory of units is essential as a first
step in identifying the differences.

Principles of Household Variation in Menu Negotiation

Within the context of the shared community pattern, it is also important to look at the way households differ. We looked at two types
of variation: one based on household attributes (composition, stage

in the domestic cycle, differences in income, education level, and activity patterns) and the other based on unique practices transmitted through natal and affinal household lines (family traditions). The latter usually refers to more idiosyncratic and unique household definitions of sensory standards of taste, eye appeal, and texture, the outcomes of individual likes and dislikes.

The ways in which household composition affects food choices is itself an aspect of the community-shared pattern. For example, adult males, females, and children play similar roles in menu negotiation throughout the community. Households thus differ in predictable ways because of their domestic cycle stage *or* sex and age composition rather than because they operate according to idiosyncratic rules. Households of widows differ greatly from those with senior males present. Preschool children play very different roles than older children. Thus, we have to be very careful with instances of household variation since much of it may be due to structure rather than signifying a breakdown in the influence of ethnic group membership.

In this analysis, we identified the key culinary decision-maker in each household. We followed the convention cooperatively established by the Russell Sage Foundation Gastronomic Categories Project and use the designation "key kitchen person." In our community, the senior female (wife, mother) occupied this position in each household. Her role is significant not only for menu negotiation within the household (daily, weekly, and festive occasions), but also for the inter-household transmission and reinforcement of food norms. Patterns of appropriate eating are taught by mother to daughter and after marriage by mother-in-law to daughter-in-law. Ideas about food are also strongly influenced by this role bearer's network of friends and acquaintances with whom shopping, food preparation, and meals are shared and food is exchanged.

Variation in household composition, including the structure ("nuclear," multi-generational), size, and roles occupied by various members, contributed to differentiated eating. Although the households we worked with are presently nuclear, this had not always been the case. Experience in multi-generational households (primarily wife's parents) leads to a shift in responsibility from wife to mother and intergenerational negotiation about eating events.

We found that the most important structural variable in the household is the presence or absence of a senior male, for menu negotiations rely heavily on his preferences and activity patterns. His presence also requires precedence in seating arrangements and service order. If absent, his role will be filled by another member of the household or a guest, e.g. a son, potential son-in-law, other male relative, or friend.

Generational cohort differences within a group may also influence characteristic eating patterns. The historical period during which socialization of adult household members occurred is significant for taste preferences, patterns of procurement, notions about motherhood and nurturance, and beliefs about health and nutrition. Individual household differences in the content, timing, and manner of consumption are also related to the household's stage in the domestic cycle. We worked with families who presented a bi-modal contrast in the stage in the domestic cycle. Several of the families have adult children whose aesthetic preferences and activity patterns produce variations in the culinary decision-making process. The others are composed of dependent school-aged children and infants. Both the *variation* in ages, number, and gender of children and the *compatibility* of their preferences and activity patterns (within a household) contribute to differences in the nature and locus of menu negotiations.

The activity patterns of various household members — senior male, adult, and school-aged children — must also be considered in the analysis of differentiated eating. Likewise, the activity patterns of the senior female (employment outside the home, participation in voluntary organizations, and other social relationships) create contrasts in the scheduling and content of eating events.

Attention to particularistic (non-shared) household norms and traditions provides a very different dimension to the analysis of household differences. We found that each household has a distinctive aesthetic and metaphysical tradition which is a combination of the general set of rules and practices of both natal and affinal households and idiosyncratic individual characteristics. These include preferences for certain sensory qualities (and food items), concerns about diet-related health status, and the importance of religious symbolism. Finally, the key kitchen person in a household may have varying degrees of expertise (self-identified and reputed) as a cook. In this community, and others where food is an important component of social interaction and is definitive of a woman's role competence, this distinction may have important consequences. The relative expertise of the key kitchen person (as a cook) is often related to the pattern of hospitality in individual families.

Individuals other than the key kitchen person and the senior male can also exert idiosyncratic pressures on food decisions. Such pressures are the result of individual taste preferences and individual needs generated by activity patterns. The individual's role in menu negotiation is also very significant when it comes to introducing items, dishes, and formats from other food systems. Household members are influenced outside the home, in school and at the workplace, by peers from other communities. These social ties reinforce the attractiveness of models, available in restaurants or in the media, which might be rejected without social mediation. Children as well as adults have many experiences eating outside of the centrally controlled kitchen of the home, and these experiences contribute to household menu negotiation and ultimately to household differences.

We have previously discussed the meal system in this community which distinguishes between gravy and platter meals of the ordinary weekday and provides appropriate formats for weekends and several levels of festive occasions. How is this shared community pattern mediated by household differences and individual preferences?

Households differ significantly in selecting the content for formats. While the party format calls for the most American selections, all other formats are mixed and potentially include both Italian and American items. Families differ in the degree to which they favor either type. Buffet-style content offers great choice. Some of the households we worked with consistently used only Italian items in their buffet-style format, while others tended to mix items. An important variable taken into account is the specialties of members of the extended family, because these specialties become family traditions as individuals develop reputations for particular dishes. Taste variables which enter into these decisions are the preferences of the planner (key kitchen person) and her perception of what foods are universally liked. Household or intra-household dislikes are obviously incorporated in decisions and tend to be avoided. The buffet format is more defined and offers fewer choices than the buffet-style form. Sandwiches of meats and Italian gravy and roast beef in American gravy, as well as combinations of both American salads and Italian vegetables, are standard items. The dessert course in both buffet and buffet-style formats is the broadest and most open. Desserts are a domain in which Italian items are much less frequent than in other segments of food events.

The important factors in content selections of weekly meals are activity patterns and individual status. Strong likes and strong dislikes are both considered. Husbands hold a particularly powerful place. Their preferences are most often the primary filters for decisions about basic menu structure. However, relative strength varies across households. For example, one wife almost always accedes to her husband's desires while another verbally describes her freedom from her husband's control but still acts to please him in many instances. A food strongly disliked by the husband will usually not become part of a basic meal structure while a favorite dish of the husband is often part of the menu even though other household members will not eat it. In spite of the senior male's influence, there is also a basic norm of equity in meal planning. Effort is made to see that all other household members get their preferred foods at least once during the week. Thus a child's strong preference — if not disliked by the senior male — can become part of the basic meal structure. The fact that a child complains of being ignored or is acknowledged to have been neglected can strongly influence decisions about meals, even so far as to override the rules for Friday and Sunday meals. Finally, the key kitchen person herself occasionally seizes the upper hand and makes content decisions with regard to her own likes, cravings, mood, or desire for cooking experimentation.

We have said that sex is important in ranking the priority of preferences of the adult household members, but sex is not that significant among younger age groups. In fact, young children's preferences are relatively unimportant. As a child grows older, his preferences become more influential. Babies are given what adults think is good for them. Children show preferences for sweets and other treats, but these are not given in response to preferences but at strategic times in order to control and manipulate their behavior.

There is a significant generational difference between cohorts in likes and dislikes. The generation raised before World War II likes many traditional Italian one-pot dishes which their offspring will not eat. There is a repugnance among the offspring in all the households (adult children and school-age children) for foods that suggest their natural forms. Pig's knuckles, organ meats, and smelts are popular with the householder generation but not among their offspring. The younger generation requires that food be disguised and processed with heads, extremities, and skin removed. However, they also avoid mixtures like the one-pot in which the parts may be too mixed and thus unrecognizable. They want food transformed from its natural state yet easily identified. It is likely that this preference is shared by all generational cohorts socialized in the 1960s and 1970s in the United States.

In most households, there are strong likes and dislikes for particular ingredients and they serve to modify significantly the composition of gravies, salads, and other universally present dishes in the Italian-American structural repertoire. Strong spices, particularly garlic and onions, are used very differently from household to household. Each household has a very distinct gravy taste and texture, and differences are well known and subjects of conversation. Visual attributes of food are very important. Red color was one of the most significant attributes used in judging gravies, and the contrasts and presence of red, white, and green in gravy meals was frequently noted. Family members are very verbal about aesthetic qualities: color, texture, greasiness, and spiciness.

Summary and Conclusion

The relationship between ethnicity and food is not simple. Ethnic food systems cannot be defined as uniformly "conservative" nor can they be described as quickly disappearing except for holiday traditions.

From the previous discussion, several important principles emerge as a framework for the comparative analysis of the differentiated food systems of American subgroups. While many Americans are not members of neatly bounded groups which maintain shared rules for food patterning, we can best understand the nature of food systems by first focusing on those groups which are relatively bounded community enclaves and yet still participate to some degree in the American national system. Such groups can be defined by common ethnic or regional origin. Other groups exist, based on age or occupation, which can also be studied as having shared food systems. Such a focus on shared food systems will ultimately help us to explain the principles of choice and selection of menu formats and content negotiation even for those households embedded in diverse, loose-knit ties of kinship and friendship.

The level of a group-shared food system is indeed evasive to the observer unless he looks specifically for it and looks at the highest level of analysis, the meal cycle. Sampling meals at random, days of the week at random, or times of the year will lead the observer to describe America as a set of individualistic households each making random selections from the vast, differentiated food supply. Choices will seem to be responses to the external constraints of time or money or to idiosyncratic likes and dislikes rather than to shared sociocultural rules. The observer will miss the essential organization of the entire group-patterned system because the locus of the structure is a spatio-temporal cycle of meal formats rather than food items or recipes. Items and recipes are very significant for truly isolated and closed communities like the Amish, for isolated subsistence-oriented farm communities, and for the migrant group in the arriving generation. However, contact with supermarkets, communication media, restaurants, school lunches, and industrial workplaces tends to lessen the importance of content and increase the importance of the structure embedded in the meal cycle as a marker of group-patterned systems. The issues of continuity and change cannot be explored without a focus on meal formats and meal cycles instead of items and dishes.

The week, the weekend, and the seasonal and life-cycle feasts all must be investigated. However, the common assumption that more ritualized and less mundane events will tend to be more rigidly patterned and conservative over time need not be true. As we have seen in our group, the weekly pattern is quite uniform while format choice is open for many feasts, and the major wedding feast format is often non-traditional in form and content.

Moreover, household variability does exist as a widespread phenomenon in even relatively closed and bounded communities. This can very often be mistaken for the lack of a shared pattern and lead to the conclusion that the old systems have broken down in the face of the choices resulting from the American melting pot and "horn of plenty." However, household differences themselves are predictable for the community system according to such variables as the composition of the household, stage in domestic cycle, generational cohort, and activity patterns. This is a further indicator of the continuity of a community pattern in which household roles are ranked and accorded specific rights in menu negotiation. Such rights would probably be different in another sociocultural subgroup. Thus, any study must first identify the group-shared rules and then examine the patterns of household menu negotiations, the decision-making actions mediating between shared rules, situational pressures, and personal preferences.

In addition to such shared patterns, idiosyncratic sensory preferences and beliefs about food do exist within the community. This accounts for many of the differences in item frequencies and recipe style across household lines and is a result both of linear transmission of family traditions and the unique contacts of household members with friends and workmates outside the family and community. Such non-shared elements do not negate the tremendous importance of the shared structural patterns. In fact, an attempt to explain the dynamics of non-shared elements will enable us to understand better those American households which are only loosely related to tight community norms which influence their eating.

Such a focus on whole systems and cyclicality also enables us to understand better the processes of continuity and change in food systems, since structural features are often the vehicles for the introduction of new content. For example, in the Italian-American weekly pattern, new "American" items entered largely into the platter format rather than the "gravy" meal. The buffet format was a festival vehicle for mixing stylized elements of gravy meals with those of platter meals. In other kinds of change, new formats might themselves be proliferated alongside the old, as with the development of restaurant formats each with their own rules of appropriate use. Still another type of change occurs when structural rules themselves are inverted or manipulated in some way, as in the creation of the weekend mini-cycle.

To understand the processes of differentiation in American eating patterns at the level of *shared sociocultural rules*, it is necessary to focus on interacting social units above the level of household and on culinary units above the level of the food item or dish. The meal format and meal cycle are units which must be further developed. Once we have begun to understand the relative impact of community-shared systems of defined food events and the processes of their transmission and reinforcement through time (from generation to generation) and through social space (from household to household), we will understand that the differences in food intake in the United States are not merely the result of income, age, sex, location, and idiosyncratic food preferences acting upon an infinite array of foodstuffs, but the result of the interaction between these factors and a complex set of definitions and meanings attached by sociocultural groups to the acts of food choice and the creation of meals.

ACKNOWLEDGMENTS

Much of the research discussed in this paper was supported by Temple University. The first support was a grant of National Science Foundation institutional funds awarded by the Graduate Committee of the College of Liberal Arts, Temple University. This was followed by one study leave and three Faculty Senate grants-in-aid from Temple University. The participant observation phase in 1978–79 was conducted with the generous support of the Program in Culture of the Russell Sage Foundation as part of the Project on Gastronomic Categories directed by Dr. Mary Douglas.

NOTES

1. Various aspects of this field study are presented in the following: Karen Curtis, "Food and Ethnicity: The Italian-American Case" (M.A. thesis, Temple Univ., 1977); Karen Curtis, "A Comparison of Foodways in Two Italian-American Communities," paper delivered at the Northeastern Anthropological Association (Providence,

R.I., March 1977); Judith Goode, "Modifying Ethnic Foodways: The Effects of Locality and Social Networks," paper delivered at the Northeastern Anthropological Association (Middletown, Conn., March 1976); Judith Goode, "Foodways as an Ethnic Marker: Assumptions and Reality," paper delivered at the Northeastern Anthropological Association (Providence, R.I., March 1977); Judith Goode, "Ethnic Dietary Change: Variation in Nutritional Consequences," paper delivered at the American Anthropological Association (Houston, Nov. 1977); Janet S. Theophano, "Feast, Fast and Time," *Pennsylvania Folklife,* 27 (1978):25–32; Janet S. Theophano, "Creolization as a Concept for the Study of Foodways," paper delivered at the American Folklore Society (Philadelphia, Nov. 1976); Janet S. Theophano, "The South Philadelphia American," paper delivered at the American Folklore Society (Detroit, Nov. 1977); Judith Goode, Karen Curtis and Janet Theophano, "Change in a Food System: External Influence or Internal Process?" paper delivered at the American Anthropological Association (Cincinnati, Nov. 1979); Goode, Curtis, and Theophano, "Group-shared Food Patterns as a Unit of Analysis," in Sanford A. Miller, ed., *Nutrition and Behavior* (Philadelphia: Franklin Institute Press, 1981), 19–30.

2. The major work done under the auspices of the National Research Council had this emphasis. See Committee on Food Habits, *Manual for the Study of Food Habits,* National Research Council Bulletin No. 111 (1945). Specific examples of such work include: G. Gizzardini and N. Joffe, "Italian War Time Problems of Food & Nutrition" (National Research Council: Committee on Food Habits, 1942), mimeograph; Margaret Mead, *Food Habits Research: Problems of the 1960's* (Washington, D.C.: National Academy of Sciences, 1964).

3. John Bennett, "Food and Social Status in a Rural Society," *American Sociological Review* 8 (1943):561–59; John Bennett, Harvey Smith and Howard Passin, "Food and Culture in Southern Illinois," *American Sociological Review* 7 (1942):645–60; Mary de Give and Margaret Cussler, "Interrelations Between the Cultural Pattern and Nutrition," United States Department of Agriculture, Extension Service Circular No. 266 (Aug. 1941); Margaret Cussler and Mary de Give, *Twixt the Cup and the Lip* (New York: Twayne, 1952).

4. Melford Spiro, "Acculturation of American Ethnic Groups," *American Anthropologist* 57 (1955):1240–52.

5. Norge Jerome, "On Determining Food Patterns of Urban Dwellers in Contemporary United States Society," in *Gastronomy: The Anthropology of Food and Food Habits,* ed. Margaret Arnott (The Hague: Mouton, 1974).

6. Karen A. Creuziger, "Tea for Two (Hundred)," (M.A. thesis, Univ. of Pennsylvania, 1980).

7. John Bennett, "An Interpretation of the Scope and Implications of Social Scientific Research in Human Subsistence," *American Anthropologist* 41 (1946):553–73; Norge Jerome, "On Determining Food Patterns of Urban Dwellers."

8. Herbert Gans, *The Urban Villagers: Group and Class in the Life of Italian Americans* (New York: Free Press, 1962).

9. Toni F. Fratto, "Cooking in Red and White," *Pennsylvania Folklife* 19 (1970): 2–15.

10. Elisabeth Rozin, *The Flavor Principle Cookbook* (New York: Hawthorn Books, 1973).

11. K.C. Chang, ed., *Food in Chinese Culture: Anthropological and Historical Perspectives* (New Haven: Yale Univ. Press, 1977); E. Anderson and M. Anderson, "Cantonese Ethnohoptology," *Ethnos* 37 (1972):134–47.

12. Mary Douglas, "Deciphering a Meal," *Daedalus* 101 (1972):61–81; Mary

Douglas and Michael Nicod, "Taking the Biscuit: The Structure of British Meals," *New Society* 30 (1974):744–47.

13. Lucy Gillett, "Factors Influencing Nutrition Work Among Italians," *Journal of Home Economics* 14 (January 1922):14–19; Bertha Wood, *Foods of the Foreign Born in Relation to Health* (Boston: Whitcomb & Barrows, 1922); Gertrude Mudge, "Italian Dietary Adjustments," *Journal of Home Economics* 15 (April 1923); Almeda King, "A Study of the Italian Diet in a Group of New Haven Families" (M.A. thesis, Yale Univ., 1935); Dorothy Bovee and Jean Downes, "The Influence of Nutritional Education in Families of the Mulberry Area of New York City," *The Milbank Memorial Fund Quarterly* 19 (1941):121–46; G. Gizzardini and N. Joffe, "Italian Food Patterns"; M. Cantoni, "Adapting Therapeutic Diets to the Eating Patterns of Italian-Americans," *American Journal of Clinical Nutrition* 6 (1958):548–55; Phyllis Williams, *Southern Italian Folkways in Europe and America* (New York: Russell and Russell, 1969).

14. Norge Jerome, "Diet and Acculturation: The Case of Black-American In-Migrants" in *Nutritional Anthropology*, eds. Norge Jerome, Randi Kandel, and Gretel Pelto (New York: Redgrave, 1979).

15. The development of the catering industry in the Philadelphia region involved specialization from the base of corner grocery store catering to a few large establishments. The growing enterprises recognized that they could not survive if they were oriented to a single ethnic group. Thus, even Italian-American proprietors developed standardized menus in which format and items were largely shared across groups.

PART II

*Food in the Performance
of Ethnic Identity:
Field Studies*

4

Metaphor and Changing Reality: The Foodways and Beliefs of the Russian Molokans in the United States

Willard B. Moore

In 1903, partly in response to their prophets' warnings of impending disasters, approximately 3,500 members of the Russian religious sect who called themselves Molokans moved to the United States and established colonies in southern California, the Guadalupe Valley of northern Mexico, Arizona, and Oregon. The Molokans are not orthodox Catholics, but protestant spiritual Christians who broke from the dissenting Duxobor and Xlysty groups in the mid-eighteenth century and have continued as an independent religious body in southern Russia since that time.[1] The story of the Molokan journey from the Transcaucasus to the United States and their difficult transition from a rural life to an industrialized, technologically oriented, and pluralistic but relatively tolerant society is not unlike that of many eastern European groups. The elements which made the Molokan experience unique are their world view, the culture and adaptive strategies developed here by them, and their ethno-religious interpretations of their identity apart from non-Molokans. Among these, their strategies for maintaining a spiritual separation from the rest of the world are especially important.[2]

Prior to emigration, the sectarian population of Tsarist Russia was large, and Molokans were but one of many sects which included Baptists, Adventists, *Skoptsy*, Old and New Israelites, and the Duxobors. The Molokans themselves consisted of several branches, the main ones being the *Obščie* (communalists), the *Postojannye* (Steadfast), and the *Pryguny* (Jumpers). It was from this latter branch that the vast majority of Molokan immigrants derived. While there are several small *Postojannye* Molokan communities in the western United States, the term "Molokan" in this essay will apply only to *Pryguny.*

The ethnic and religious boundaries of this sect are co-terminus. Molokans today accept no converts, prefer to speak Russian at religious events, and are generally aloof with outsiders, though they are extremely hospitable toward individuals with sincere inquiries. Their "kosher" dietary laws and their modest concern for the secular world beyond their need to make a living are part of a world view which is briefly summarized in the Russian terms, *svoj* (ours) and *ne naš* (not ours). Through examination of the group's foodways we can better understand its strategies for reducing ambiguity among its members and for clarifying its distinctiveness from the outside world in the eyes of God.

Among the approximately fourteen thousand Molokans in the United States there is wide variation in the process, involvement, interpretation, and meaning of cultural expressions and customs. Still, certain institutions receive recognition by all Molokans: foodways, costume, singing, prophecy, and the concept of *poxod* or Exodus into spiritual refuge; these function as foci of social and spiritual interaction. Some are metaphors which, in the context of Molokan life, reduce social and spiritual ambiguity and provide avenues for revitalization.

For many Molokans, the previously secular customs are now so integrated with religious and social expression that feelings of incompleteness and disorientation are manifested if the customs are abbreviated or omitted from ritual or from specific parts of daily life. From years of considering these practices at several levels of consciousness there has emerged a sense of style, an extrapolation of themes, forms, and qualities deemed appropriate for manipulation within the perceived range of possibilities for aesthetic expression. For still other Molokans, the customs are colorful and unique, but their associative value is primarily subjective. That is, preparation of a meal, decoration of costume, or style of singing may remind them of specific traditional performers, usually relatives in the extended family. For them, the customs are important but they no longer retain their full historic or spiritual breadth. Moreover, these individuals may no longer see these modes of expression as viable for their own ethno-sectarian identity. Whatever the case, these cultural institutions serve as markers which, when examined at the level of symbol and metaphor, reveal the variation of interpretation and sense of reality held by Molokan community members.[3]

As an ethnic sect, the Molokans have consciously maintained and elaborated distinctive food traditions which bridge secular and spiritual life through their skill in unifying Old and New Testament teachings in a single belief system. Their tradition reflects the dialectical tension between preservation of group identity along Old Testament lines and Paul's adjuration to embrace all men as brothers. This dialectic in Molokan life is central to our understanding of their foodways within the entire symbol system and as a metaphoric process.

Molokan Foodways

The Molokans have retained their distinctive southern Russian dialect and a costume reminiscent of early folk culture in rural Russia. Despite some changes, their rites of passage are very much like those brought here by their forefathers in 1904–1912. But just as these basic cultural modes of expression and communication have adjusted to a new environment, so have Molokan foodways. Basically similar to Russian peasant fare and heavily influenced by years spent among non-Russians in the Transcaucasus region, Molokan food is strikingly different from Orthodox Russian cuisine of the middle and upper classes.[4]

The daily diet still consists mainly of bread, various gruels, noodles, pancakes and pastries, eggs and dairy products, fresh and cooked vegetables, tea and juices, meat and fish. Molokans have preserved somewhat less successfully the food methodology and the complex of material culture tools which their forefathers used in Russia or during the early years in this country. Today, both urban and rural Molokans may smoke their seasonal catch of fish, but the use of modern freezers has largely replaced this method of preservation, as well as the practice of storing vegetables in straw-lined, underground bins. Molokans still tend to use bread as the symbolic, if not the caloric, center of the meal (as is the case generally in Slavic and European folk cultures), but the traditional outdoor Russian oven is no longer a part of the scene. Elders who were born in Russia or who were part of the early colony in the Guadalupe Valley of northern Mexico or the later settlement in Arizona in the 1920s clearly remember the ovens their mothers used, but few of the modern generation have any idea of what they looked like. Only the stories remain of how good the bread tasted.

A conscious, day-to-day effort to remain separate from the larger society places increased emphasis on the ideological uses of food as a means of maintaining social distance. The tensions of Molokan ethnic and spiritual identity extend through two dimensions of time: backward to the ancient Hebrews, to the early apostolic Christians, and to the martyrs of their own Russian sect; and forward to the millennium and a return to a metaphorical place of refuge called "Zion." Salvation is dependent upon faith and upon adherence to biblical codes. For the most part, spiritual and physical survival requires a striving toward spiritual purity and ethnic unity on a conscious level. This consciousness is implemented, in part, through adherence to most of the Levitical dietary laws of the Old Testament. The origin of Molokan observance of this part of scripture lies in the Russian nativistic reform movement of more than three hundred years ago which was characterized in part by a search for original meaning in the symbols and codes of early Christians.

Much of the non-Molokan world is considered "unclean," but the consumption of pork is singled out as the worst transgression, possibly because in previous settlement experiences their neighbors were often pork users: Russians, Ukrainians, or Mexicans.[5] Today, most Molokans purchase their meats from the four Molokan-owned markets in Los Angeles or obtain bulk meat from rural friends or from relatives who raise their own animals and slaughter them properly. In earlier decades, according to oral tradition, certain Molokan males held status as particularly adept at calming animals just prior to slaughter, praying over them and, in this way, minimizing the blood content of the meat after butchering.[6] But buying practices today vary with the ethno-religious intensity of the individual. Many liberal Molokans purchase meat from a "reliable" butcher or even at a supermarket. The deeply ingrained aversion to pork products and to those who use them has obviously been selected as a behavior control device in both religious and social situations.

Although the everyday fare of Molokan families frequently includes items from the formal church dinners, they normally eat American-style cuisine (beef ribs, turkey, corn-on-the cob, casseroles, and pies). Annual get-togethers sponsored by the United Molokan Christian Association include a steak dinner and a picnic each summer at which men prepare *šašlik,* a traditional dish learned in their former home in Transcaucasus Armenia. Also from Armenian foodways, but with origins in Iran, comes *lavash,* a crusty, thin, oval bread not carried in Molokan markets but popularly purchased from Los Angeles Armenian bakeries. Popular dishes from other ethnic groups such as pizza, burritos, or almond chicken demonstrate both individual tastes and an attempt to blend and to compromise with the dominant culture or with other ethnic groups, where possible on a secular level. Even non-Molokan Russian foods such as beef Stroganoff and Siberian *pel'meni* (meat and vegetables stuffed in small egg noodles and boiled in chicken broth) are prepared and served at home but never in a religious context. While their Russian Duxobor brethren in Canada extend their pacifist beliefs to the lives of animals and thus embrace vegetarianism, the Molokans generally do not. Meat avoidance is an individual choice, though at certain rites the ritual meal is meatless.[7]

Clearly, these borrowings are viewed as safe means of dietary enrichment. As accretions to Molokan foodways, they will undoubtedly be retained and supplemented variously, depending upon family members' ages, commitment to their sectarian identity, and individual family histories. For example, families whose grandparents helped settle the Molokan colony in northern Mexico might exhibit a retention of some Mexican dishes, while those Molokans who immigrated from Iran in the 1950s may continue to prepare certain traditional Middle Eastern foods such as *pilaf.* As noted earlier, these families' sense of style may be both eclectic and subjective, given their respective histories.

The Molokans' parochial stance, wherever possible, against commercially prepared foods on the grounds of pollution aligns them, coincidentally at least, with other Americans who are skeptical of additives and preservatives in their diet. The abhorrence of chemical contamination is a natural extension of those taboos against foods which represent the non-Molokan, and more explicitly, government authority. As in other areas of food prohibition and acceptance, Molokans vary in their tolerance of these products and this variance parallels, to some extent, the factional lines of the sect. As he discussed the variety of opinion about the topic, one Molokan male declared: "Well, that other *sobranie* is very strict, y'know. They won't even buy C&H sugar for their tea. Well, they claim that the sugar is filtered through animal bones and they figure that maybe the company uses the bones of pigs to filter the sugar. And they don't want anything to do with that!"[8]

As with many non-Molokans, this skepticism extends also to commercial pharmacology. Most older and more conservative Molokans prefer first to employ traditional Russian homeopathic methods of cure or, in serious cases which evidence emotional causes or which have symptoms which indicate that the root of the trouble lies in the violation of community norms, to attempt faith healing.[9]

Conservative members of the sect believe that adherence to the Old Testament laws is part of their responsibility in the covenant of a chosen people with God. To associate with the outside world where the degree of observation of these laws is an unknown factor is to endanger and perhaps defile this inheritance. Young Molokans are brought up to avoid intense involvement with outsiders lest this behavior should lead to defection or even marriage outside the faith.

The controls are not, of course, completely effective. One informant stated that, "Nearly every large family has lost one child to the outside world."[10]

Foodways and Communication Networks

Social cohesion cannot be maintained through negative attitudes alone. Every rite of passage in the Molokan religious context is observed by a formal dinner or food sharing in some established form, usually at church or sometimes at home. The formal community dinner (*obed;* plural: *obedy*) is prepared by teams called *partii* which are organized along patrilineal kinship lines with older women acting as head cooks and overseers of the church kitchen. These meals are a major social occasion and a significant spiritual experience, and they are a successful means of bringing together all levels of the community for interaction. Even persons who have otherwise left the community maintain contact and probably some measure of security by attending these dinners.

Molokans usually refer to these dinners as a *žertva* (offering) or as a "love feast," a term common to Dunkards and other Christian sects as well. The *obedy* are prepared to mark the rites of passage such as marriage, the dedication of a child, or the funeral dinner following a burial. The organizational pattern and structure of this meal are worth examining in detail. When time allows, such events are announced in advance in the community newsletter. News of the death of a Molokan, however, is passed through the community by word of mouth and by telephone. Immediately, the wives and grandmothers contact one another and, in a matter of hours, women are making plans to go to the church and prepare food. Out of respect for age and skill, certain women are asked to take charge of specific tasks connected with the preparation of the meal. The position of head cook (*strjapši*) is especially prestigious.

On the day before the *delo* (doing) the women and, usually, several retired men gather at the church and roll out *lapša* (noodles) made from wheat flour, eggs, and salt. This highly skilled operation is of interest for several reasons. First, it is a time when a woman displays her abilities in Molokan food preparation style. With a *skalka* (rolling pin), she must roll a large lump of dough into paper-thin pancakes approximately thirty inches in diameter. The pancakes are then quickly dried on a stove top, folded in half twice to form a wedge, rolled, and quickly sliced laterally with a sharp knife. The *lapša* are kept covered until the day of the dinner when they are boiled in beef broth, though sometimes they are cooked in milk in deference to vegetarian guests. The speed and dexterity of the rolling, folding, and slicing of the *lapša* reveal the woman's skill and knowledge.

Second, the making of *lapša* provides an opportunity for community women from various *sobranie* (churches) and family lines to work together for a common cause. They sing psalms and spiritual songs which they have known all their lives and, at the conclusion of the task, sit down to a simple luncheon surrounded by huge baskets of golden noodles, symbols of their collective accomplishment. Personal differences or prideful misunderstandings can be smoothed over by the need and desire to work together, if not by the solemnity of the occasion. One male elder put it this way: "We could never buy a machine to do this work. Then there would be no love between the sisters. Now, if there is a squabble, they are forced to come together and talk it out in the presence of all the others."[11] Unfortunately, this tradition has eroded somewhat in urban Los Angeles. There, some church groups and families purchase machine-made *lapša* from a Molokan market and the degree of social interaction is thereby lessened. But as the *style* of commercially prepared *lapša* becomes more and more appropriate, behavior and behavior control mechanisms must adjust correspondingly. Most families now own their own *lapša* machines, and status achievement via this food custom has become home-centered. Yet this enculturating experience for the young women of the church continues as Molokan women of all ages gather twice each year to make *lapša* for benefit sales.

Male members of the Molokan communities are more passively involved in folk cookery, but the occasion of an *obed* is no less valuable for them, especially the young. Men and boys sit in groups around the plain wooden tables, chopping the vegetables for *boršč* (borshch, vegetable soup) and discussing a wide variety of topics which concern their beliefs and their daily spiritual lives. Where did we come from? What was it like in Russia under the Tsar? Why do we adhere to this or to that custom? What was meant by the prophet who spoke out in meeting last Sunday? A well-informed Molokan once explained: "We don't use books much. We learn about ourselves while we work. If you want to hear about the past, come into the kitchen. That's where the real Molokan education takes place!"[12]

After a Molokan funeral, the members of the immediate family must go home, bathe, and change clothes as an act of ritual purification. They are then ready to return to the church and join their brethren in the *obed.* [13] It is in the formal seating arrangements at the tables, a pattern which Molokans have absorbed from childhood, that the dominance of the male members and the status accorded various sub-groups is fully recognized. The minister, his assistants, and the male elders are seated at the first table, actually an extension of the small, plain table which serves as an "altar" and on which lie the Bible, prayer and song books, and the *Dux i žizn' (Book of Spirit and Life).* [14] Younger men or those with less status or responsibility in the church sit at the far end of this table and at the second table as befit their ages and roles. Women may sit with husbands at the second or third table, but women often sit together, especially the wives of the husbands who occupy the first table. Young people and any non-Molokan visitors sit at the table farthest from the elders.

Outside the kitchen, women occupy an equally important role in the formal structure of religious ritual as singers and prophetesses. Moreover, there are two tasks for women which, according to Molokan custom, cannot be fulfilled by men; these tasks are a clear example of how Molokans find religious and social expression in the serving and consumption of food. During the religious service which precedes the dinner and at the point where the prayer service begins, a woman brings from the kitchen a fresh loaf of Russian bread and a dish of salt. She places first the bread and then the salt on the table. After the prayers, a blessing is asked, the prophets prepare themselves to receive the blessing of the Holy Spirit, and singers begin an appropriate song. As soon as the Holy Spirit is manifested, usually in jumping or the raising of hands by all or part of the congregation, the minister places the bread on the Bible, sprinkles the salt on the bread, and holds it above the heads of the petitioners. Bread and salt, ancient Russian symbols of life and mutual amity, of growth and preservation, establish the sacred milieu. The bread and salt are eaten during the meal, and they remain on the table until the meal's conclusion.

As soon as the congregation is seated to begin eating, the minister and the elders are served by one or two older, married women who sit at the minister's left hand. Called *nalivašicy* (pourers), they pour tea, slice bread and see to the elders' every need. These two tasks are considered great honors and they are always reserved for women of good character with respected positions in the community.

According to tradition, the meal begins with hot tea served in glasses and deep saucers. With lemon, sugar, or preserves, one flavors the tea to taste, pours the tea into the saucer, and drinks it between bites of fresh bread, tomatoes, raisins, and cucumbers seasoned with fresh lemon juice and salt. To set the empty glass upright in the saucer is to ask for more; when one lays the glass on its side in the saucer, it is a sign that the person is finished with that course.

The second course, *boršč* or *lapša*, is eaten with traditional Russian wooden spoons, and sometimes a person will use a small piece of bread to convey the spoon to the lips without dripping. The third course is boiled beef, the broth from which has been used in the preparation of the previous course, and it is served simply on platters. The final course may consist of watermelon, bananas, apples, oranges, or pastries. Aside from the soup course, Molokans eat with their fingers at these ritual dinners, a conscious expression of simplicity, humility, ethnic and spiritual equality, and corporeal cleanliness.

These table "mannerisms" are passed on from generation to generation, reinforcing the group ethic and teaching restraint and respect. For example, between the blessing and the first bite of food, it is traditional to speak to the hosts' generosity and to wish him (or her) good health and the Lord's blessing for the rest of his days. This comment is always initiated by the eldest or most honored male present (who is seated at the head table) and is echoed in chorus by all others. One never puts one's elbows on the table nor slouches nor introduces unseemly topics in the table conversation. Even "please" and "thank you" are avoided as superfluous remarks since the food is actually a gift from God and the "thanks" have already been appropriately expressed. Ideally, one eats in a quiet and reflective manner at such spiritual gatherings, though it is often the case that some tables engage in conversation more lively than is desired. Occasionally, an elder rises to suggest a more restrained demeanor. As in other areas of traditional Molokan life, the young learn from their elders, and tradition or scripture is cited as the basis for practice.

Such a meal may go on for hours with psalms or spiritual songs sung between courses and brief *besedy* (discourses) offered by the various attending elders and honored guests from other areas. The immediate family of the person in whose name the dinner is given traditionally remained on their feet, not partaking of the food with their guests. Theirs was the role of host and hostess and they remained in a position which symbolically displayed their willingness to serve others before themselves. This posture is more difficult than one realizes. In the case of a funeral dinner, the family has borne the grief of the past three days (since the passing of the deceased) and must now show that "spiritual food" is, for the time being, enough to carry them through.[15] Today, the host and hostess are encouraged by the minister to join their guests after the prayers and acknowledgments. Such examples of restraint and stamina are rare in our modern world, but no true Molokan would consider doing otherwise. It is no wonder that the family's offering to the community is called a *žertva* (offering or sacrifice). For the Molokans, as with other peoples, food is a necessary mechanism for community solidarity in both a social and a ritual sense. Eating together is a deeply social act that erodes factionalism and enhances group identification and mutual permeability.[16] The gathering of the community at dinner following a funeral, for example, is a sign that death, in fact, has not weakened the group. The abundance of food and the joyful singing are signs to the contrary.

One of the clearest examples of relationship expressed through food custom is in the old Russian tradition of *pridanoe* (bride's marriage-portion or dowry) as it appears in Molokan weddings today. A loaf of bread, used at the *molenie* (prayer service) in the bride's home prior to the wedding, is wrapped in a white table cloth along with a dish of salt, two tea glasses, saucers, a platter, a small tea pot, and spoons. The entire affair is tied up in an *uzel* (bundle) and taken to the church ceremony by the bride's mother. At the proper time in the ceremony, while a special song is being sung, the matron of honor (*svaška*) presents the *uzel* to the minister, unwraps the cloth and sets the food and utensils before the elders and guests. The minister acknowledges the gesture and the *svaška* must then re-stack the items and re-tie the four corners of the cloth before the final verse of the song is concluded. Following the wedding, the groom's mother retrieves the *uzel* from the *svaška* and delivers it to the couple's residence. There, the bread and salt and other items are used at a *molenie* at which the minister and invited guests take part in the blessing of the couple in their new home.

Molokans generally agree that *pridanoe* is an old custom, perhaps one which symbolized the transfer of the bride's allegiance from her parents' home to the domain of her new husband and, ultimately, to her new mother-in-law. Today, Molokans interpret this act as an acknowledgment by the bride of her duty at setting a proper table, her acknowledgment of the Lord as provider, and her recognition of the importance of prayer and other forms of spiritual expression which are to be used in her new life before, during, and after eating.

Bread and salt as symbols of welcome are carried by the groom's parents from the church when they meet the wedding party prior to the ceremony. As the party responsible for preparing and serving the *obed*, the groom's family arrives at the church early and oversees the preparations for as many as two hundred or more guests. When the young couple, their attendants, the bride's parents, and their relatives and guests arrive from the *molenie* at the bride's home, the groom's mother goes into the church kitchen and brings a loaf of bread and a dish of salt (used in the *molenie* at her home) out to the wedding party. With her husband, she greets their "new daughter" and invites them all to enter and to begin the ceremony. The groom's mother then carries this bread and salt to the altar, thus announcing to the assembled elders and guests that the bridal party has arrived and that the service is about to begin. This same bread and salt is used in the blessing as described above.

Every close-knit community must learn to share its goods and will attach social and symbolic significance to such activity. The network of social interaction concerning foodways extends beyond the formal *obrjady* (rituals) of the church to the home. Here the ethnographer finds somewhat less emphasis on old-world traditions and more on style. At home, Molokans are generous to a fault, and visitors from rural areas will nearly always bring gifts of fresh produce or meat to their urban hosts, while the urban visitor might appear at her rural cousin's door with a platter of freshly baked *načinki* (pastries). The hostess responds (and receives recognition as a proper wife) by having on hand a variety of home-made edibles to serve with tea. Mutual respect is further inculcated by serving as few commercially prepared products as possible and by sharing the family's fruit preserves, home-salted sauerkraut, *kisloe moloko* (yogurt), home-cultivated honey, or home-canned pickles. Taken by themselves out of context, such sharing is not unlike the practice in the homes of many Americans with agrarian roots. The distinguishing element among the Molokans is the notion of avoidance of commercial products (an extention of avoiding the non-Molokan world in general) and the continuity of Russian foodways in a new land. In some respects, this behavior includes the presentation of American foods in a Russian style.

The parents and elders of the Molokan communities, and especially those more conservative sub-groups within the sect, spend a great deal of time inculcating their young with concepts of avoidance and purity. As in other cultural matters, there is a wide range in the degree of success in this matter and such variety is part of the complexity of intra-ethnic differentiation. In the home and at socio-religious events, foodways are a vehicle for establishing prescribed tastes and internalized reactions in children and teenagers. In large part, the instinctive sense of belonging and respect for the family and for the brotherhood is closely intertwined with a young Molokan's carefully developed attitudes toward conduct at meals, food preference, poise, and hospitality. Young people's groups in the various churches prepare and serve a community dinner for the adults on certain occasions. In this way, they show their interest in this tradition and learn the practical aspects of its fulfillment.

One of the best examples of young adults practicing Molokan foodways, and of integrating them with other aspects of enculturation, is the *spevka*. A *spevka* (from the Russian verb, *pet'*, to sing) can be loosely translated as a "singing class." The group sits at a dining room table, practices psalms and spiritual songs for an hour or more, and then partakes of a simple meal: tea in the Russian style, pastries, fruit and vegetables, and dairy products. As it is with kitchen work at church, the *spevka* is a forum for questions and answers about Molokan heritage and modern practice of the faith. It is an opportunity to demonstrate what they have learned from adults to the peer group. It is also an important opportunity to meet and to establish proper relations between girls and boys in a context approved by the community.[17]

Young Molokans do not lead totally cloistered lives, however. The community newsletters recognize athletic ability, leadership qualities, and even scholarly achievement outside the community. As much as possible, adults attempt to provide attractive activities for teenagers, and the admonitions of the elders against movies and going to the beach are heard less frequently today than in the 1940s and 1950s. A teenaged Molokan once described one of the less formal, but equally important, meetings of his friends at a local drive-in restaurant in Los Angeles:

Yeah, we always met down at K_____'s on the strip. And you could always tell where the Russians parked. You could walk by and see the sunflower seeds on the ground. They would sit in their cars and order *čaj* (tea) and eat *semečki* (sunflower seeds) and throw the hulls out the window. It was a place to be by ourselves and we were still acting right.[18]

Two of the four Molokan-owned food markets have a very special place in the history of the Molokan settlement in the Boyle Heights area of East Los Angeles, called "Flats." Today they serve not only as providers of "kosher" foods and Russian delicacies but also are places to meet friends and to post notices of community events. Adult Molokans recall the many times when credit to needy families was extended by these stores (and often simply not recorded) during hard times. In Molokan parlance this generous consideration was called "buying *na knižku*" (literally, "on the book," meaning "on credit"). Today, the community returns the favor with a steady and growing patronage; and these markets, together with the two new Molokan stores, continue to play a large role in the dynamics of Molokan food-related behavior.

Cultural Institutions:
Costume, Rites of Passage, and Food

With the understanding that *culture is integrated,* one can look at some of the Molokans' most prominent church-related cultural institutions and the extent to which they hold parallel values and meanings with ritual foodways. These institutions are consciously preserved, adapted, and manipulated to represent both their unique ethno-religious culture and the many ways in which individuals can interpret that culture with some latitude and yet avoid ambiguity within the group. The structural relationships of these institutions are understood by members of the communities, and it is in this "understanding" and in the reduction of ambiguity that the creation of symbol and metaphor begins.

Most visible among the Molokans is their ritual costume which is worn at all socio-religious occasions, whether in church or at home. Patterned essentially on the utilitarian dress of nineteenth-century Russian farming people, it consists today of three basic elements for women: a *kosinka* (head scarf), a dress or two-piece "outfit," consisting of a *jub* (skirt) and a *kofta* (blouse), and lastly, a *fartuk* (apron). The male costume is more a costume-complex, consisting of a Russian-style *rubaška* (shirt), which is unique in its high collar enclosing the throat with four buttons down the left side beginning at the shoulder, and a silk *pojas* (corded belt) tied around the waist and knotted at the left hip.[19] Males wear ordinary slacks or suit pants and dress shoes with the *rubaška.* The second element in the male costume is a beard, ideally worn long and untrimmed in the Hasidic fashion. Many, however, trim their beards to a spade-like shape or are clean-shaven. The third element of male costuming is hair style.

Interviews with Molokans about costume design and use in former times revealed that in Russia, and during the hard times of the early settlement years, costume was seldom thought of in any conscious or symbolic way. Cloth, colors, and patterns were chosen for utilitarian purposes. Women's dresses and men's shirts were frequently dark, patterned, or striped so as not to show dirt. Sturdy fabrics were selected for warmth and long wear. The apron was widely worn by women to protect the dress from soil and wear, especially when kneeling in church or at work.

Modern Molokans' costumes are quite different. Men and women attend religious and social gatherings in "outfits" cut from the same cloth and color, usually white or pastel. The favorite material is a light synthetic which is comfortable in southern California churches or in homes with modern heating plants. They are easily laundered in modern washing machines and most individuals own five or more outfits. The *kosinka* or head scarf has changed from a large, practical garment offering warmth and protection in wet weather to a highly decorated hand-made lace scarf. The apron today usually matches the *kosinka* in style and material and is essentially a decorative but still highly symbolic item.

Taken as a whole, the complete costume and its evolution from a utilitarian to a decorative complex tell us much about how Molokans have changed and how they have not changed. Since their religious boundaries are also their ethnic boundaries, it is considered important to continue wearing "Russian" clothing styles at religious services just as it is important to continue using the Russian language, especially in singing and when reciting vows. However, if we arrange these costume elements in some meaningful relationship, a new message appears. If a woman comes to the church kitchen to prepare an *obed,* she will probably wear a plain cloth dress of contemporary American cut, plus a *kosinka.* It is obligatory that her head be covered in church, even in the kitchen, and most married Molokan women continue the Russian custom of wearing a head scarf out-of-doors for both practical and symbolic reasons. The *kosinka,* then, is a basic and necessary element in female costume.

The next most important element is the "outfit," the skirt and the blouse. Unmarried girls seldom own or appear in this garb at any gathering. For them, the ordinary American dress plus the *kosinka* are sufficient. The "oufit," then, is, by and large, a mark of a married woman and is always made specifically for its wearer. The skirt is ankle-length; the blouse is fitted with wrist-length sleeves; and the bodice and sleeves are usually decorated according to individual taste and expressive intent with small sequins or pearl buttons and lace.

The third item in importance is the apron or *fartuk.* Though some claim that wearing the apron is merely a matter of personal choice, it tends to be omitted by young and middle-aged women, but it is worn as a decorative item by elderly women, usually widows, by important female singers in the *sobranie,* and by prophetesses.

The most important basic item in the men's costume is the Russian shirt or *rubaška.* Very rarely will a Molokan male appear at any religious or social event, picnics and other informal outings excepted, without such a shirt, always buttoned up and never without the silk *pojas* or corded belt. The men's shirt is undecorated, and the cuffs may be styled in an individual manner.

Traditionally, men stop shaving at marriage, but today a few beards are evident among the more dedicated teenaged boys or among those who admire current popular style. Informants have declared that one major reason for wearing a beard is that it serves as recognition of and respect for their forefathers' sufferings. However, there are numerous older men without beards or with only a mustache. Any neat and modest hair style is appropriate for men, but older men, church elders and prophets, as well as more conservative Molokans, part their hair in the middle as did their Russian forefathers.

In tabulated form, then, the elements of Molokan costume appear thus in order of completeness:

Female	Male
Kosinka (scarf)	*Rubaška* (shirt with belt)
Jub i Kofta (skirt and blouse)	Beard
Fartuk (apron)	Hair parted in middle

The order of the elements in each list denotes adherence to tradition (as interpreted by community members today) and connotes progression in age, ascribed as well as desired social position, respect, and authority. Ministers, prophets, and other elders tend to wear all elements of the traditional costume-complex as befits their status, their degree of participation in religious ritual, and their commitment to an unambiguous relationship with God.

Molokan rites of passage, church services, marriage negotiations, and periodic family gatherings for memorial services or visits are observed as uniquely Molokan in form, content, and style. These gatherings mark periods of transition, separation, and incorporation.[20] In light of the Molokans' struggles for pollution avoidance and an unequivocal relationship with God, these rites also reflect periodic reduction in ambiguity, with both the community and with the Spirit. At birth, a Molokan child, himself an untested being, faces many unknowns, both physical and spiritual. Receiving a name is the first, formal step toward reducing ambiguity and it is initiated by his parents. Later, the Molokan youth initiates another step by choosing a Molokan marriage partner; together, they reduce both social and spiritual ambiguity by adhering to traditional group values and behavior. The funeral, a rite of separation for the deceased (but a rite of transition and incorporation for the survivors), is the final reduction of ambiguity. The unknowns of earthly life are replaced by the ultimate

Unknown, which, by virtue of faith, dogma, and the covenant with God, is at once the least mysterious stage of all. Thus, from birth, Molokans steadily reduce metaphorical dependency until, at death, the total Other is achieved and earthly metaphors are meaningful only to those who remain behind.

As with costume, these rites and gatherings connote a significant sequence in emotional, spiritual, and social completeness parallel to the tabulation shown above. For example, one of the earliest Molokan rites of passage is the dedication of a child during which the infant is formally named and dedicated to the beliefs of the sect. Despite the obvious religious basis of this activity, the tone of the event is joyful and future-oriented. Such gatherings may be small affairs held at home or larger gatherings at a church. Sometimes several families dedicate their babies in one church service. A full *obed* is served, but it is at such events that innovations in the traditional menu are sometimes attempted. For example, barley soup is substituted for *boršč* or fancier pastry is offered. This latitude in content and structure, and the fact that infants, parents, and relatives are all important in the event, encourages family and community members to interact in a relaxed and informal manner.

By contrast, a marriage ceremony is attended by large numbers of well-wishers from various communities, but young married and unmarried friends of the bridal couple are a more visible segment among the attenders. A full *obed* is served and certain elders are always called upon to make speeches concerning the couple and their obligations to each other and to the faith. This is an opportunity to inculcate the young, unmarried attenders with the concern for maintaining cultural cohesion and social stability. The focus of this event is the bride and groom, and the concerns of the guests are mainly future-oriented. Still, there is, as always, a strong undercurrent of memory and recollection of the couple when they were younger and of other, previous weddings, including one's own.

Russian folk tradition and Molokan spiritual codes demand that weddings serve as a clear rite of incorporation, thus strongly reducing ambiguity on several levels. *Obrjady* (rituals) are strictly observed, and great emphasis is placed upon completing the ceremony without errors. Russian is spoken whenever possible, though the young people's English tends to predominate. The tone of the event is joyous and, though the couple's responsibilities in the ceremony are somewhat rigorous, the large numbers of well-wishers create a mood of jocularity and goodwill which is typically Russian and highly infectious.

Most structured and least ambiguous of the Molokan rites of passage is a funeral, attended by family and friends and marked by high emotion. Every community member tries to attend funerals regardless of family relationship to the deceased. A full *obed* is served, elder Molokans are more in evidence than younger, and the role of the elders is more prominent. Spoken discourses (*besedy*) focus on but one figure, the deceased, and tend to be concerned with both the biblical or historical past and with the millennial future. There are more manifestations of the Holy Spirit as the community unites spiritually in this last major opportunity to communicate both inwardly and outwardly their sense of loss in the present, the richness of the past, and their prayers for the future. The attending community partakes of the *obed* solemnly and reflectively; and the symbolic and metaphoric roles of food in the rite are celebrative in a far different way than at a wedding. In short, more people achieve a deeper unity if for no other reason than the recognition that the fate of the deceased is the ultimate fate of all.

In tabulation, the institutions of Molokan costume and rites of passage are:

Mode	Costume (Female)	Costume (Male)	Rite
Least structured:	*Kosinka*	*Rubaška*	Dedication of child
Moderately structured:	Skirt/Blouse	Beard	Marriage
Most structured:	Apron	Parted Hair	Funeral

These elements correspond to a progressive increase in structure, stability of content, status, age, and spiritual involvement.

The cultural institution most germane to this essay is the formal dinner, called *obed.* Dinners follow a traditional pattern as follows:

Čaj (Tea, served in glasses), raisins, bread, and sliced vegetables;
Soup (*Boršč* or *lapša* or some close innovation);
Meat (Beef, chicken, or lamb);
Fresh fruits and pastries.

Again, one finds here a socio-religious institution patterned after an earlier Russian food custom which was more utilitarian than ritualistic. Elders have stated that this meal has a special order that was satisfying to the farm worker who returned from long hours of continuous labor or to the traveler who had come a long way through the Caucasus Mountains to visit another Molokan. This custom, too, can be broken down into component parts which are used for various kinds of social or religious interaction, *but always in sequence*. Tea, bread, jam, and sliced vegetables seasoned with lemon juice and salt are a typical snack for an afternoon guest of no particular status or for an elder who drops in unexpectedly. The bread is always fresh, home-baked (if possible) white bread. Sweet rolls (*načinki*) are invariably prepared by the hostess in her own kitchen.

A typical meal for a family, especially in the past when meat was too expensive, was bread, vegetables and fruit, milk or cheese, plus *boršč* or soup. Only a particularly festive or spiritually significant occasion required that meat be served.

The *obed* is always accompanied, in church or in a private home, by hours of conversation and frequent songs, either psalms or *duxovnye pesni* (spiritual songs), which are uniquely Molokan in form and style. The psalms are slower, more sedate, and thoughtful; and they are sung in the early stages of the meal, setting the proper tone as they do at the opening of a church service. The more spirited *duxovnye pesni* come later, often during or after the meat course. Though spiritual expression (jumping, prophecy, or the raising of hands in praise) may occur at any time, significant manifestations of the Spirit *tend* to be seen during the latter part of the dinner when people are standing in song. It is at the end of such a dinner that all the elements of Molokan culture seem to coalesce, bringing the emotional, spiritual, and historic tides in each individual to a crest. Intensely emotional remarks are delivered in Russian by bearded elders, with spiritual brothers and sisters in traditional garb filling every table; the cadence of highly spiritual songs reminds the gathering of their past and their future and creates a sense of *edinomyslie* (one-mindedness). This unity is both spiritual and cultural, and it is based upon a sense of progression through ritual from simple to complex, from partial to full participation, from marginality to centrality, from beginning to completion.

"Completion," for this analysis of Molokan expressive culture, means an inner unity which comes with the blessing of the Holy Spirit or a striving for that blessing, a striving for a sign. Theoretically, this process is metaphoric and it is necessarily ephemeral. If *every* living act were acknowledged by the Spirit, the millennial state would be achieved, paradise regained, and total integration with God attained; only the deceased have attained this integration. During this premillennial period, the Molokan sect revitalizes itself through intermittent, ritual acts within a recognized structure or paradigm. These acts are important from the level of an individual's conscious feeling of belonging (through costume, song and prayer, and foodways), to the total group's ability to interact continually and meaningfully within a single system. Part of that system is the structural relation of the cultural institutions outlined here.

In tabulation, the institutions examined may be shown cumulatively as reflective of the Molokan sense of completion:

Female	Male	Food	Oral	Spiritual Event
Kosinka	*Rubaška*	Tea	Psalms	Dedication of child
Outfit	Beard	Soup	Speeches	Marriage ceremony
Apron	Hair	Meat	Spiritual songs	Funeral service

The Molokans are a complex society, manifesting wide disparity internally as to the veracity, meaning, and modes of expression of symbolic and metaphoric images, processes, and ideas. As demonstrated in the analysis of major cultural institutions, certain elements connote completion and commitment far beyond the social and spiritual depth of some members. For them, wearing the costume, occasionally attending church services, and, of course, appearing at certain *obedy* are all they deem necessary. For many others, wearing the costume and observing food taboos in an actively spiritual manner, attending services regularly, and demonstrating a willingness to learn and use the Russian language, at least in religious song, signify the maximum ethno-religious expression. A small number of Molokans consistently and persistently incorporate virtually every institution into their daily lives. Some Molokans demonstrate their commitment to the community through youth and adult club activities. They publish the community newsletter, organize sports, and coordinate "secular" events such as the annual steak dinner each June. Finally, a small number of Molokan-born individuals have, with their families, left the community, joined other churches; they now attend only the funerals of relatives, the most obligatory of Molokan religious services.

Predictably, these gradations of spiritual and social involvement reflect the extent to which individuals think of themselves as "Molokan" as compared to other categories such as "Christian" or "American." The individuals who casually observe dietary traditions and divide their social lives between the Molokan world and outsiders may be seen as drifting toward denominationalism, identifying more with a "Christian" life. They tend to maintain Russian folk customs minimally, as no longer integral to their personal tastes or to their social and spiritual lives. Frequently, the excuse is given that the older form of a ritual puts too many demands upon the family or that a certain custom no longer is meaningful to younger family members. At the other extreme, more conservative Molokans stridently emulate the image of a Chosen People and, more important, they are overtly political in their ever-evolving sectarian attitudes toward the outside world and with their own brethren. They prefer to call themselves "Molokans," "Russian Molokans," or "Spiritual Christian Jumpers." Many from this segment of the community support *poxod* from the United States; their use of the Russian language is more extensive; and their observance of traditional foodways is painstaking and legalistic.

The ability of the Molokans to create dense visual, aural, kinesthetic, and celebrative symbols is an example of an unusually well-ordered strategy for ethno-religious expression. Since the outside world sees little of these cultural institutions, in process or in form, one must conclude that their function is internally directed. Because the order of this process is known, status is sought and conferred through the manipulation of and participation in the celebrative acts. Degrees and intensity of expression denote ethno-religious affiliation and modes of interpretation of that affiliation. As culture is dynamic, these acts, forms, and processes will surely change; and it is the intra-group metaphoric action which supplies the evidence of how they change.

Thus, the sustaining power of food in both a physical and in a metaphysical sense can be understood only through careful examination of cultural history, manifest customs, and the underlying behavioral and emotional patterns of group members who strive to define and to redefine their identity and the identity of their culture group through manipulation of foodways. Together with historical and ethnographic documentation, analyses of symbol and metaphor can clarify behavioral patterns and strengthen our grasp of ethnic and religious affiliation.

ACKNOWLEDGMENTS

The field research for this study was supported by a grant from the Center for Urban Ethnography, University of Pennsylvania. The author is grateful to Dr. Stephen P. Dunn and Ethel Dunn of the Highgate Road Social Science Research Station for their encouragement, support, and cooperation in sharing research materials. My thanks to the Dunns, to Anne R. Kaplan, and to several members of the Los Angeles Molokan community for reading earlier drafts of the essay and for offering many helpful suggestions. All interpretations and conclusions in this essay are the responsibility of the author. For more complete analysis, see the author's "The Spiritual Christian Molokans in the United States: A Cognitive Analysis of Metaphors and Symbols," Ph.D. diss., Indiana Univ., 1983.

NOTES

1. Pronounced Mál-e-k'n. The major works on the Molokans include Pauline V. Young, *The Pilgrims of Russian-town* (Chicago: Univ. of Chicago Press, 1932, re-issued by Russell and Russell, 1967); Sidney Rochelle Story, "The Russian Molokans of the Guadalupe," (Ph.D. diss., Univ. of California at Los Angeles, 1960); John K. Berokoff, *Molokans in America* (Whittier, Calif.: Stockton-Doty, 1969); Willard B. Moore, *Molokan Oral Tradition: Legends and Memorates of an Ethnic Sect,* Folklore Series No. 28 (Berkeley: Univ. of California Press, 1973); Willard B. Moore, "Communal Experiments as Resolution of Sectarian Identity Crisis," in *Communes Historical and Contemporary,* ed. Ruth Shonle Cavan and Man Singh Das (New Delhi: Vikus Publishing House, 1979), 92–112; Ethel Dunn, "American Molokans and Canadian Dukhobors: Economic Position and Ethnic Identity," in *Ethnicity in the Americas,* ed. Frances S. Henry (Chicago: Aldine Press, 1976); and Ethel Dunn and Stephen P. Dunn, "Religion and Ethnicity: The Case of the American Molokans," *Ethnicity* 4 (1977):370–79. For a review of Soviet scholarship on the Molokans, see Ethel Dunn, "Russian Sectarianism in New Soviet Marxist Scholarship," *Slavic Review* 1 (1967):128–40.

The transliterations of Russian words in this essay are based on the international scholarly system for Russian and Slavic Studies as presented in J. Thomas Shaw, *The Transliteration of Modern Russian for English-Language Publications* (Madison: Univ. of Wisconsin Press, 1971). The following brief guide will be helpful: i is pronounced as ee in see, u is pronounced as oo in shoot, š as sh in shoot, č as ch in church, y as i in it, x as ch in Bach, j as y in yes, ž as z in seizure, and c as ts in lots.

2. See John A. Hostetler, *Amish Society,* 3rd ed. (Baltimore: Johns Hopkins Univ. Press, 1980), 75–92. Also, see John A. Hostetler, *Hutterite Society* (Baltimore: Johns Hopkins Univ. Press, 1977), 140–48.

3. See Sydelle Brooks Levy, "Shifting Patterns of Ethnic Identification among the Hasidim," in *The New Ethnicity, Perspectives from Ethnology,* ed. John W. Bennet, 1973 Proceedings of the American Ethnological Society (St. Paul: West, 1975), 25–50. See also Frederik Barth, ed., *Ethnic Groups and Boundaries* (Boston: Little, Brown, 1969), 29; James P. Spradley, ed., *Culture and Cognition: Rules, Maps, and Plans* (San Francisco: Chandler, 1972), 25–26; and Robert Murphy, *The Dialectics of Social Life* (New York: Columbia Univ. Press, 1971).

4. For example, ritual foods are used and, sometimes, named differently. The traditional Easter bread, called *kulič* by Orthodox Russians, is called "*Paxsa* bread" by the Molokans. Vodka and other festive alchoholic beverages are never acknowledged as proper.

5. Accounts of these settlements may be found in Oscar Schmieder, "The Russian Colony of the Guadalupe Valley," *Publications in Geography,* Univ. of California, Berkeley (1928); Story, "The Russian Molokans of the Guadalupe"; Berokoff, *Molokans in America;* and Moore, "Communal Experiments." By contrast, from the 1930s until the mid-1950s, three substantial Molokan villages operated successfully in what is now northern Iran. Molokans who emigrated to California from these villages are known as "Persians." Witnesses to the early stages of Soviet collectivization, the Persians bring to their American communities a very recent Russian village experience, fluency in Russian, and some variation in ritual.

6. As blood is the essence of life itself, and only God may spill it without sin, extreme care is taken to minimize blood flow in slaughtering. See Theodore Gaster, *The Holy and the Profane* (New York: William Sloane, 1955), 206–208; and *The Code of Maimonedes,* Book X, trans. Herbert Danby (New Haven: Yale Univ. Press, 1954).

7. There is some evidence that Molokans at one time considered becoming vegetarians. See Ethel Dunn, "American Molokans and Canadian Dukhobors," 111.

8. Personal interview with Molokan elder, 1969.

9. See Moore, *Molokan Oral Tradition*, 70.

10. Personal interview with John K. Berokoff, 1970.

11. Personal interview with J.E. Poppin, 1971.

12. Personal interview with George J. Samarin, 1970.

13. See Moore, *Molokan Oral Tradition*, 36. Since the body of the deceased is soulless, it is polluted, and the family's bathing and change of clothes is a necessary symbolic cleansing.

14. *Dux i žizn': kniga solnce (Spirit and Life: The Book of the Sun)*, ed. I.G. Samarin, 3rd ed. (Los Angeles: Young People's Church, 1947). This book contains the edited writings of Maksim Gavrilovič Rudometkin, Luk'jan Petrovič Sokolov, and David Evseevič as well as the narratives and prophetic plans of Efim Gerasimovič Klubnikin. *Dux i žizn'* is comparable to *The Book of Mormon* or, for Quakers, the *Journals of George Fox*.

15. Some families choose to fast prior to such memorial dinners. In those cases when they eat separately, at the close of the ceremonies, the portions they eat are called *povtorimye* (literally: "repeats").

16. See George De Vos, "Psychology of Purity and Pollution as Related to Social Self-Identity and Caste," in *Ciba Foundation Symposium on Caste and Race: Comparative Approaches*, ed. A.V.S. de Reuck and Julie Knight (London: J.&A. Churchill, 1967), 310. See also Michael Kearny, "The Social Meaning of Food Sharing in Mexico," *Kroeber Anthropological Society Papers* 43 (1970):32–41.

17. Molokan song traditions will be discussed in Stephen P. Dunn, et al., *The Kingdom in the City*, in progress.

18. Personal interview with Molokan youth, 1971.

19. Many interviewees testified that the significance of the corded belt is stated in Ephesians 6:14: "Stand therefore, having your loins girt about with truth. . . ." See also, Rudometkin, *Dux i žizn'*, 284. Older Molokans are loathe to wear neckties with American style shirts, calling them *sobačij jazik* ("dog's tongue"), a term connoting foolishness and gaudiness.

20. Arnold Van Gennep, *The Rites of Passage* (Chicago: Univ. of Chicago Press, 1969), 1–4.

5

Why Migrant Women Feed Their Husbands Tamales: Foodways as a Basis for a Revisionist View of Tejano Family Life

Brett Williams

In the array of artifacts by which Tejano migrant farmworkers identify themselves, the tamale has no serious rival.[1] It is a complicated culinary treat demanding days of preparation, marking festive — sometimes sacred — occasions, signalling the cook's extraordinary concern for the diners, and requiring a special set of cultural skills and tastes to appreciate and consume appropriately. Tamales are served wrapped in corn husks which hold a soft outer paste of *masa harina* (a flour) and a rich inner mash prepared from the meat of a pig's head.

Only women make tamales. They cooperate to do so with domestic fanfare which stretches through days of buying the pigs' heads, stripping the meat, cooking the mash, preparing the paste, and stuffing, wrapping, and baking or boiling the final tamale. Women shop together because the heads are very bulky; they gather around huge, steaming pots to cook together as well. Tamales are thus labor-intensive food items which symbolize and also exaggerate women's routine nurturance of men. The ritual and cooperation of tamale cookery dramatically underscore women's shared monopoly of domestic tasks.

For middle-class women, such immersion in household affairs is generally taken as a measure of a woman's oppression. We often tend to equate power and influence in the family with freedom from routine family tasks and find such tamale vignettes as those below disconcerting:

—At home in Texas for the winter, an elderly migrant woman, with her daughters-in-law, nieces, and goddaughter, spends several weeks preparing *200 dozen* tamales to distribute to friends, relatives, and local taverns for Christmas. The effort and expense involved are enormous, but she regards this enterprise as a useful and rewarding way to commemorate the holiday, to obligate those she may need to call on later, and to befriend the tavern owners so that they will watch over her male kin who drink there.

—In Illinois for six months a year, migrant women take precious time out from field labor to prepare elaborate feasts, with many tamales, commemorating the conclusion of each harvest (in asparagus, peas, tomatoes, pumpkins, and corn) as well as dates of biographical significance to others in the camp. An especially important day is the *quinceñera,* or fifteenth birthday, on which a young girl who will most likely spend her life in field labor is feted with tamales, cakes, and dancing all night, just as though she were a debutante.

—A young migrant, with the full support of his wife's kin as well as his own, sues his wife for divorce in a smalltown Illinois court. His grounds are that she refuses to cook him tamales and dances with other men at fiestas. A disconcerted Illinois Judge refuses to grant a divorce on such grounds and the migrant community is outraged: women argue with special vehemence that to nurture and bind her husband a proper wife should cook him tamales.[2]

Incidents like the last, focused on women, their husbands, elaborate domestic nurturance, and the jealous circumscription of sexuality in marriage, again seem to reveal the most repressed and traditional of females. Because migrant women are so involved in family life and so seemingly submissive to their husbands, they have been described often as martyred purveyors of rural Mexican and Christian custom, tyrannized by excessively masculine, crudely domineering, rude and petty bullies in marriage, and blind to any world outside the family because they are suffocated by the concerns of kin.[3] Most disconcerting to outside observers is that migrant women seem to embrace such stereotypes: they argue that they *should* monopolize their foodways and that they should *not* question the authority of their husbands. If men want tamales, men should have them. But easy stereotypes can mislead; in exploring the lives of the poor, researchers must revise their own notions of family life, and this paper argues that foodways can provide crucial clues about how to do so.[4]

The paradox is this: among migrant workers both women and men are equally productive wage earners, and husbands readily acknowledge that without their wives' work their families cannot earn enough to survive. For migrants the division of labor between earning a living outside the home and managing household affairs is unknown; and the dilemma facing middle-class wives who may wish to work to supplement the family's income simply does not exist. Anthropologists exploring women's status cross-culturally argue that women are most influential when they share in the production of food and have some control over its distribution.[5] If such perspectives bear at all on migrant women, one might be led to question their seemingly unfathomable obsequiousness in marriage.

Anthropologists further argue that women's influence is even greater when they are not isolated from their kinswomen, when women can cooperate in production and join, for example, agricultural work with domestic duties and childcare.[6] Most migrant women spend their lives within large, closely knit circles of kin and their work days with their kinswomen. Marriage does not uproot or isolate a woman from her family, but rather doubles the relatives each partner can depend on and widens in turn the networks of everyone involved. The lasting power of marriage is reflected in statistics which show a divorce rate of 1 percent for migrant farmworkers from Texas, demonstrating the strength of a union bolstered by large numbers of relatives concerned that it go well.[7] Crucial to this concern is that neither partner is an economic drain on the family, and the Tejano pattern of early and lifelong marriages establishes some limit on the whimsy with which men can abuse and misuse their wives.

While anthropology traditionally rests on an appreciation of other cultures in their own contexts and on their own terms, it is very difficult to avoid class bias in viewing the lives of those who share partly in one's own culture, especially when the issue is something so close to home as food and who cooks it. Part of the problem may lie in appreciating what families are and what they do. For the poor, public and private domains are blurred in confusing ways, family affairs may be closely tied to economics, and women's work at gathering and obligating or *binding* relatives is neither trivial nor merely a matter of sentiment. Another problem may lie in focusing on the marital relationship as indicative of a woman's authority in the family. We too often forget that women are sisters, grandmothers, and aunts to men as well as wives. Foodways can help us rethink both of these problematic areas and understand how women elaborate domestic roles to knit families together, to obligate both male and female kin, and to nurture and bind their husbands as well.

The Setting For Family Life

To understand migrant family foodways, it is important to explore first the economic circumstances within which they operate. The two thousand Tejano migrants who come to Prairie Junction, Illinois, to work in its harvest for six months a year are permanent residents of the Texas Rio Grande Valley, a lush and tropical agricultural paradise.[8] Dominating that landscape are great citrus and truck farms, highly mechanized operations which rely on commuters from across the Mexican border for whatever manual labor they need. Lacking jobs or substantial property at home, Tejanos in the valley exit for part of each year to earn a living in the north. Agricultural pay is low and employment is erratic, guaranteeing no income beyond a specific hourly wage and offering no fringe benefits in the event of unemployment or disability.[9] As a consequence, migrant workers must be very flexible in pursuing work and must at the same time forge some sort of security on their own to cushion frequent economic jolts. Migrants use kinship to construct both the security and the flexibility they need to manage a very marginal economic place.

In extended families, all members are productive workers (or at the very least share in childcare duties), and migrants find a great deal of security within families whose members are mutually committed to stretching scarce resources among them. Kin call on kin often for material aid, housing, and emotional support; they cooperate in field labor and domestic tasks and freely share food, money, time, and space. Because resources are only sporadically available to individuals, depending on kin eases hard times. In turn, most persons are sensitive to their relatives' needs not only because they care about them but also because they recognize the great value of reciprocity over time.

Migrant families are not easily placed in a convenient anthropological category for they implicate relatives in binding ways while allowing husbands and wives a great deal of freedom to move and settle when they need to, and to return whenever they like. This relative independence of nuclear families allows them to scatter and regroup when pursuing erratic opportunities to work, but always underlying their travels is a sense of a long-term place within a wider circle of kin. I call migrant families *convoys*, for they should be conceptualized as a process rather than a structure; they literally join persons in travel, in work, and through the life course, sharing food as well as the most intimate of concerns.

In the rural Texas settlements (*colonias*) where most migrants spend jobless winters, and in the stark barracks of Prairie Junction where they work each summer, convoys come together (1) to produce and share food for economic survival, (2) to surround food with ritual in order to save one another's dignity in degrading situations, (3) to reaffirm their cultural identity through marking and crossing boundaries with outsiders, and (4) to gather and bind kin, including spouses, to accompany them through life.

Strategies for Survival: Routine

Just as tamales ritually underscore women's domestic commitments, the everyday preparation and sharing of food routinely reaffirms family ties and allows families to work as efficiently and profitably as possible. Especially in emergencies, the sharing of food attests to migrants' visions of their lives as closely, mutually intertwined. The discussion which follows explores the foodways of the Texas *colonias* and the Prairie Junction migrant camps, the routines which surround them, and the ways they mobilize in crisis.

A newcomer to the Texas *colonias* is struck first by the appalling poverty in which migrants live there. Most are too far from the valley's urban centers to share in such amenities as running water, sewage disposal, or garbage collection. Hand-constructed shacks usually surround a primitive central area where fruits and vegetables grow, goats and chickens roam, and children play. The homes have many hastily-constructed additions and ill-defined rooms, attesting to the mobility of the individual family members and seemingly indicating an impermanence to domestic life. This feeling of impermanence is belied, however, by the ongoing family-scale agricultural and pastoral system through which kin produce and share their own food over the Texas winters. Individuals may come and go; but through the extended family migrants adapt as peasants to those times when there is no income. The *colonias* offer evidence of creative domestic cooperation in stretching and sharing food within families and in the continuing migration of family members north from Mexico and back and forth to Illinois to work. These kin know that they can always find food from the winter gardens in Texas.

It is in this context that one can appreciate Sra. Compartida's great Christmas feasts of 200 dozen tamales for relatives, friends, and people she considers resources or contacts. She has worked for most of her life to allow her relatives in Mexico to join her, and in her old age she finds herself surrounded by kin who help her and whom she can count on. She feeds them still and is known especially for the beans and flour tortillas which she always cooks for those she welcomes home. She is clearly at the center of a convoy of cooperating kin whom she has organized and continues to remind of their obligations to one another.[10]

Sra. Compartida has worked for wages throughout her life and continues to do part-time housework when it is available. But, like other migrant women, she is a wife who appears much too submissive to her husband: she offers him extraordinary care, cooks everything he eats, and quietly abides his beer-drinking although she disapproves of it. On the other hand, her efforts on behalf of her family have compelled Sra. Compartida to learn English and cultivate respectable skills at negotiating bureaucracies such as the immigration service. Her husband clearly depends on her as his ambassador, not only among kin but also with the outside Anglo world. They cooperate in setting their particular relationship apart through constructing roles in which he pretends to be boss, proclaiming extreme jealousy and expecting that she nurture him in elaborate ways. Yet one cannot dismiss their interaction by stereotype, for Sra. Compartida's authority and influence as mother, aunt, god-mother, sister, and grandmother are so definite that she simply will not fit a category. Tamales help her maintain that influence, and she uses them to express affection and obligate others, as well as to gather a network of tavern owners who watch out for her husband when she cannot be there.

Domestic cooperation extends to the Illinois migrant camps, long barracks of small single rooms originally designed to accommodate prisoners of war. The camps offer domestic convoys highly inappropriate living situations, for they allot these single rooms to conjugal families, and through separating kin dramatically defy their routine commitment to shared domestic tasks. Because observers often prefer that each family convene in a tidy still-life world, migrant family life in the camps has been portrayed by some as very chaotic.[11] Kin realign in this inappropriate space to share domestic duties, care for children, cook cooperatively, allow husbands and wives conjugal privacy, and meet recurring emergency needs. While a conjugal family might remain basically committed to a particular room, kin move in and out of one another's rooms throughout the day, often carrying pots of food or other supplies. Children gather with elderly caretakers in a central outdoor spot (for the small rooms are stifling), and it is sometimes difficult to identify their mothers and fathers. Other kin who have settled temporarily in town visit the camp frequently, bringing food and children back and forth with them.

Women cook together routinely, sharing and stretching short supplies, combining scarce ingredients to preserve what they can of traditional Tejano tastes. They transport clay pots, tortilla presses, and chiles from their homes to the camps each year, and replenish short supplies throughout the summer as kin travel back and forth to Texas.

Thus, surrounded by Illinois cornfields, women simmer beans in the barracks, save tomatoes from the fields for sauces when they can, and do their best to stretch the family's wages to support a large group of relatives.

Strategies for Survival: Crisis

If the tamale symbolizes elaborate celebration and nurturance, the tortilla is probably most symbolic of the last bit of food a woman has to share. Simply, quickly, expertly made by migrant women, tortillas are treated very much like bread. Women roll a dough from *masa harina* or plain white flour, lard, salt, and water, flatten it with a press or by hand, and fry it on a dry griddle for just a few minutes. It is the least expensive and most basic of their food items, and when women worry (as they often do) that their supplies have dwindled to the ingredients for tortillas, they are speaking of real want. Tortillas stand for emergencies, and it is through such crises that one can see perhaps most clearly how migrant family foodways work.

One family which has weathered many crises typical of migrant life is the Gomas. Their domestic convoy stretches through four generations and across several marriages, and their members are dispersed in Texas and Illinois but remain closely involved in one another's lives. The woman most central to this family is middle-aged and lives with her husband and their teenaged children off-and-on in Prairie Junction. Joana Goma and her husband have never been able to last for long in Illinois, for it is difficult for them to find work there, and they move back and forth to Texas often, sometimes leaving one of their children there for a time or returning with other young relatives so, as she puts it, "I won't have to be lonesome for them all winter." Each summer some two dozen of the Goma's relatives arrive to work through the migrant season, and during that time Sra. Goma mobilizes on their behalf the resources of her Illinois networks — legal aid, public assistance, transportation, and a less formal example, a service station owner who will cash paychecks. She has worked hard to stretch and secure this network, often initially obligating friends through food. By sharing her locally famous taco dinners, Illinois residents act as though they are kin, and through time she finds that she can call on them for help as if they really were.

Although Joana Goma's marriage also appears quite traditional, with food and sex recurring metaphors for conjugal loyalty, she is the center of a world on which her husband and his kin depend. [12] When her sister-in-law was disabled because her hands were poisoned by pesticides, Sra. Goma saw to it that her own sister assumed the woman's cooking and housekeeping tasks. When her sister's nephew was stricken with hepatitis, Sra. Goma untangled the complicated legal procedures whereby a local hospital was compelled to provide free medical care for indigents, secured his bus fare to Texas from Traveler's Aid, and organized an investigation of the camp's drinking water. But these smaller, frequent emergencies are less telling than a more dramatic tortilla crisis in which the Gomas powerfully affirmed the importance of family to migrant workers.

One summer, Joana Goma's husband's brother, his wife, and their five children could not find work. They were penniless and planned to stay for several months, hoping there might be employment in a later crop. Joana brought her husband's employer to their home in the middle of the night "to see for himself all those little children sleeping on the floor," thinking that she might persuade him to offer her brother-in-law a job. The employer stalled, and she worked at securing public aid for the family. This process is a lengthy one, and she soon found her household with no money or food left but tortillas, which they lived on for several days while Joana visited local ministers to ask for loans. On the day the welfare check at last arrived, her father and mother were critically injured in an automobile accident in Texas; and Joana and her children traveled there immediately, financed by this check.

Migrant family life may appear chaotic as kin realign inside and outside the camps, travel when they need to give support, and share what they have down to the last tortilla. Joana and her husband will never be rich, for they are unwilling to cast off the demands of kin. They love them, and they also seem to know that they are happier and more secure in the long run if they embed their marriage in a larger family circle. Again, Joana appears the most submissive of wives, but as a sister, daughter, and in-law she is the most highly regarded member of the family.

Ritual and Affirmation

Beyond the routine domestic order and beyond using food in emergencies as a metaphor for the ways in which person's lives are intertwined, migrants give food special significance in ritual. Some observers have noted that migrants' rituals seem both wasteful and tawdry, at best a mere release of tension for the poor.[13] From a certain perspective migrant ritual seems absurd: women waste valuable working time preparing a feast to commemorate a harvest which is not really theirs and which in fact signals a slack time between crops; or women cook extravagantly to celebrate a young girl's birthday in what appears to be a tragic display of false consciousness about the course of her future life. Further, migrant rituals are tainted by the unavailability in Illinois of their preferred foods and crops: sometimes women must substitute barbecued chicken and potato chips for the tamales, chili, and beans which have for centuries marked such occasions and are deeply rooted in an oral tradition shared by women through recipes. Even so, such feasting seems to testify to migrants' involvement with kin in ways that reach far beyond the ritual moment.

Susana Sangre is the youngest of five sisters dispersed throughout Texas and Illinois. She stays fairly permanently with her mother, father, and small nephews, whom she cares for when she is not working in the fields. As her fifteenth birthday approached, her sisters gathered in the camp bringing tamales from Texas. With the help of their mother and other women, the Sangre sisters spent almost a week digging great barbecue pits, soaking pinto beans to cook, and purchasing items such as cakes and potato chips in local stores. On the evening of Susana's birthday, almost everyone in the camp gathered to kiss and congratulate her, present her with inexpensive storebought gifts (most often handkerchiefs or jewelry), and feast and dance all night. She wore a long pink bridesmaid's dress, while the guests remained in their work clothes. Although her outfit seemed incongruous, it clearly reflected her honored status at the event, as did the great whoops and cheers which surrounded her as she opened each gift, initiated the dancing with her father, and graciously endured the evening's jolly courting. The effort and expense incurred by Susana's family were enormous, and one might argue that they should not delude her through such feasts about the significance or possibilities of her life.

The *quinceñera* feast does signal the importance of her life to *them*, and the lavish ritual expressions which surround occasions such as this work to bind kin, recreate obligations, and promise reciprocity. Most persons know that they too will be commemorated at the appropriate times, and that their lives are significant to others as well. Further, through ritual, migrants dramatically defy the degrading "total institutions" in which they spend half their lives: the monotonous surroundings and crowded, unsanitary conditions which tacitly proclaim their worthlessness.[14] Celebrating the harvest proclaims their part in it and denies that they are its slaves. And to prepare their own foods when possible is to reaffirm the dignity of Tejano identity in an Anglo world which offers it little respect, as well as to root the celebrants in a long and great tradition mediated—made present— by the family.

Strangers and Friends

Tamales are distinct and unique by place: Texans prepare them differently from Californians, Salvadorian migrants to this country often disdain those made in Mexico. Tamales testify to rich oral tradition, for the most part women's tradition, about how to buy and cook them. Although many Anglos in the Southwest enjoy Mexican food and have in part transformed the tamale into a regional artifact, for Tejano migrants the real thing is deeply theirs, rooted in their homes, and kept alive by the women who prepare, distribute, and teach others about it.[15]

In Prairie Junction this distribution is critical not only in knitting together families, but in negotiating relations with outsiders as well. Such negotiations may be crucial to family life—as, for example, when migrants befriend Anglos who have the skills, power, or resources to help their kin in various ways. In these negotiations it is evident how misleading it is to proclaim family life an isolating, stultifying, belittling activity for women, as women use food to make friends and allies as well as to identify outsiders who will or will not commit themselves to the Tejano family's concerns. Women ply prospective friends with tamales and tacos, taking an acceptance of the hospitality they offer both as a show of respect for Tejano culture and as a tentative commitment to kin-like relations.

Ethnic boundaries, of course, remain important.[16] Migrant workers do not expect that prospective Anglo friends will relish these foods as Tejanos do. Migrants joke that "gringos' stomachs are too weak" and claim that they must smuggle chiles into Illinois restaurants so that they can season Anglo food properly. Many appreciated the respectful, self-deprecating remarks of a young poverty program lawyer who found that he could not eat the tacos women offered him without a healthy dose of ketchup. While potential friends should be open to traditional Tejano food, it is best appreciated by Tejanos themselves. Significantly, those Tejanos who ingratiate themselves to Anglos are labelled "Tio Tacos," the Spanish equivalent of Uncle Toms: thus, food becomes a metaphor for those who seem untrue to their ethnic identity.[17] Migrants use foodways to preserve a sense of who they are in an alien cultural setting just as they mobilize foodways to approach and appraise friends, and, again, it seems that women purposefully monopolize those skills necessary for plying and obligating others and for keeping ethnicity alive.

The most active cook in Prairie Junction is also married to the president of a self-help organization whose goal is to help those migrants who wish to "settle out," or leave the migrant stream and try to build a life in Illinois. Although Sra. Mezclado's husband wields the official community action power among Prairie Junction's Tejanos, she is the one who mobilizes several dozen women to cook the large benefit dinners on which the organization depends for funds. Sr. Mezclado's networking philosophy is consistent with the mutual assistance tenets of Tejano family life: he and his organization hold that no conjugal family can "settle out" without aid in procuring furniture, housing, and employment. Yet even in this context of outreach beyond the family, Sra. Mezclado continues to monopolize the foodways, and, with other women, to use food to identify and enlist the support of friends. Although she seems obsequious in the home, her husband acknowledges her authority and often speaks of women generally as living representations of the Lady of Guadalupe.[18] Sr. Mezclado is especially obedient to his own mother who, when she visits, rouses him early every day for church and insists that he keep a large statue of the Lady enshrined on his television set. Other men mock these traditional religious activities because they see Sr. Mezclado as an otherwise thoroughly modern man, but he argues that his mother is *"la jefa* [the boss]. I just can't say no to her." Again the marital paradox: while acknowledging the influence of women like Sr. Mezclado's mother, both spouses insist upon constructing a marital relationship which severely circumscribes sexual nuances, grants the husband seemingly whimsical authority, and offers the wife an unchallenged monopoly over domestic life.

Gathering Kin: Men, Women, and Marriage

Families and family foodways must be worked at, and among migrants it is women who most vigorously do so. Women are much more likely than men to be involved as liaisons among kin, in stretching networks to draw in kin-like persons who can be helpful, providing the props which allow persons to preserve their dignity in demeaning situations, and negotiating ethnic boundaries.

While young, women begin to build domestic convoys whose members will accompany and sustain them through life. Marriage is a crucial step in that process wherein women find both husbands and many more kin who will share their lives. Even very young and seemingly modern women uphold traditional roles when they marry. One such woman, Dolores Abierta, works in the migrant children's educational program as a teacher's aide. She feels flattered that her husband circles the school in his pick-up truck to watch over her when he can and that he forbids her to swim or wear shorts in public. He also "presses on my stomach when my period is late," "holds me in his lap and lets me cry like a baby," and "loves my cooking." Dolores takes great pride in the fact that "when we got married he was skinny and I was fat. Now it is the other way around." She also respects the limits he places on conjugal life and appreciates his concern that sexuality be confined by marriage: "Before we got married my brother-in-law's cousin used to come into my room and bother me. Now he leaves me alone."

Dolores makes it very clear that she will not allow any of her four brothers to marry women who will not obey them, cook their meals for them, and be ever ready for their sexual overtures. She polices her brothers accordingly, and she is especially wary of Anglo women, "who don't know how to be a good wife." At the same time, she gathers her kin around her: bringing her crippled mother from Texas to live in the migrant camp, giving her husband's cousin the car so "he'll have wheels," arranging for her husband's mother to change rooms so that they can be closer together and so that Dolores can learn from her how to cook tamales.

Within their convoys of kin, women's special nurturance of their husbands makes a good deal of sense. Not only do they bind men more and more closely, but also both women and men cooperate in setting marriage apart as something special within a wide circle of people sharing resources as well as the most intimate of concerns. Sexuality is no longer a larger issue. And while women cook often for many people, in marriage the obligation is immediate and forthright and binding: their husbands must have tamales.

NOTES

1. There is a great deal of ambivalence among scholars and the people themselves about the appropriate ethnic label for migrant workers from Texas and of Mexican descent. Many migrants refer to themselves as "Tejanos" (or Texans), others prefer the term "Mexicans," others "Mexican Americans," still others "Chicanos." "Tejano" is used here, because it seems to capture the migrants' sense of themselves, as bicultural with the caution that some migrants might prefer to be identified in other ways.

2. These incidents are reported from the author's personal participant-observation in Texas and Illinois.

3. Cf. Leo Grebler, Joan Moore, and Ralph Guzman, *The Mexican-American People* (New York: Free Press, 1970); William Madsen, *The Mexican-Americans of South Texas* (New York: Holt, Rinehart, and Winston, 1973); Harlan Padfield and William Martin, *Farmers, Workers, and Machines* (Tucson: Univ. of Arizona Press, 1965).

4. Recently a number of scholars have begun to revise earlier views which held that the poor were virtually without culture, that the family life of the poor in particular was dysfunctional; cf. Carol Stack, *All Our Kin* (New York: Harper and Row, 1974), and Stanley West and June Macklin, eds., *The Chicano Experience* (Boulder, Col.: Westview Press, 1980). However, few scholars have used foodways to focus on the culture of the poor.

5. Cf. Judith K. Brown, "A Note on the Division of Labor by Sex," *American Anthropologist* 72 (1970): 1073–78; Louise Lamphere and Michelle Rosaldo, eds., *Woman, Culture, and Society* (Stanford, Calif.: Stanford Univ. Press, 1974); Peggy Sanday, "Toward a Theory of the Status of Women," *American Anthropologist* 75 (1973): 1682–1700.

6. See note 5 above.

7. Cf. W. Eberstein and W.P. Frisbee, "Differences in Marital Instability Among Mexican-Americans, Blacks, and Anglos: 1960 and 1970," *Social Problems* 23 (1976): 609–21; *Census of the US Population* 19 (Washington, D.C.: U.S. Department of Commerce, Bureau of the Census, 1970).

8. The name of the town and personal names are pseudonyms.

9. For more on this subject, see Ernesto Galarza, Herman Gallegos, and Julian Samora, *Mexican-Americans in the Southwest* (Santa Barbara, Calif.: McNally and Loftin, 1969); Lamar Jones, *Mexican-American Labor Problems in Texas* (San Francisco: R&E Research Associates, 1971); John Martinez, *Mexican Emigration to the U.S.: 1919–1930* (San Francisco: R&E Research Associates, 1971); Carey McWilliams, *North from Mexico* (New York: Greenwood Press, 1968); David North, *The Border Crossers* (Washington, D.C.: Department of Labor, 1970); Brett Williams, *The Trip Takes Us: Chicago Migrants on the Prairie* (Ph.D. diss. Univ. of Illinois at Urbana, 1975); Brett Williams, "Chicano Farm Labor in Eastern Illinois," *Journal of the Steward Anthropological Society* 7 (1976); Dean Williams, *Political and Economic Aspects of Mexican Immigration into California and the U.S. since 1941* (San Francisco: R&E Research Associates, 1973).

10. Sra. Compartida has fostered almost a dozen children, most of whom were separated from their parents as infants. Recently, she has taken both her six-year-old grandniece and her very old and dying mother to live with her. One example of her kin-gathering activities occurred when she saw a young man in an orchard with, as she put it, "my husband's face," convinced him that he was her husband's nephew who had been separated from the family as a small child, took him home and reincorporated him in the family with great celebration and a tamale dinner.

11. See especially William Friedland and Dorothy Nelkin, *Migrant* (New York: Holt, Rinehart, and Winston, 1971), treating Black migrants on the east coast.

12. He frequently threatens to "run off with a little 'mojadita' (the diminutive female term for 'wetback')," she, to "throw him out and let him cook for himself, just like he did my cat." She also likes to boast about the time her doctor "played my legs, right in front of Pedro."

13. Friedland and Nelkin.

14. "Total institution" is a term used by Erving Goffman in *Asylums* (Garden City, N.J.: Doubleday, 1961). It refers to those institutions which are qualitatively more encompassing than most, segregating and degrading their inmates in dramatic ways, often by denying them ordinary access to the props and routines by which they build their lives.

15. For example, Gerald Ford was ridiculed by the San Antonio, Texas, press when, during his presidential campaign there, he attempted to eat a tamale without first removing the corn husk.

16. Cf. Frederik Barth, *Ethnic Groups and Boundaries* (Boston: Little, Brown, 1969), who argues that ethnic identity is realized most dramatically in the negotiation of boundaries among groups.

17. One such "Tio Taco" is criticized by others for avoiding his Tejano friends and trying very hard to align himself with his fellow (Anglo) factory workers. That he does this by taking big plates of tacos to the factory every day is especially offensive, for this is women's work. And that the Anglo workers do not reciprocate by attending the migrant organization's benefit dinners seems to indicate that "they don't care enough about our food to pay for it."

18. The Lady of Guadalupe is Tejanos' most beloved folk saint. She emerged in Mexico at the time of the Spanish Conquest, appears faintly Indian, and has been carried all over the world by Mexican migrants who turn to her frequently for help with many varied matters. As a saint, she is much like an earthly woman: she has no direct power of her own, but she has a great deal of influence as a liaison with Christ and because of this is both loving and approachable.

6

Food and Celebration:
A Kosher Caterer as Mediator
of Communal Traditions

Leslie Prosterman

Food is not only a component of Jewish celebrations but may also be a framework around which the celebration is built. When people gather on ritual occasions, food (or the ritual absence of it) is often central to the event: the display of a wedding cake; fasting at Yom Kippur, the Day of Atonement; clearing the house of non-ritual food before the Passover festival commemorating the Exodus from Egypt; or the use of food as symbol in a Passover *seder* feast and ceremony.[1] Those special occasions involving an extensive concern with providing food for a large, diverse group of guests often require the services of a kosher caterer.[2]

The kosher caterer mediates the stored information, skills, and technology of the professional with the shared knowledge, individual and communal desires, and expectations of the client. In so doing, he demonstrates an important point: tradition is as much a component of creativity as is innovation. Contrary to the commonly accepted sense of tradition as a conservative, static, and consistent force, the kosher caterer's function emphasizes the dynamic qualities of tradition.[3]

The caterer's role is significant because he allows us to see folklore in action. Traditional items, ethnic markers, and the private framework based on the home are not used the same way, in the same place, or at the same time in every celebration. The caterer creates a new and acceptable celebration each time, using those elements in resonance with the innovative, cosmopolitan, and public considerations necessary to the participation of a wider audience. This is a system of relationships, not absolute values. Even when using the same caterer, members of a Jewish community do not have a single way of celebrating with food. In one synagogue the same caterer might be presented with five families who might want stuffed cabbage for an hors d'oeuvre, no matter what the occasion. Another family from the same synagogue might request a different serving style and choice of foods for a wedding than for a bat or bar mitzvah (the celebration of religious and ethnic maturity for Jewish children, usually at age twelve or thirteen). Each celebration is a constellation of elements that derive their significance from their relationship to other elements in that event.

A caterer must formulate consciously ideas about food and convey these ideas to the public. Sidney Kowit is a kosher caterer whose clients were long-term residents of the Jewish community in North and Northeast Philadelphia.[4] His professional life has been focused on food and celebration. He knows many codes of food preparation and related behavior, and he interprets and acts upon them every time he makes a caterer's decision or suggestion. His perceptions of food behavior include information from widely diverse sources: his own and his wife's background, the national origins of his clientele, restaurateur's standards, the food service industries, the union, cookbooks, and the glossy food and trade magazines. He must organize this knowledge in relation to his clients' wishes to form an appropriate celebration.

Mr. Kowit described his decision-making processes as he discussed client interviews:

Your customer is the person whom you are serving—you must reflect your customer, not you. Very few customers will come to a caterer and say: "Make me a party, the kind *you* would enjoy." Because invariably they will speak of their likes and dislikes. You'll ask them, what party have you attended that you enjoy, what didn't you enjoy? And then you will create their dinner *simkhe* [joyous occasions] in accordance with what *they* will approve of.

Mr. Kowit's clients would come to his office to look at menus, inspect the catering facility, review prices, decide on service and decor, and discuss all the aspects of the celebration that were important to the participants. Often, it was the mother who made most of the decisions. However, sometimes it was the twelve-year-old in the group or someone's hairdresser who had the influence or the ideas for a hockey theme, for example, and the caterer has to work within that framework. Sometimes, Mr. Kowit made suggestions from his own repertoire, from restaurant experiences, and from friends' accounts of their own experience. It could be a flicker of the eyelash or a thumping of the foot that told him that the customer had one or two specific ideas or requirements that must be worked into the whole dinner:

Well, say you're a customer and you're sitting with me—and you're planning a wedding and you say to me, "Well, the boy comes from Texas and I'd love to have something of down home on the table." Well then, comes the question, what is normal for Texas? If the answer be, they like to eat meat on the bone. Or, if the kids who come in planning their wedding [are] almost barefoot, you might suggest a Henry VIII, with just a sharp knife and meat on the board. Not nice for a wedding but could work for many other kinds of parties.

After the clients describe their wishes, that information must be negotiated with the expertise of the cooks, with the expectations of the guests, and with the structural, ritual, and aesthetic requirements of the event. The result must be in the client's style and be accessible and comprehensible to all the client's guests. The caterer is ultimately responsible for the choice of appropriate elements and for the combinations of those elements into an event which satisfies as many people and styles of *simkhe* as are required.

The caterer must locate all elements of the celebration in accordance with his client's wishes along the continuum formed by the seemingly opposed concepts of tradition and innovation, ethnic and cosmopolitan, and private and public. Though the first two sets of categories are clear enough in common usage, the third set merits further elaboration. The *simkhes* that Mr. Kowit caters may be either public or private. A public event involves more guests than would comfortably fit into a client's home, or more people than one would care to cook for oneself; usually these are people other than close friends and relatives and, often, people who are outside of one's immediate social or religious group. This kind of celebration is usually attached to rites of passage.

A private event indicates an affair that has no outsiders present either as guests or preparers, although the caterer might send in a few dishes. Although a caterer is called in for public events, his model is the private celebration. This paradox influences all of his preparations. Some of the criteria for the public parties the caterer manages are: qualities of intimacy and being *heymishe* (homelike), the inclusion of some of the ethnic Jewish ways, along with indications of being up-to-date and having cosmopolitan savoir-faire. Calendrical events often are celebrated privately.[5] Mr. Kowit commented on the home as the desirable prototype for the catered event:

So where people, Jew, Gentile, black and white, may have occasion for celebrations with food and liquor, and with enough people so that their homes are not large enough to accommodate the party, we become the home away from home, and we as caterers become physically possible, because in many instances the number of guests far exceeds the ability of the home or apartment to contain the party.

The caterer's constant negotiations with clients reveal how essentially active and flexible are the elements that make up a celebration. Traditional small-group, privately oriented expressive culture does not constrain people to repetitive action. Rather, these elements in general allow people to act in the larger world by giving them a system of recognizable reference points and the confidence of a secure cultural base from which they can expand. Sidney Kowit's discussion of his duties and theories of catering provides a basis for understanding his role as mediator in celebrations. His own background and his recital of changes in catering illustrate the historical context in which he works.

Mr. Kowit was born and raised in South Philadelphia. Mr. Kowit says: "My mother tried very hard to have a kosher home and a Jewish home. My father, like many men who worked away from home, did not adhere to the dictates of *kashruth.*"

When his father opened a luncheonette in North Philadelphia in 1933, the whole family moved to that area to help him, calling themselves commercial caterers. They prepared breakfast, lunches, and sandwiches for factory workers.

Mr. Kowit married in 1941, and he and his wife, Tessie, went into business for themselves, also in a luncheonette in North Philadelphia. A year later they entered the field of social catering by what he describes as an accident. A friend of his mother-in-law's needed a Sweet Sixteen party, which they catered. After that, he says, "We were faced almost immediately with, we saw your affair, we enjoyed it, can you do my daughter's bat mitzvah, can you do an engagement party, our children are gonna get married, can you do a wedding?"

Mr. and Mrs. Kowit developed most of their skills as apprentices in a traditional manner, but his son went to a restaurant school for his training. They were in great demand for kosher Jewish social functions. His mother-in-law, her friends, Tessie, and he cooked everything and distributed it to synagogues prior to the Sabbath or on a Sunday.

It got to the point where Mom and her ladies couldn't handle the meat and poultry any more, so she and her ladies backed into the Jewish niceties, like liver, fish, *knishes* [dough filled with meat, potatoes, rice, cheese, or buckwheat and served hot], *kugl* [pudding], *strudl,* and we hired help to do the roasting and the soups. . . .

The Kowits operated their catering business in this rather informal fashion for about a year.

And then we bumped into the problem that when you go into a synagogue, this one was on Deanna Boulevard, the *shames* [sexton] approached me with the question, "Who is your *mazhgiekh* [supervisor of religious Jewish dietary observance]? Who gives you supervision?" And the answer was, "We have none. We're coming to a synagogue, everything we prepare is kosher." And he quietly and with a nice smile on his face said, "By whose standards?" And I said, "By *my* standards." And he said, "Well, I'm not questioning your standards but in order for you to be able to say you're a kosher caterer, you need religious supervision that says so." And we were faced with the choice of either staying in the luncheonette business or going into social kosher catering and bought two properties on Lehigh Avenue, 1317–1319, and set up a commissary kitchen there. And we lived above it.

A commissary kitchen is a place where the food is prepared before it is taken to the site where the event is to be held. In 1957, Mr. and Mrs. Kowit built their own facility, the Shelron, where they could decorate as they wished and serve on the premises. This was their establishment until they retired at the end of 1978.

Mr. Kowit makes a distinction between institutional and social catering. Institutional catering is providing standard food each time, without too much "presentation" and with minimal attention to ritual requirements or variety in food and service. Social catering includes considerations of presentation such as music, decoration, the choice of silver, china, glass, linen, kinds of service (set table, buffet, but-lered), and the timing of courses. Fine gradations of tastes, textures, combinations of foods, and the satisfaction of ritual requirements are essentials in this category. Social catering is for events. There must be a reason for a party: "But rarely would you call in a professional caterer and pay him his tab for his food and equipment only just to have a gang over."

His list of events is as follows: rites of passage or life-cycle events such as weddings, bar and bat mitzvahs; confirmations/graduations; engagements; Sweet Sixteens; *bris* (circumcision ceremony); *ben zakhor* (ceremony to express joy at the birth of a child); *pidyoynes haben* (redemption of the first-born child from service in the Temple); gathering events such as organizational meetings; gatherings before a trip or other event; office parties; and finally, calendrical events, such as Passover, Rosh Hashanah (Jewish New Year), and Yom Kippur.[6]

Mr. Kowit uses the home as the model for his activities, and he maintains a repertoire of traditional and ethnic ways of celebration;

but he must also put together an event which is appealing to a much wider range of people than one would find "at home." He characterizes it this way: "We model everything on what you'd have at home — it's just on a larger scale. The parts of the evening are the same. After a dinner you might go out to the living room for dessert, ergo, a sweet table. Difference is, heavier presentation and done by a pro."

He is modest about his skills because the difference he mentions is very complicated and requires a lot of knowledge and finesse. He must adjust his kitchen staff's abilities and knowledge to meet the needs of the various customers. "When you ask about national origins in the kitchen, they all came different and with their own levels of seasoning and variation. Invariably, you change the peculiarities of the kitchen staff to those of the chef."

The satisfactory resolution of the diverse styles of the kitchen into one food pattern that can be diversified again to meet clients' needs shows the flexibility and imagination required by the caterer. There are two sides of the operation: the performers and the audience. The caterer should be a director who will keep everyone happy as much of the time as possible. The caterer does not have a set routine or response for each occasion. The suppleness of mind needed to accommodate all of these attitudes, and the subsequent action he takes at appropriate places, exemplifies the delicate position he occupies. There are issues of display, reciprocity, fashion, sophistication, comfort, and standards of competence, all of which are intensified by the public and professional nature of these affairs.

The wording of both invitations and menu must reflect the caterer's skill and justify the cost of the services provided. Accurate interpretation of relevant information on the invitation depends on the shades of meaning of the designations for events. Terms for food celebrations include reception (a formal event), party (less formal), and assorted words for meals such as luncheon, dinner party, or cocktail hour. The caterer uses this language to help his customer define the nature of their event to their guests. The caterer can judge the nuances of the language to be used in relation to times of day, the nature of the event celebrated, what will take place, and the economic and social bracket of the guests, as well as their probable experience in reading this kind of language.

Wording on the menu, and, further, the process of food combination indicate the specialized work of the caterer. "The issue is," he says, "the need for a piece of meat not to be called a piece of meat. You find some fancy word or language that gives it a little class, as you might call it. Ergo, Beef Wellington." This is beef encased in a pastry crust. Plain beef is not sufficiently elegant (unless it is prime ribs which are expensive and difficult to prepare in quantity), because it does not show effort on the part of the caterer, and it does not keep very well while waiting to be served. Beef wrapped in a crust shows thought, and it stays warmer and juicier than would a slab of beef exposed to the air. Similarly, plain slices of tomato are not as festive-looking or as juicy as tomatoes which are hollowed out and stuffed with baby peas.

The above dishes are examples of work "done by a pro," with access to restaurant technology and a knowledge of fancy, complicated presentation. The caterer must make people feel comfortable and intimate while reconciling the desire for identification with the home, tradition, and ethnicity (often for *Bubbeh's* [Granny's] sake); he must also provide ample justification for the money spent and for the effort made on the behalf of the guests by the hosts. The final criteria are that the event must be fun and the food delicious and appropriate.

Mr. Kowit describes the evolution of the catered meal from the early 1940s to the present, showing stability and changes in taste. In the early 1940s: "It was half a grapefruit, *gefilte* fish [chopped fish with seasoning and cooked in water or broth], *mandl* [egg drops], a quarter or half chicken, peas and carrots, *kugl,* candied sweet potatoes, and a block of ice with apple *strudl* was dessert. Now that *was* the standard meal." [This covered almost any festive meal after World War II.]

As the forties ran into the fifties, the issue became how can we make it nicer, and the half a grapefruit became a fruit cup, and then got served in a half a pineapple shell and *gefilte* fish was changed to baked fish and then the caterer, instead of serving baked fish alone, served baked fish or chopped liver, and the baked fish in a thin tomato sauce became one with a Creole sauce with little brown potatoes cooked with it, and then from the *gefilte* fish and the baked fish did the chopped liver creep in. Now, choice of liver with baked fish or liver with *gefilte* fish. Chicken broth with noodles and *mandl.* Why not barley mushroom, or split pea or vegetable? The quarter chicken became prime ribs of beef, boneless chicken, the candied sweet potatoes with peas, peas and carrots, I've seen so much of it, green beans came into being, the candied sweet potatoes ran into small over-brown potatoes, or a scooped baked potato. And why not *kugl* on the side and a plate of liver *knishes* or potato *knishes? Kasha* and bows [buckwheat groats and noodles] was a nice starch and then came the word—stuffed *derma* and *kishka* [intestines]. So it's not unusual to have oven-browned potatoes with green beans and almonds and condiments like sweet and sour cabbage, half-green pickles, condiment bowls with olives, radishes, and celery were normal, and then fruit forms that were covered with *parveh* chocolate and painted in the color of the fruit itself, so it became decorative. [*Parveh* is a term applied to food which cannot be classified as milk or meat and which may be eaten with either, without in-fringing on the dietary laws.] Parfaits and sundaes, once again made with *parveh* ice, became fashionable. And it didn't take too long before pastries, *parveh* pastries such as strawberry shortcake, cream puffs, eclairs, Napoleons came as an alternate to dessert. So that menus change. But back in the fifties, in order to be nice, you had to serve more food. So rather than the five-course meal of fruit, fish, soup, main course, and dessert, now the question became, maybe we should have chicken livers with mushrooms in a patty shell between the soup and the main course. It became popular to see how much food could be put on the table. In the sixties the trend changed. In the sixties did we slowly see the meals getting nicer, meals getting lighter in weight, the salad came into being. And it soon became a question of, did you have fruit, appetizer, soup, salad, you took three, dropped one. In the summer you dropped the soup, in the winter you dropped the appetizer. And today we have gone even further than that in that we only serve two courses before the main, whether it be fruit, salad, main course, and dessert — and the salads are no longer a wedge of lettuce. Salads are made of spinach and mushrooms, a Caesar salad, and many names that were created just to make changes. My thought to you is that the niceties of boneless chicken — we serve it ten-twelve different ways — came into being as opposed to the quarter of a chicken. And today, the lighter meal is more prevalent than the heavy.

Mr. Kowit's description of his roles and theories of catering and his presentation of the varied ramifications of food service over the years indicate the compelling need for a skillful mediator. The kosher caterer mediates on several levels simultaneously. He establishes the creative coexistence of the traditional folk world and mainstream culture. That seeming dichotomy is illustrated by the continua of traditional and innovative, ethnic and cosmopolitan, and public and private. Elements which are traditional are not necessarily ethnic — for instance, wedding cake is traditional at American weddings, but its use is not necessarily identified with one culture group. The use of a waiter for the hors d'oeuvres may be cosmopolitan, but it is not particularly innovative.

The different elements which must be properly located on these continua are: vocabulary, ritual propriety, structure, and aesthetics. Vocabulary as used here refers to the actual items of food. Ritual propriety is the system of keeping kosher. Structure is the relationship of parts of the events and the sequence or combination of foods. Aesthetic is defined by the caterer as "niceness," as in "have a nice piece of fish," "it was a *nice* party." He uses "nice" in referring to such aesthetic considerations as weight and quantity of food, and elegance of presentation. The identification of degrees of tradition and innovation, ethnicity or cosmopolitan behavior, and privacy or publicity depends on the use of changing food items, the aesthetic system, the structural position in the organization of the event, and the requirements of ritual propriety.

Food items are often marked with ethnic identification. Jews and non-Jews often request certain foods as being ethnic. "After all, what do we go to a Jewish caterer for?" The list is predictable to those familiar with Jewish cooking: *nahit* [chick peas], especially for a *bris* or *ben zakhor;* wine; sponge cake or honey cake; *kishka, kasha* and bows; *knishes; kreplakh* [a boiled dumpling or pocket stuffed with meat or cheese]; chopped liver; chicken broth with *mandl; matzah* [unleavened bread]; *farfl* [noodle or *matzah* dough chopped into small grains]; *matzah* balls [*matzah* crumb mixture shaped into dumplings]; noodles; roast chicken; *strudl; prokis* [stuffed cabbage]; and smoked fish. As Mr. Kowit says, these foods are sometimes included for the sake of the grandparents, sometimes for exoticism, and sometimes for their ethnic and religious identification. Even though "most people don't have the experience of eating these foods at Mama's table too often," apparently everyone always requests that some of these foods appear at some time in the event.

Reconciling this desire for traditional foods with the need for change and sophistication is difficult. It is not just a matter of inserting a *knish* here and *kugl* there. The foods have to be appropriate to their setting so they do not clash with the concept of the particular course they are in or with the foods they accompany. They have to remain distinct enough so that people obtain the satisfaction of identifying a food as ethnic and traditional. For instance, a *knish* usually is not considered a proper side dish to Chicken Kiev or a Salade Nicoise. It can be put very well with a selection of hors d'oeuvres, although if the hors d'oeuvres are all Chinese-kosher, a *knish* would be inappropriate and the caterer and client might decide to serve *strudl* on the sweet table instead. At a wedding, one traditionally has wedding cake, but this custom must be reconciled with the fashion of having a light fruit dessert — perhaps the cake may be boxed to take home later.

Another problem is the craving people have for variety, especially from a professional whom they must pay. The ethnically marked and traditional foods are distinctive and limited enough that they attain the status of a bad joke ("What do you say it'll be boneless breast of chicken again?"). The caterer must not repeat so often that his returning customers and audiences get bored. These distinctive food items must be used always in small, judiciously chosen quantities placed carefully in the structure of the event. They must not conflict with the always changing and expanding repertoire of fashionable party foods which comprise the rest of the food selection. The caterer constantly has to balance choices available to him and the client in order to unite an acceptable sequence of food items. However, for the more intimate calendrical celebrations modelled on the Sabbath, like Passover, Yom Kippur, and Rosh Hashanah, there tend to be more of these ethnic or traditional foods on the menu, even on the catered occasions.

Negotiations with customers to satisfy ritual dietary propriety are closely related to those just described for vocabulary items. Some kosher parties are ethnic only in that they are supervised and ritually kosher. The meats have been properly butchered, and the kitchen and cooking methods are correct. While trying out new dishes, the caterer must be a custodian of the full understanding of the system of *kashruth* and the knowledge of combinations which are ritually pure. He is under strict supervision by the *mazhgiekh,* and he is accountable for satisfaction of the dietary requirements for an entire celebratory community. The caterer, rather than his clients, accepts responsibility for the knowledge and practice of the dietary laws. There is no problem if he adheres to the traditional and ethnic foods only, because the ritually pure combinations already have been ascertained. The situation becomes more difficult when foods that are not known as Jewish or that are not associated with a particular event come into the repertoire. It also becomes difficult when a certain course or dish comes to demand a certain element, such as desserts containing cream; this necessitates the development of *parveh* cream or fancy ice shapes to simulate ice cream forms. Some form of accommodation has to be developed every time an unfamiliar food or element is contemplated. And, as everyone who cooks knows, it is not as easy as merely dropping out an offending item or adding an acceptable one. Every element has to exist in harmony with the others. Tastes, textures, quantities, relationships, appearances, and digestive properties must be in proper proportions and fit into the system of *kashruth.* The customer has to feel safe and daring at the same time:

If you see a Chicken Kiev or Cordon Bleu in a restaurant and you want to emulate it, it becomes difficult for a caterer to make kosher. Cheese, ham, and chicken don't go together. You must create a dish with the same title in quotes, but with definitions that immediately tell the customer, "Well, we call it Chicken Kiev, but . . . ." This is the nature of catering and imagination becomes most important.

If one item changes, everything else may have to change. The customers must be aware of these changes. The customer can order a full Chinese meal and still remain kosher, with a sizable amount of work on the part of the caterer. That is, of course, an extreme, as is the fully "Jewish" meal. The caterer must take the Chinese and the Jewish and the "festive foods" and put them into the ritual framework together. He convinces the guests that they are traditional in their religious observance and in relation to their heritage and innovative in their tastes. He works out the ritually pure combinations of new and unfamiliar foods.

The structure of a meal involves combinations and sequences of food components, space, and time. The structure of the event/meal is presented by Mr. Kowit as: hors d'oeuvres, usually at a buffet table or butlered, then a lapse of time and then the meal, which consists of appetizer, soup or salad, entree, and dessert. These are eaten at a table, served by a waiter, or obtained from a buffet and brought to the table by the guests. Often, after another lapse of time, a sweet table is displayed. The guests then eat the confections, either choosing their own sweets or being served from the selection on the table. There are shifts in types of food service and place of eating. Either the table changes or the mode of butlering changes. The progression in tastes goes from sharp, salty, tangy and spicy, to a melange of tastes and textures, to the sweets. Liquor can be served with the first group. It is usually not served with the second group, although recently wine may be provided. Wine or hot tea and coffee are served with the third group. One might eat hors d'oeuvres and sweets off a plate while standing and conversing, but one usually sits down to eat the entree. The rare exception is the stand-up buffet.

You try to serve your hors d'oeuvres for the first period of time, half an hour to an hour. Then open a buffet with heavier foods. We also like them butlered because many older people will come and sit down and won't bother to go to a table. Then they're ready to go to the heavier table. Most people appreciate it if you regiment the way they eat. Pauses between courses and a limited amount of time for each.

Some of the slots are more ethnically marked than others. For instance, Mr. Kowit's Jewish clients have little affinity for liquor; they would not drink hard liquor with their sweets especially, and they have less affinity for sweets than some other groups. So one might not have an open bar and a sweet table at the end of a meal. But it is absolutely necessary in this area to have an hors d'oeuvres slot — Mr. Kowit says his Jewish clients always want a full serving of hors d'oeuvres, no matter what else is on the menu. One could fill the hors d'oeuvres slot with Chinese egg rolls or Italian ravioli, but hors d'oeuvres must be present in some form. Again, this structure must be consonant with expectations of satisfactory eating patterns (enough courses, the right parts of a meal) and ritual propriety. The caterer must be able to fill the third slot of a tri-partite meal if his customers feel that is the proper structure, but they might not want a sweet table. Perhaps the wedding cake or bat mitzvah cake can go in its place. Alternatively, the sweet course may be left off but the meal will end with coffee for closure. The first course must always include food rather than only drink.

Jewish groups tend not to like casseroles or stews served to them by a kosher caterer, perhaps because they do not show enough effort or preparation, or they may conceal violations of ritual law. At the same time, the customers and technological exigencies demand some combination of food to show the caterer's art and to keep the food appetizing. Even at organizational meetings, people will only accept stews and casseroles from a gentile caterer or restaurant. From a kosher caterer they want distinct entities combined in a sophisticated manner.

Aesthetics is the last category requiring mediation. Mr. Kowit described a time when "niceness" meant that food was plentiful at an event and that expensive, rich, and heavy ingredients were used. "Niceness" meant more-than-enough solid food. However, fashions have changed over the years, and with different ideas of health and beauty, heavy presentation has begun to be less appealing aesthetically. The issue is connected to display and reciprocity. When asked if a sweet table after dinner was necessary to the guests because they were still hungry, Mr. Kowit said the sweet table is usually only half-consumed, but there is a need to look impressive, both to the guests on behalf of the host and to the host on behalf of his money and celebration. "The amount of food that's served . . . should be a reflection of what would do honor to the hostess. The manner of service, the niceties of service, are as different as there are caterers." The caterer is also responsible for satisfying the "New American" [immigrant] or old-fashioned psychological craving for quantities of food within the modern standards of restrained elegance. Some food portions are judged by weight and some by visual effect. His Jewish customers are inclined to want a fairly substantial amount of food displayed across a table even if they do not want to eat it. A joke illustrates the relationship between visual and gustatory needs:

A "New American" patronized a certain restaurant. The proprietor served two slices of bread with each meal. The customer requested more bread. The proprietor obliged with two more slices. The next time the customer came in, he requested of the waiter even more bread. The proprietor told the waiter to satisfy the customer. This went on for several days. Finally, the next time the customer wanted more bread, the proprietor said to the waiter, "Take a loaf of bread, split it, butter it and give it to him." The waiter did so. Then the customer beckoned to the proprietor, who asked if everything was all right. "Fine," said the customer, "but how come you're back to only two slices of bread?"

Even though the criteria of "niceness" demand less food be eaten, there must be *enough* (never an exact amount), and it must be elegantly displayed and served.

Many wedding cakes are beautifully decorated and take weeks to put together — what does the cake taste like inside? It doesn't matter — it was how beautiful it looked, not how good it tasted. Or the cake is done around dummies and the cake itself is in boxes. Many times this is just for looking, not eating. Usually for weddings — costly, beautiful, and not edible. It's visual rather than eating.

The perennial problem of the caterer is typified in his attempt to reconcile aesthetics with the practicality of serving the cake. The present aesthetic emphasizes the lightness and elegance of the food. However, the well-stocked table is visually and psychologically appealing: even if guests do not consume all the food, they may feel slighted and hungry if they think there is not enough. Traditional aesthetics demand large quantities of heavy food while innovative aesthetics require small amounts of light food: the caterer compromises on this continuum according to the specific needs of the particular celebration.

There are numerous points where all these elements must be reconciled. The caterer has to have many strategies for mediating these oppositions. It is impossible to delineate all the situations and all the strategies because they change for each occasion. The greatest qualities a caterer can have seem to be flexibility and imagination in working with his repertoire.

For instance, a problem that fuses aesthetic and structural concerns is how to combine the various parts of the meal, the amount of food provided, and the timing of its presentation. This example shows a situation that was a bit strained due to differences in expectations connected with age:

Last Saturday we did a bar mitzvah where the mother and father were "young swingers" in the sense they like to dance, to drink, and they don't find a particular need for a long, heavy meal. They're in their early forties. Their parents are in their late sixties. Their parents were very disappointed with the fact that for hors d'oeuvres we had egg rolls and pizza and half-sized hot dogs and rolls, and hot soft pretzels and mustard, as well as the normal butlered hors d'oeuvres that were served. For main course, we had a Nicoise salad, boneless breast of chicken with stuffed tomatoes and asparagus, and we had a Pear Hélène for dessert. Then we followed it with a dessert table: fresh fruit, mousse, jello and pastries. And this wasn't brought out for two hours. And to the grandmothers, it was terrible the way the evening was dragged out. You never had enough to eat. To the young people, it was wonderful, because you had plenty of time to dance, drink, and have a good time and weren't bored with sitting at the table constantly. It is very difficult to satisfy three or four generations at the same party. A party is more than just eating—it is being entertained, made to participate.

Celebrations are only successful if there are satisfied participants. One reason for traditional expressions of culture, for ethnic markers, and for creating a homelike atmosphere is to indicate what is going to happen and what tone will be adopted so that the guests can share in the proceedings. There cannot be a celebration unless enough people know the rules. There must be a relaxed setting and a shared understanding of the event to attain the desired result. Familiarity is a clue to that understanding. The public, innovative, and cosmopolitan categories also have a place in the celebration. Cosmopolitan considerations function in a similar way to traditional and ethnic ones; not everyone at the catered event is from the same religious and social group, and there have to be elements that are accessible and appealing to everyone. Few people who use caterers live in a circumscribed world. Therefore, they want identification with a larger existence for themselves and for the sake of their guests. People like change and variety, which makes innovation a necessity. Also, the events for which people use caterers are those that require a certain amount of tangible status. Public display is used to show joy as well as the social status of the host and pride in the event celebrated. Many of these occasions are signals for the appropriate, and perhaps even obligatory, service of the caterer.

The caterer demonstrates the relationship of folklore and tradition to change.[7] He is one example of a mediator who requisitions elements from different areas and constructs an affair appropriate to each occasion. Tradition must be balanced with innovation, ethnicity with cosmopolitanism, and private with public models. In so doing, he uses tradition innovatively, employs ethnic markers in a cosmopolitan way, and establishes an intimate, meaningful world in a public setting. He displays the creative process that puts traditional expressive culture in a dynamic framework and uses these expressive forms in a variety of fashions. He shows how change in folk culture, indicated through food and celebration, is a positive force. Tradition, among other things, *is* action. What we think of as unchanging "folklore" or tradition must be reassessed every time it appears in a new configuration, as a creative, meaningful force in specific response to people's lives.

ACKNOWLEDGMENTS

This paper could not have been written without the generous contributions of knowledge and time by Sidney Kowit. I owe other special debts of gratitude to Claire Farrer and Judith McCulloh for their help. Many thanks for comments and suggestions are given to: Henry Glassie, Marjorie Hunt, Barbara Kirshenblatt-Gimblett, Robert Leibman, Philip Nusbaum, Brian Rusted, Janet Theophano, Chava Weissler, and M. Jane Young.

NOTES

1. Hebrew terms are spelled in accordance with the forms used in the *Encyclopaedia Judaica*, ed. Cecil Roth (Jerusalem: Keter Publishing House, 1972). Some Hebrew terms appear in the Ashkenazic pronunciation consistent with the caterer's Ashkenazic usage, e.g. *bris, simkhe*. The spelling of Yiddish terms follows Uriel Weinreich, *Modern English-Yiddish, Yiddish-English Dictionary* (New York: YIVO Institute for Jewish Research, McGraw-Hill, 1968).

2. Most of the Jewish dietary laws, or the laws of *kashruth*, come from the books of Exodus and Leviticus. The observance of the dietary laws is known as keeping kosher. These laws include such proscriptions as not mixing milk with meat in cooking or eating, and not eating certain foods, the most common of which are pork and shellfish.

3. The theoretical framework in this paper is informed by the work of Frederik Barth, Mary Douglas and Claude Levi-Strauss. The studies that are particularly helpful are Frederik Barth, *Ethnic Groups and Boundaries: The Social Organization of Culture Difference* (Boston: Little, Brown, 1969); Mary Douglas, "Deciphering a Meal," *Daedalus* III (Winter 1972):61–81; and Claude Levi-Strauss, *The Savage Mind* (Chicago: Univ. of Chicago Press, 1966). Readers familiar with Levi-Strauss's discussion of the *bricoleur* will recognize its role in my concept of the caterer's activities.

4. This paper deals specifically with one man's experiences with his Jewish clients. His wife Tessie, whom he describes as "the backbone of the back room," preferred that Mr. Kowit be the sole purveyor of information in this context. Mr. Kowit reports that though most of his clients were Jewish, in about 1972 he began to acquire other clients belonging to Polish, Eastern European, Italian, Afro-American, and other cultural groups. He always prepared food according to the dietary requirements, whether or not his Jewish clients kept kosher and whether or not his clients were Jewish. "In many fashions we're able to convert or serve the different ethnic groups' foods in such a fashion that they're not conscious of the fact that we're kosher caterers." Many of his clients were of middle-income level, Jewish, and from north or northeast Philadelphia. Other demographic data were not available.

5. Janet Theophano, personal communication.

6. The three calendrical holidays which are catered most often in his kosher Jewish world might be explained by the already public nature of a *seder*. It involves a ritual dinner to which strangers traditionally are invited. The public "American Jewish" nature of Yom Kippur and Rosh Hashanah, which are marked in the American mind as *the* Jewish holidays (along with Chanukah), could contribute to their inclusion on the catering list. These observations are from a personal communication from Chava Weissler. Also, these three holidays are very busy periods where much time is passed in the synagogue. Women now are spending less time at home and presumably more time in the synagogue and inviting more people to celebrate the holidays, hence the need in some places for a caterer.

7. For discussions of tradition and change within the context of native American cultures, see Dell Hymes, "Folklore's Nature and the Sun's Myth," *Journal of American Folklore* 88 (Oct.–Dec. 1975):345–69; and Keith Basso, *Portraits of "The Whiteman"* (New York: Cambridge Univ. Press, 1979).

PART III

Food as the Rhetoric
of Regionalization:
Field Studies

7

A Wilderness in the Megalopolis: Foodways in the Pine Barrens of New Jersey

Angus K. Gillespie

The New Jersey Pine Barrens, which cover nearly a third of the nation's most industrialized state, shelter both endangered wildlife and vast, untapped natural resources. Characterized by sandy soil and cedar swamps dotted with scraggly pine trees, the south central region of the state is considered unsuitable for conventional upland agriculture and has been out of the mainstream of national development for the last three hundred years. At first glance, the 1,700-square-mile Pinelands seem undistinctive and uninteresting. From the air, this tract of land, larger than the state of Rhode Island, appears flat and underdeveloped, broken only by a few long, straight highways. From an automobile the view is still unimpressive. Many visitors from Philadelphia or North Jersey drive through the Pine Barrens on their way to Atlantic City or other shore resorts and are completely unaware that this apparent "wasteland" holds any special charm.[1]

Although they are in the midst of the nation's most densely populated state, south of New York City and east of Philadelphia, the Pine Barrens have remained largely invisible and unheralded, even to most New Jersey residents. The boundaries of this region are not sharply defined, and the Pine Barrens have not been celebrated in the same way as, for example, the Big Thicket in Texas, the Badlands in South Dakota, or the Dismal Swamp in Virginia and North Carolina. For those who take the trouble to look, however, there is a modest body of literature on the Pine Barrens.[2] Perhaps the finest book on this topic, certainly the best-written, is John McPhee's *The Pine Barrens*. The reader comes to know the Pines through the eyes of Fred Brown, McPhee's principal informant. The book is already regarded as a minor classic.

Driving through the Pine Barrens, the occasional visitor who stops his car and looks around will probably be disappointed. The scrubby trees all look alike. However, old-timers will look for cedar or maple, which are signs of water, while oaks indicate dry soil. Surprisingly, there are more than a dozen species of oak here. What the pines lack in species diversity, they make up for in their forms—sometimes tall and straight, sometimes crooked and twisted. The largest remaining stand of Atlantic white cedar trees in the East is here, as is the third-largest cranberry industry in the nation. Underneath the million acres of Pinelands forest is a precious resource, seventeen trillion gallons of extraordinarily pure water, filtered through the soil, lying only twenty feet or less beneath the surface.[3] Indeed it was water that led Joseph Wharton, a nineteenth-century Philadelphia financier, to assemble the 95,000-acre Pinelands tract. He intended to pipe the water from the Pines to Philadelphia for profit. The New Jersey state legislature learned of his plan and blocked the scheme before it could be put into effect.[4] To this very day, preservation efforts are typically justified because of the water resource.[5]

The overall population density of New Jersey is 1,000 people per square mile. The Pinelands region now has about 400,000 residents or 235 people per square mile.[6] As recently as the late 1960s in one section of well over 100,000 acres, McPhee reported that there were only 21 people.[7] The Pinelands are sparsely settled and thus appear to the visitor to be lonely and desolate. There, however, is a network of small homogeneous communities in the woods whose members have stepped out of society at large. These people are called "Pineys," for many years a term of disparagement. Now that the land is seen as a valuable resource, however, this negative attitude seems to be changing. Some long-term residents now embrace the term "Piney" with pride. These people exhibit a strong sense of place and local patriotism. In this connection, it is interesting to note that cultural geographer Yi-Fu Tuan has coined the term "topophilia" (a Greek construction meaning, literally, "love of place").[8] The term can be readily applied to the Piney attitude toward their landscape.

In the early years of settlement, people did not come to the Pinelands because of love of place. Rather, people came to get away from everybody else. Thus Tories escaped to the Pines during the American Revolution. Quakers who were unwilling to live up to the Quaker standards of behavior fled here. So did Hessian deserters from the British Army, as well as French Huguenots. In the eighteenth century, American Indians began to take refuge here. In addition to these groups came an assortment of pirates, smugglers, and outlaws of all kinds.[9] This colorful and romantic background has attracted the attention of journalists and folklorists, social workers and poets. These outsiders often came to the Pines with preconceived notions. For example, in a long poem "The Pineys," Gerald Stern wrote:

> I saw the Piney at first as merely a stray
> Historical mixture, some lopsided fault,
> Like the pure product of America gone crazy,
> Or something out of Faulkner or Caldwell that touches
> Our lower hearts but later I saw this line
> Was much too primitive to do them justice.[10]

How do the Pineys describe themselves? Attachment to the land and self-sufficiency are key virtues most often mentioned. The Pineys try to avoid dependence on the outside world as much as possible, bypassing the mainstream cash economy and providing for themselves largely by foraging. Ideal Pineys, in theory if not always in fact, wrest their livelihood from the woods in the west, the sea in the east, and the gardens in their backyards. Some of their tools and techniques, tailored to conditions in New Jersey, are not found in quite the same form anywhere else in the world. In the Pine Barrens, for example, you can find a "sneakbox," a boat designed to keep a lone duck hunter hidden in marsh grass, or a "Jersey garvey," a craft whose high gunwales allow its crew to tong for clams even when the waves are high. Such boats are custom-made by local craftsmen who learn their trade not from manuals, but by observing and imitating the generation of boatbuilders who came before them. Most Pinelands lore is transmitted in this fashion. The oral tradition is strong in the Pine Barrens, an area where people still spend long winter nights trading songs and stories.[11]

The importance of foodways in the Piney culture is made apparent by its prominence in so many of their stories and anecdotes. Cookbooks are rare; most recipes are passed down orally from mother to daughter. Traditional successful hunting, gathering, foraging, and preparing strategies are thus not only shared but refined over the years by all members of the local culture. This essay will address not only the way Pineys gather and prepare their food but also the ways in which food mores inevitably express important cultural aspects of the community.

The Pines have provided no celebrated restaurants, no famous dishes, and no franchised food marketing concepts. A number of compilations of recipes have been assembled — one by a university press — and it is possible that in time the Pines will have greater national recognition.[12] One way to view the cookery of the Pinelands is in terms of two apparently contradictory observations—on the one hand, it is much like rural cookery in the rest of the country; and, on the other hand, it is unique within the state of New Jersey. This contradiction was explained by John W. Sinton: "We must also understand that most of the Pine Barrens cultures are not clearly distinct from other rural cultures elsewhere in the United States. What makes Piney culture distinctive is that it continues to exist in the midst of a sprawling megalopolis."[13]

The people of the Pinelands see themselves as distinct and separate from the rest of the people of the state of New Jersey. Thus their foodways have taken on symbolic value to them, and their distinctive cuisine has become a badge of identity. Essentially, the food of the Pines comes from four sources: the woods, the water, the garden, and the store. The Pineys are able to move from one environment to another with enormous ease because of their intimate knowledge of the land. Not only do they move easily from place to place; they also move from season to season with complete confidence. In drawing out life stories from Piney informants, the researcher is impressed by the fact that, typically, the same person would know about all the different environments. The Piney acquires these skills early in life and continues to use them until they become second nature to him.

Pineys are as a rule hospitable. The custom of hospitality is part of their identity and tends to break down their isolation and bring them into relations with the larger group. Hospitality is readily extended to neighbors, close relatives, distant relatives, even acquaintances. Food is both a mode of incorporation and a medium of exchange for social bonding. On this matter Gladys Eayre of Forked River, a lifelong resident of the Pines whose family history has been intertwined with the Pines for over 200 years, said:

Everybody who came to the house had to eat something, regardless of whether it was meal time or not. It was customary to offer somebody something. We made sure they did it, because if they went away without eating, that was bad. There was always a piece of cake or pie, or perhaps a little chowder left on the stove. There was always something cooking, a pot of soup or something.

Most of the cooking back our way was on wood stoves and the fire was always going. There was always a pot of coffee brewing or stew or soup. And homemade bread. If you didn't have anything else, you just whipped up a batch of biscuits and bulldog gravy—flour and water and grease with salt and pepper. It's good. We had our meat and potatoes and vegetables and fish and clams. We ate pretty high on the hog, but we didn't have any money.[14]

Some outsiders, by the very nature of their occupations, are in an adversary position with the Pineys. It is difficult to feel hospitable to a revenue agent if you make a little of your own home brew. It is difficult to feel hospitable to a game warden if you take the official hunting season with a grain of salt. Other outsiders, because of their roles, are at least overtly treated with extreme courtesy—hunters, for example, who hire the Pineys as guides, and fishermen who charter Piney boats. As a general rule, Pineys are well-disposed to outside visitors taken one at a time.

Indeed the custom of hospitality is a great boon to the researcher. To be sure, there is always a temptation on the part of a knowledgeable rural dweller to take advantage of the naiveté of the city slicker, and many local stories document how a Piney will tell the most outrageous lie in a straight-forward manner. If the city slicker takes the bait, the story becomes more and more elaborate and preposterous. But in spite of this storytelling tradition, Pineys are generally courteous to their visitors. This courtesy is shown by their sharing of food with outsiders. Sam Hunt of Waretown, an old timer who builds boats, banjoes, and furniture in his own small shop, expresses what would seem to be the prevalent attitude towards outsiders:

No, I don't dislike any human being. If they come around here . . . they come from all over, you know . . . I just find out what they do and they find out what I do, and we get along fine. I always offer people a drink, even though I don't drink myself. I prefer lemonade. I always keep lemonade in the refrigerator. I don't have much use for cities myself. I never did like cities. If I have my way, I will always live right here in the woods, but I've been to cities like New York and Philadelphia. City people come here; I always show 'em a nice time.[15]

Despite the hospitality that Pineys show to outsiders, there are basic points of stress and conflict between the Piney and the outside world. Pineys as a group resent the increasing urbanization of their environment. To the extent that outsiders are viewed as having contributed to development, with its attendant ills of roads, sewers, regulations, police, and taxes, outsiders are the enemy. To the extent that outsiders have contributed to the breakdown of the physical and social environment, they are unwelcome. This concept emerges again and again in studying foodways in the Pines, since foraging and self-sufficiency are cornerstones of Piney folk culture. If the environment is disrupted, then the culture is disrupted. Put another way, if the larger culture or government regulates or forbids certain interactions with the environment, then the culture is disrupted.

The ways Pineys gather and prepare their foods express their self-sufficiency. The Pineys identify themselves through their food. This strong sense of identification is not unlike that described by Roger Welsch on the Omaha, Charles Joyner on Blacks and Soul Food, or by Alicia Gonzales on the Mexican-American *Panadero*.[16] The Pineys employ food as a metaphor to respond to and to control their interaction with the larger outside culture. It is interesting to note in this connection that self-sufficiency for the Pineys could be expressed in a variety of ways. They could, for example, make their own clothes or make their own shelter; but, for the most part, they do not. Why then is food the medium for the expression of the cultural value of self-sufficiency? To answer this question, the researcher must take a close look at the values of the culture.

Who are the Pineys? How do they define themselves? Like other distinctive small groups, they define themselves in large measure by saying what they are not. There is a broad range of possibilities to choose from. They could use race to define themselves. (Pineys are white; therefore, nonwhites cannot be Pineys.) But race never emerges as an important category. They could use ethnicity to define themselves. (Pineys are Anglo-Celtics; therefore, all other "foreign" ethnics are not Pineys.) Here again, this is not the case.

Perhaps the most relevant dichotomy is city versus country. Pineys are country people; they are not "city slickers." Food hunted or gathered from the natural world provides the Pineys with independence from the larger civilization. Obtaining their food in this way also allows the Pineys to pass on the cultural values of independence to their children through the customs and traditions of hunting, gathering, and preparation. Most importantly, the unique Piney foodways provide a symbol of their difference from surrounding urbanized cultures. The Pineys represent nature; the city slicker represents civilization.

Their everyday approach to foodways encapsulates this assumption. In an era of supermarkets, the Pineys rely on early food gathering methods. Hence, hunting, fishing, and gathering are the most esteemed ways of going about getting food. Agriculture, largely in the form of the family garden plot, is the next best mode. The least desirable, and most "citified," mode is the general store, or worse yet, the supermarket. The supermarket is an extension of the city, which embodies all the negative values of industry, pollution, and overpopulation. Thus, the Pineys' attitudes about food articulate and dramatize the city/country dichotomy in a quite striking fashion.

Foodways and the Woods

To understand the Pines we must leave the highways and enter the woods. Now we begin to get a feeling for the area's sheer vastness — a million acres of forests with small trees. Imagine four-wheeling through miles and miles of sand-track roads which form a labyrinth through the woods. Imagine rounding a bend at dusk and encountering several deer. Startling experiences of this sort heighten the visitor's sense of the Pines as a special place, a wilderness area set within the urban megalopolis of the northeast. Of course, naturalists tell us that it is not really a wilderness at all. The special character of the Pines is partly due to natural causes — its location on the outer coastal plain, its sandy soil, its abundant water, and so on. But human intervention — especially periodic fire — has played a major role in shaping the character of the vegetation and the face of the landscape.

The Piney prides himself on his all-providing self-sufficiency, and wildlife resources are part of the picture. Hunting is manifestly an integral part of Piney culture. Unregulated hunting in years past has wiped out the black bear, the wolf, and the beaver. Even the deer — the principal wildlife resource in the Pine Barrens — was nearly wiped out by 1900. In recent decades, however, the State has attempted to bring game populations up to what the habitat can accommodate. In addition to deer, small game is taken during a three-month season beginning in November. Cottontail rabbits and bobwhite quail are the most popular. Ruffled grouse, gray squirrels, raccoons, and foxes are less commonly hunted.[17]

It is not necessary to be dependent on an employer or the money economy if you can support yourself and your family by living off the woods. If the woods offer a generous meat supply — accessible to those with the knowledge and skill — then the battle for self-sufficiency is tipped in the Piney's favor. The importance of deer hunting in Piney culture emerges in one story after another. These stories have persisted for a long time. Folklorist Herbert Halpert did considerable field work in the Pines in the later 1930s and early 1940s. Some of the very best stories Halpert collected deal with hunting.[18] For the folklorist, it is gratifying to find that these stories have not completely died out. Remarkably enough, some forty years later a few of them still persist.

It is nearly impossible to write about the Pine Barrens and not deal with hunting. When John McPhee, a gifted writer and frequent contributor to *The New Yorker,* turned his attention to the Pine Barrens, he was just as stunned as any other New Jersey resident when he discovered a wilderness within a couple of hours' drive from his house in Princeton. McPhee's principal informant, Fred Brown of Hog Wallow, was a man who embodied the values of Piney folk culture. It did not take long for McPhee to discover the Piney attitude toward deer hunting:

> In Atlantic City not long ago, a man bit into a hamburger and found that it was full of buckshot. He was really eating a venisonburger, and the meat had come from the Pine Barrens, where deer poaching has been going on for exactly as many years as there have been fish-and-game laws. [19]

What makes Fred Brown's story so memorable is that the story serves as a perfect metaphor for the incompatibility of the country and the city. To find buckshot in a hamburger is a ridiculous convergence. This absurd incongruity serves the narrator's purpose in pointing out to the audience that the Pines are separate and distinct from the mainstream culture of the rest of New Jersey.

McPhee went to some pains to draw distinctions between commercial poaching, "market gunning," and local consumption. McPhee once overheard one of his informants placing an order for deer meat over the telephone:

> "I don't call it poaching when you're putting meat on the table," the woman went on. Most people in the Pine Barrens would agree with her. They know that it is against the law to kill deer out of season—the shooting season is six days long and comes in December—but they seem to feel that the law was made to control sportsman hunters, and not to deny a native right to the people of the woods. [20]

This attitude makes sense, but it puts game wardens on the spot. How do you tell a Piney from a poacher? Pineys I have talked to say that commercial poaching, with few exceptions, is done by outsiders. Still no one doubts that it does occur. McPhee tells a revealing little story:

> Last year in Toms River, which is just outside the Pine Barrens, Fred Brown went into a short-order restaurant and ordered a hamburger. When it came and he had taken a bite of it, he said to the man behind the counter, "That hamburger wasn't raised on corn."
>
> "What was it raised on?" the man said.
> "Acorns."
> "Keep quiet," the man said, and he gave Fred a second deerburger on the house.
> "The second one was deer and pork mixed," Fred told me. "And that is good. Hell, yes." [21]

In addition to subsistence hunting and "market gunning" (poaching for profit), Pineys sometimes serve as guides for outsiders. The guides are knowledgeable outdoorsmen, who, in exchange for free room and board for a week as well as a small salary, show outsiders around during the official deer hunting season.

The hunting role is interesting since it shows how a survival activity can be transformed into a sports activity. It shows how traditional roles and skills can be used to satisfy the needs of the outside culture. It also provides the Piney with some small power since the outsider clearly needs help. Further, outside sportsmen may begin to realize that the loss of the Pinelands would be a loss for everyone, not just the Piney. The Piney's attitude toward what he is doing differs from that of the city slicker. Of course, there is an area of convergence: man against the elements. But the Piney tries to live it out as life while the sportsman lives it out as play.

Foodways and the Water

The highest point in the Pines is on the so-called Forked River Mountains with an elevation of some 400 feet. It seems ridiculous to call these small hills mountains. The practice, originally perhaps ironic, however, is firmly fixed in local tradition and on detailed maps of the area. Years ago the New Jersey Forest Fire Service used to maintain one of their red-and-white painted steel towers there. The tower is gone, but the mountain is still approachable in a four-wheeler. The visitor can drive up there and stand on top of a vehicle and look in all directions. To the west, there is nothing but the woods for miles and miles. It is an eerie experience to see nothing but the blue sky above and the green trees below, marred only by an occasional sand track gouged out through the woods. To the east, there is the Barnegat Bay—appearing as vast as the Atlantic Ocean itself. Here, for a few minutes at least, one has the entire Piney worldview: to the west, the woods; to the east, the bay. This dual environment is reflected constantly in Piney culture—in songs, in stories and in foodways. Thus to the basic diet of venison, add waterfowl, shellfish, and other seafood.

A complete account of Pine Barrens aquatic ecosystems must take into account freshwater environments including bogs, swamps, lakes, creeks, streams, rivers, and estuaries. As a general rule, these environments are less important than the bay and the ocean are for food, except for snapping turtles. Because of the acidity of the water, most of the streams and creeks offer poor fishing. In most cases the fish are simply too small to be useful as food. Despite all these limitations, the Piney still manages to find food resources in these fresh waters.

In this connection, it is revealing to contrast the Piney's attitude with that of the sport fisherman visitor. For example, one fish that does attain a respectable size is the chain pickerel, which is very bony. It is popular as a game fish, but most sport fishermen just toss them back. One Piney informant who often dines on chain pickerel said: "Sure, it's bony; you just have to be careful."[22]

A similar example can be found in the case of the catfish. The usual tourist visitor sport fisherman does not care for catfish. One reason for this avoidance may be that the catfish lacks scales and hence does not seem to be a "real fish." But the Piney routinely utilizes the catfish as a food source; indeed it is probably the primary freshwater resource. Catfish cause some trouble because they have to be skinned and the barbs are believed to be poisonous, but they are easy to catch and easy to clean. They are plentiful in places like Bamber Lake. Merce Ridgway of Waretown, a lifelong resident of the Pines, describes the white meat of the catfish as "fresh water chicken."[23]

A third example of divergence of taste between the visitor and the Piney is the eel. Although eels are quite common in the Pine Barrens, most visitors avoid them altogether. This pattern of avoidance is easy to explain: they look like snakes. Eels are so common and easy to catch that there is a considerable commercial market for them. Very few are sold for domestic table use, except to a few immigrant groups, notably Italians. The bulk of the eel harvest is used domestically as bait for fishing or is exported to Europe for food. Although most Americans would not consider the eel to be suitable food, the Piney is willing to eat it. Merce Ridgway says that for as long as he can remember he has been preparing eels for his family's use. It is simply a matter of catching them, removing the skin with a pair of pliers, cutting them up into four- or five-inch sections, breading them, and frying them in a cast-iron skillet. Merce's father remembers that years ago, "They used to be as big around as your arm."[24]

The point to be made in looking at the chain pickerel, the catfish, and the eel is that the Piney is a forager, not a sportsman. Fishing is not play; it is part of a pattern of self-sufficiency. In some areas of the Pines, the Piney and the sport fisherman may fish side by side. This happens in areas where the acidity of the water is not high and the fish are more familiar. Such areas include the Mullica River, Toms River, Great Egg Harbor, and the Morris River—especially in their lower tidal portions. Here both Piney and sport fisherman may catch sunfish, large-mouth bass, and white perch. Another area of convergence would be some of the larger lakes which the New Jersey Division of Fish, Game, and Shellfisheries has stocked with trout and large-mouth bass.[25] While it may appear in such locations that the sport fisherman and the Piney are doing the same thing in the same place, in fact their goals are quite different. One is pursuing recreation; the other, survival.

Piney interaction with saltwater environments—the Atlantic Ocean and Barnegat Bay—is far more involved than their interaction with fresh water and their interaction with the woods. Just as deer may be harvested for subsistence, or market gunning, or for sport with outside hunters being led by Piney guides, so it is with saltwater fishing. Sometimes the fish are taken in small numbers for subsistence, sometimes in large numbers by Pineys who are commercial fishermen, and sometimes in relatively small numbers by outside sport fishermen who are escorted in party boats captained by Pineys.

To fish successfully here, it is necessary to acquire considerable knowledge about which fish are out there and in what season of the year. For example, in the winter, one can find ling, whiting, and cod in the ocean. During that same period of time, one can find flounder in the bay. In spring, the fishermen begin to find striped bass in the ocean. Later in the summer and on into the fall, they will find fluke, bluefish, weakfish, and even tuna. Pineys who are particularly good at fishing sometimes go into the business of taking tourists and sportsmen out on party boats. Marinas with party boats can be found all up and down the coastal Pinelands, including the towns of Forked River, Waretown, and Barnegat.

Although commercial fishing is not directly connected to this narrative, it should be pointed out that some Pineys are involved in large-scale commercial fishing. Here trawlers go far out into the ocean looking for menhaden, bonita, or tuna. Especially profitable are large numbers of bottom-fish such as blackfish, porgies, hake, fluke, and cod. Commercial fishing has recently fallen on hard times, but old-timers remember well the days when fleets of deep-sea fishing boats would bring giant catches of menhaden to a large processing plant on a small island off Manahawkin and Tuckerton. The fish would be ground up and made into fertilizer. Commercial fishing may never again be what it once was, but for many years it was part of the Piney way of life. A commercial fisherman can be his own boss (if he owns the boat). If he feels like staying home, he stays home. Of course, in actual practice most of them go out every day, but the point remains: nobody can make him go.

Herbert Halpert found that stories of fishing and waterfowl gunning were just as plentiful as stories about hunting. Most of these were tall tales about the great numbers of fish caught and ducks shot. Storytelling used to be an accepted pastime in the Pines. One artistic convention was that the stories, while they may have had some nucleus of truth, were to be exaggerated for the sake of amusement and that the teller had to present the story, however outrageous, as true. So many of these tall tales have to do with fishing that the term "fish stories" could stand for the whole genre.

Fish stories deal with familiar themes: the size of a given fish (especially one that got away), physical evidence in lieu of the fish itself, the size of a catch, the value of a catch, and so on. Duck-hunting stories contrast nicely with deer-hunting. To some Pineys, venison is not really a prize food because it reminds them of the Depression. It is considered "poor man's food." Instead, the prime attractions are the waterfowl. The species most commonly taken by hunters are wood duck, black duck, mallard, and green-winged teal. Other species include pintail, blue-winged teal, American widgeon, ring-necked duck, hooded merganser, and Canada goose.[26] Also popular were the formerly numerous marsh birds, or rails, which used to inhabit the Wading River and the Mullica River. Rails are known locally as "coots." The rail population is down today because motorboats have badly damaged the shorelines of the rivers. Quail enjoy a sort of immunity from hunting, possibly because they are known to eat garden bugs.

Foodways have a tremendous impact on Piney material culture. For example, the prevalence of duck hunting has resulted in the production of a unique type of boat mentioned earlier, the Barnegat Bay sneakbox. As the name implies, the boat is constructed to enable the hunter to move in on ducks in a stealthy manner. It is a small, one- or two-man craft, very low to the water, of a boxy or rectangular construction. It is just big enough for two hunters, their guns, and their dogs.[27] Another unique type of boat mentioned before is the garvey, used for clamming.

Foodways and the Garden

The deerhunter and the bayman are colorful and romantic characters. It takes no great leap of the imagination to see the deerhunter in the American tradition. Like his ancestor, Natty Bumppo-Pathfinder-Leatherstocking-Deerslayer, he stalks through the woods with all the cunning of an Indian. In a similar vein, we see the rugged bayman, his skin bronzed by the sun, setting forth before dawn in his sturdy garvey to gather clams, depending only on his own physical strength

and his knowledge of the bay. These lonely and stoic masculine call-
ings are easy to see through a nostalgic haze. These seem appropriate
activities for a group of people we have been told are descendants of
Tories and Huguenots, escaped criminals and vagabonds, runaways
and fugitives. Although these images are attractive and hard to shake,
the fact is that gardening is of paramount importance to the people
of the Pines.

Shooting deer and gathering clams are, in essence, foraging activities. As such, they are subject to all kinds of unpredictable vagaries
and shortages. But a garden, being an agriculture activity, albeit on
a small scale, is a fairly steady and reliable source of foodstuffs. Of
course, not all Pineys are gardeners. And of those who do grow gardens, not all do it well. But those who maintain successful gardens
are tremendously respected. How could anyone grow a garden, not
to mention a successful garden, in such admittedly poor soil, where
even the pine trees seem to have a hard time? The secret lies in constant mulching and fertilizing. With this kind of constant renewal,
some family gardenplots in the Pines have been productive for more
than a century.[28]

Gardening is not a hobby; it is serious business. You usually do
not go away and leave it in order to take a two-week vacation. You
have someone, usually a relative, take care of it. The Piney gardener
is more sophisticated about his gardening than his suburban amateur
counterpart. The gardens are diversified. If something fails, there will
be something else to rely on. The visitor quickly notices that the gardens are not bug-ridden and nasty. The Piney gardener goes out and
picks off the bugs, one at a time. Insecticides are dismissed as expensive contaminants.

Given the seriousness of gardening in the Pines as a means toward
self-sufficiency, it is not surprising that Halpert collected a number
of tales dealing with planting customs, giant vegetables, and voracious
pests. Jim Albertson relates a more modern version:

Well, a friend of mine one time tried to grow cantaloupe one year. He
planted the seeds and fertilized and everything. He really tried to get some
cantaloupe going. Well, he noticed one morning he come out there was chipmunks in the garden, and he tried all kinds of ways to scare them away. You
wouldn't call it a scarecrow. I guess you would call it a scare-chipmunk. He
tried the cannon, the gunshot. He shot at them and everything, and it seemed
after a few days it was very successful. He didn't see the chipmunks any more,
and the cantaloupe were doing quite well. By the end of the season he had
these big beautiful cantaloupe. His mouth was just watering thinking how
delicious they were gonna be. He went out to pick a couple of 'em. He picked

the cantaloupes off the vine, and they were suspiciously light. And when he turned the cantaloupes upside down there was a hole in the bottom of each of the two cantaloupes he picked. He had answered the question of where the chipmunks had gone. They had burrowed into the cantaloupes and had eaten out the insides and were using them as nests! Just the shells were left. The cantaloupes for all intents and purposes were gone.[29]

There is even a song dating back to the 1940s which describes in vivid detail the difficulties encountered in raising a garden. The song resulted from the efforts of American folklorist Dorothea Dix Lawrence. It seems that she was trying to line up singers and musicians for the National Folk Festival. According to Janice Sherwood, a lifelong resident of the Pines, Miss Lawrence had recruited her uncle, W.J. Britton, known to Janice (and nearly everyone else) as Uncle Bill. Miss Lawrence was delighted with Uncle Bill's musicianship since it seems that he knew a number of old Anglo-American fiddle tunes. There was only one problem: though Uncle Bill knew many songs, none of them dealt with the Pine Barrens directly. Miss Lawrence encouraged Uncle Bill to try his hand at composition. Because of modern scientific fieldwork principles, most contemporary folklorists would undoubtedly avoid such a practice. The resulting song, however, is very agreeable. Though he had never tried anything like this before, Uncle Bill sat down and wrote "Home in the Pines," a fine song still sung today by his niece Janice Sherwood and other members of an old-timey string band centered in Ocean County and known as the Pineconers:

> When you settle in the pinewoods down by the Jersey shore
> You're gonna have the hard time knockin' at your door.
> When you plant yourself a garden against the time of need
> You're gonna be mighty lucky if you ever raise your seed.
>
> So folks I'm gonna tell you if you crave to settle here
> You needn't bring your city clothes along.
> For what ere you turn your hand to make you daily bread
> It's ten to one it's gonna turn out wrong.
>
> The soil is doggone sandy, the insects try your soul
> For first they eat your beans up and then they eat the pole.
> The deer will leap your garden fence in the middle of the night
> If you want to save your cornfield you got to get up and fight.
>
> So it's work all day and gun all night; there is no time to sleep
> Except when you are leaning 'gainst the rail.
> And if you kill the pesky deer that's eating up your beans
> The warden wants to throw you in his jail.

Now when you go and dig some clams to sell when you reach shore
You'll find that the people just don't eat clams no more.
But when the season changes and clams just can't be found
You'll find a buyer waiting each time you turn around.

Oh the deer eat up your garden and the clams you cannot sell
Your luck just turns a little worse each day
But you've got to stay and take it until the bitter end
For you haven't got the means to get away.

But folks in spite of all this, there's something about these woods
That you will feel if here you ever roam.
And when you see our sunsets and breathe the balmy air
You'll never want to leave your Jersey home.[30]

Nearly everyone who tries to raise a garden in the Pines has difficulty with the deer. Janice Sherwood told me that her family had the same troubles as Uncle Bill. It seems that Janice's grandfather, Jackson Britton, was the caretaker at Lacey, or the Rutherford Stuyvesant tract, a vast area of some 14,500 acres. The family lived there from 1909 until 1950. At one point, Edward Britton, Janice's father, decided to make a large garden of sweet potatoes. Unfortunately, the deer love sweet potatoes. Edward Britton tried everything. At first, he tried to keep the deer out by putting up kerosene lanterns, but found it just made it easier for the deer to see what they were doing. Next he tried putting a cowbell on a long string. It fell to Janice's grandmother, Sarah "Sally" Britton, to wake up every once in a while to pull the string. Grandmom soon got tired of that. Finally Ed Britton rigged up two storage batteries with alarm clocks and automobile horns. The clocks were set so that they would go off when the minute hand went past twelve o'clock or six o'clock. The horns were rigged so that every fifteen minutes the horn would blow at one end of the field or the other. The deer could not get used to that. It was not consistent enough, and the garden was spared.[31]

Besides dramatizing the perennial conflict with the deer, the words of the song indicate clearly that agriculture, or gardening, is security against the vicissitudes of hunting and gathering. The garden is planted "against the time of need." Hunting and gathering are still preferred activities, because, on the continuum from nature to culture, gardening is a step closer to culture.

Foodways and the Store

Whether a given meal comes from the woods, the ocean, the garden, or in some combination of these, the common denominator here is the Piney's goal of all-providing self-sufficiency. Realistically speaking, this goal is simply an ideal which is seldom actually reached. The gap between what the Piney produces for himself and his family and what he needs is met by the store or, in recent years, the supermarket. In the not-too-distant past, stores were relied on chiefly for staples such as flour, salt, and salt-pork. The store was not viewed as a cornucopia of processed and prepared foods. Because purchases at the store indicated that the ideal of self-sufficiency had not been achieved, the store and the storekeeper were viewed with a good deal of hostility. There was always the suspicion that the storekeeper was "not really working" and was simply making a living through excessive mark-ups. And, to the extent that one needed to spend money in the store, one was dependent on the economy at large and the wage system. So however much the store was indeed needed, the storekeeper found himself the focal point of considerable resentment.

When John McPhee was exploring the Pine Barrens, he stopped at the Chatsworth General Store, largely unchanged since it was built in 1865. He describes it carefully:

> On the southwest corner of the town's principal intersection is the Chatsworth General Store, the entrance to which was cut into a corner of the building on an angle, so that the door itself, aproned with concrete steps, is the most prominent exterior feature of the building. The door was apparently designed to attract people from both intersecting streets, although the store has no competition for a ten-mile sweep in all directions. When I first stopped in there, I noticed on its shelves the usual run of cold cuts, canned foods, soft drinks, crackers, cookies, cereals, and sardines, and also Remington twelve-gauge shotgun shells, Slipknot friction tape, Varsity gasket cement, Railroad Mills sweet snuff, and State-Wide well restorer. Wrapping string unwound from a spool on a wall shelf and ran through eyelets across the ceiling and down to a wooden counter. A glass countertop next to the wooden one had been rubbed cloudy by hundreds of thousands of coins and pop bottles, and in the case beneath it were twenty-two rectangular glass dishes, each holding a different kind of penny candy. Beside the candy case was a radiator covered with an oak plank. Chatsworth loafers sat there. There were no particular loafers. Almost everyone who came into the store spent a little time on the oak plank.[32]

Thus the general store in the Pines functions as delicatessen, luncheonette, grocery store, hardware store, and gathering place. Still, the store is viewed with some hostility. This hostility is typically covert but emerges in disguised form in storytelling. For example, one legendary character fully explored by Halpert was old Jerry Munyhun, a wizard or magician. Halpert found a full cycle of legends about Jerry

1. Although the Pines are not known for special regional dishes, Connie's Pine Barrens restaurant represents an attempt to capitalize on the growing popularity of the New Jersey Pine Barrens as a resort area.

Munyhun, many of which reflected hostility towards iron manufacturers, mill owners, sawmill operators, bartenders, and storekeepers. In one such story Munyhun paid for an order of food in cash; but, when the storekeeper emptied the cash register at the end of the day, the money had turned into clam shells.[33] The story turns up from many different informants and in many different versions, but the theme remains the same. Jerry Munyhun stands for the underdog, the Piney, and he has the last laugh in outwitting the moneyed class, which is embodied in these tales by the storekeeper.

Nearly forty years later, Janice Sherwood of Forked River talked about the subject of foodways in general and the store in particular. She can trace her family history in the Pines back to before the time of the American Revolution, and she enjoys the role of spokesperson for the Pineys. She felt no particular hostility to storekeepers. Indeed, she viewed the old general store with fond nostalgia. She is not even particularly angry with contemporary supermarkets. What does make her mad is the population pressure which has forced a change in the self-sufficient Piney lifestyle. Janice reminisces about the old general store:

> Grandmom would go to Tom's River in the fall and buy great big enormous bags of flour, a ten-pound bag of salt, and a fifty-pound bag of sugar to get through the winter with. Today there is much more reliance on the supermarket. You're not allowed to raise pigs. It's against ordinance. You can't raise chickens, unless you have always raised them. You can't have a cow. You have to have so many acres to have a horse. The ordinances don't fit the circumstances. And the Bay is polluted over here on our side so you can't go clamming. You gotta go across the Bay to certain places to get your seafood—if you have a license. There's a lot more rules and regulations. Population is the problem.[34]

Janice is right: Population *is* the problem. Population was at the heart of the public policy debate which swirled around the Pinelands throughout the 1970s. On the one hand, there were those who advocated preservation of the Pines, which seems simple enough. On the other hand, those who opposed preservation never put it quite so baldly. Instead, they spoke in terms of "home rule" and "private enterprise." Indeed, they could make a persuasive case. If a family has owned a piece of land for years and years and has paid taxes on it, why shouldn't they be allowed to develop it for profit? And if the state wants to preserve the land, let the state buy it at a fair price. The matter was settled in 1979 when Governor Brendan Byrne signed into law the Pinelands Protection Act which enforced a construction moratorium and

2. Buzby's General Store in Chatsworth, Woodland Township, was built in 1865.

created a Pinelands Commission to draft a master plan. Governor Byrne characterized the legislation as "the bill that 100 years from now I'll be most remembered for."[35] Undoubtedly, part of the Governor's success in this matter came from the support he received from the Pineys themselves.

Efforts to Preserve the Heritage

Pineys are not comfortable with the world of interstate highways, shopping malls, and supermarkets. Instead, they are at home in communities made up of churches, granges, and volunteer fire companies. With their long isolation from mainstream culture, they have developed a regional sense of uniqueness. As the population pressure from Philadelphia and New York led developers to build more tract housing in the 1960s and 1970s, old-time residents felt increasing resentment at the changes in their environment. They were forced to ponder their relationship to society as a whole. One response was the formation in April of 1975 of the Pinelands Cultural Society.

The group's avowed aim is to preserve and foster the cultural heritage of the Pine Barrens. The group is primarily interested in preserving the old-time music of the area. But the music itself is a polemical weapon in the service of preservation. Some of the best-known performers in the Pines have been featured at concerts sponsored by the Pinelands Cultural Society. Admission to these weekly gatherings remains at $1.50 for everyone over age twelve. The society administers the funds collected, placing them into a building fund that society leaders hope will one day help them to erect a permanent music and cultural center for the Pinelands region. The very name Pinelands *Cultural* Society suggests that these people had a sense that the significance of their undertaking embodied not just the music but the whole traditional way of life of the Pine Barrens.

One of the first activities of the new society was the publication of the Pinelands Cultural Society cookbook, a mimeographed collection of recipes. The long-term residents of the New Jersey Pine Barrens, articulately represented by David Rinear, Janice Sherwood, and Gladys Eayre, feel threatened by the increasing development and urbanization of what they see as their once idyllic, rural space. The PCS cookbook represents a conscious effort on the part of its members to argue in favor of the older Pine Barrens aesthetic and value system in contrast to that represented by the newcomers, those who have migrated here in increasing numbers over the past twenty years.

3. Cranberry bog worker cleans weeds out of an irrigation ditch on a farm near Chatsworth. The cleaning is done in July; the cranberries will not be harvested until the fall.

Pinelands foodways are emphasized in day-to-day life. With increased Piney political awareness, however, it is not surprising that foodways have also begun to play a part in public and festive occasions. For example, in the spring of 1979 the organizers of the New Jersey Folklore Symposium sponsored by the New Jersey Committee for the Humanities, called on Arlene Ridgway, one of the founders of PCS, for advice on devising an appropriate Pine Barrens foodways luncheon. Adherence to tradition was reflected in the decision to serve clam chowder, South Jersey apple juice, Barnegat Bay clam fritters, turnip n' tater stew, and huckleberry pie, with the added festive touch of blueberry champagne from Renault Winery in Egg Harbor City.

This self-conscious celebration of Pinelands foodways promoted by the Pinelands Cultural Society is one aspect of a community's efforts to come to grips with what it perceives as its fading past and the urban encroachment of an all-too-real present. The PCS is concerned about the effects of industrialization and urbanization. In South Jersey the old folkways had developed and solidified for a longer period than elsewhere in New Jersey. Thus the shock of urbanization there has been greater and the reactions more extreme.[36] The members of the PCS exhibit what Tuan calls "local patriotism" — a patriotism that "rests on the intimate experience of place, and on a sense of the fragility of goodness; that which we love has no guarantee to endure."[37] The moving forces behind the Society view urbanization as a direct threat to the physical and social environment they have known for their entire lives.[38] Their awareness of their past and their drive to preserve what they can of it — in song, story and foodways — is intricately tied to their love of place and their perception of themselves as a people apart from the other residents of New Jersey.

ACKNOWLEDGMENTS

Many of the ideas presented here grew out of conversations with Barbara Kirshenblatt-Gimblett of New York University. I wish to express my gratitude to John Sinton and Tom Ayres of Stockton State College, both of whom have lived and worked in the Pines for many years. They both read an earlier draft of this paper and offered numerous helpful suggestions for revisions. Additional revisions were suggested by Linda Keller Brown, Kamala Truscott, and Paul Schiffer. My work was supported by a Summer Research Fellowship from Rutgers University.

NOTES

1. See Jack McCormick, *The Pine Barrens: A Preliminary Ecological Inventory* (Trenton: New Jersey State Museum, 1970).

2. For a review of the literature see Barbara Smith Irwin, "New Jersey Pine Barrens Folklore: A Selective Bibliography," *New Jersey Folklore: A Statewide Journal* 2 (Spring 1979).

3. John W. Sinton, *Natural Cultural Resources of the New Jersey Pine Barrens* (Pomona, N.J.: Stockton State College, 1979), 1–7.

4. John McPhee, *The Pine Barrens* (New York: Farrar, Strauss, 1968), 14.

5. On July 12, 1978, the House of Representatives in Washington approved legislation which authorizes the federal government to spend $26 million to protect the New Jersey Pine Barrens against uncontrolled development. Reps. James J. Florio, D-1st Distr., William J. Hughes, D-2nd Distr., and Edwin Forsythe, R-6th Distr., co-sponsored the legislation.

6. Shayna Panzer, "Public's Ideas Sought on Pinelands Plan," *New York Times*, 6 July 1980, 16 (N.J.).

7. McPhee, 3.

8. Yi-Fu Tuan, *Topophilia: A Study of Environmental Perception, Attitudes, and Values* (Englewood Cliffs, N.J.: Prentice-Hall, 1974).

9. McPhee, 23–26.

10. Gerald Stern, "The Pineys," *Journal of the Rutgers University Library* 32 (1969): 55–80.

11. See Pat Morris, "Jersey Garveys, Grecian Myths," *Matrix: A Report on Research at Rutgers* (Winter 1979):16.

12. Arlene Ridgway, *Chicken-Foot Soup and Other Recipes from the Pine Barrens* (New Brunswick: Rutgers Univ. Press, 1980).

13. Sinton, 166.

14. AG interview with Gladys Eayre, 15 July 1979, East Millstone, Somerset County, N.J.

15. AG interview with Sam Hunt, 4 Oct. 1979, Waretown, Ocean County, N.J.

16. See Roger Welsch, "'We Are What We Eat': Omaha Food as Symbol," and Charles Joyner, "Soul Food and the Sambo Stereotype: Foodlore from the Slave Narrative Collection," *Keystone Folklore Quarterly* 16 (Winter 1971):165–70, 171–77. See also Alicia Gonzales, "'Guess How Doughnuts Are Made': Verbal and Non-Verbal Aspects of the *Panadero* and His Stereotype," in *"And Other Neighborly Games": Social Process and Cultural Image in Texas Folklore,* ed. Richard Bauman and Roger D. Abrahams (Austin: Univ. of Texas Press, 1981), 104–22.

17. James E. Applegate, Silas Little, and Philip E. Marucci, "Plant and Animal Products of the Pine Barrens," in Richard T.T. Forman, ed., *Pine Barrens: Ecosystem and Landscape* (New York: Academic Press, 1979), 29–30.

18. Herbert Norman Halpert, "Folktales and Legends from the New Jersey Pines: A Collection and a Study" (Ph.D. diss. Indiana Univ., 1947).

19. McPhee, 139–40.

20. McPhee, 140.

21. McPhee, 142.

22. AG telephone interview with Merce Ridgway, Jr., 8 July 1980, Waretown, Ocean County, N.J.

23. Ibid.

24. Ibid.

25. AG telephone interview with Robert W. Hastings, 8 July 1980, Camden, N.J.

26. Applegate, Little, and Marucci, 30.

27. F.M. Paulson, "Barnegat Bay Sneakbox," *Field and Stream* (Oct. 1971):143, 148–49.

28. One such garden belongs to Kenneth Eayre of Well's Mill Road (County Road 532) in Waretown. The garden was started by his grandfather, Franklin Eayre. Kenneth, brother of Gladys discussed earlier, currently grows lettuce, tomatoes, cabbage, soybeans, wax beans, cucumbers, beets, parsnips, Swiss chard, onions, peas, zucchini, hot peppers, okra, celery, asparagus, basil, parsley, comfrey, Jerusalem artichokes, dill, and black-eyed peas.

29. AG interview with Jim Albertson, 10 Nov. 1981, East Millstone, N.J.

30. AG interview with Janice Sherwood, 12 Aug. 1978, Forked River, Ocean County, N.J.

31. AG interview with Janice Sherwood, 15 July 1979, East Millstone, N.J.

32. McPhee, 78–79.

33. Halpert, 252–53.

34. AG interview with Janice Sherwood, 15 July 1979, East Millstone, N.J.

35. Panzer, 1.

36. Cf. D.K. Wilgus, "Country-Western Music and the Urban Hillbilly," in *The Urban Experience and Folk Tradition,* ed. Americo Paredes and Ellen J. Stekert (Austin: Univ. of Texas Press, 1971), 137.

37. Tuan, 101.

38. Cf. Suzi Jones, "Regionalization: A Rhetorical Strategy," *Journal of the Folklore Institute* 13 (1976):105–18.

8

The Social and Symbolic Uses of Ethnic/Regional Foodways: Cajuns and Crawfish in South Louisiana

C. Paige Gutierrez

A tourist, stepping off the plane at the New Orleans International Airport, is confronted with an array of commercial products found in no other part of the United States. Airport gift shops sell the city's heritage in the form of freeze-dried gumbo mix, plastic-wrapped pralines, voodoo paraphernalia, Dixieland jazz records, and dark-skinned "quadroon" dolls dressed in ruffled antebellum hoop skirts. Scattered among these New Orleans artifacts are souvenirs of a different kind—those that are more properly associated with Cajun country, which lies to the southwest, west, and northwest of the city. Prominent among the Cajun-oriented products is the image of the crawfish (or "crayfish" or "crawdad," to the unacculturated tourist). A visitor leaving New Orleans and venturing into Cajun country will find even more commercial crawfish iconography: plastic crawfish key chains and combs, real crawfish frozen into clear acrylic paperweights shaped like the state of Louisiana, children's books featuring anthropomorphized crawfish as main characters, and expensive gold or silver crawfish pendants. The tourist will also notice that these emblematic crawfish are frequently juxtaposed with verbal expressions of ethnic/regional consciousness. The words "Cajun," "Acadian," "Cajun Country," and "Louisiana" often appear in conjunction with crawfish imagery; for example, a popular local license plate and T-shirt show an upraised fist holding a crawfish, with the accompanying slogan "Cajun Power."

Even though these souvenirs are commercial products that have appeared as a response to a rise in tourism during the past two decades, they are also indicative of a strong symbolic association involving Cajuns, crawfish, and region that reaches beyond the walls of the souvenir store. The crawfish — both as animal and as food — is the predominant ethnic and regional emblem for Cajuns and for southern Louisiana.

The word "Cajun" implies both an ethnic and a regional identity. The French who settled in Nova Scotia in the seventeenth century became known as Acadians. They prospered in Canada until 1755, when the British destroyed their holdings and ousted them from Acadia. After three decades of wandering, large numbers of Acadian refugees settled permanently in southern Louisiana, where they eventually became known as "Cajuns." Cajun lifeways in Louisiana developed in response to a physical environment that included swamps, bayous, marshes, and prairies, and a social environment that commingled continental and Caribbean French peoples, Germans, Spaniards, Blacks, Indians, Anglo-Americans and others.[1] Cajuns adapted successfully to the various physical environments of the area and acculturated much of the non-Cajun population to the Cajun lifestyle. Thus, there are many people in southern Louisiana today, who, though not descended from the Acadians, call themselves Cajuns and/or participate widely in Cajun culture.[2]

Although it is impossible to define fully the word "Cajun," it has been suggested that "a Cajun is most emphatically identifiable as an individual who is typically Roman Catholic, is rural or of rural extraction, emphasizes kinship relations over those of nonkin-based associations, and who speaks or understands both English and Louisiana French languages or has close relatives who do so."[3] In addition, south Louisiana remains the homeland even for a Cajun residing elsewhere. Cajun culture has shaped and has been shaped by geographic region. Despite the incursions of the modern world (which sometimes actually strengthen regional identity, as is the case with the oil industry and its contribution to the growth of new Cajun occupations such as roustabouting and petroleum engineering), Cajun Louisiana in many ways still conforms to Zelinsky's definition of a traditional region:

These regions are relatively self-contained, endogamous, stable, and of long duration. . . . An intimate symbiotic relationship between man and land develops over many centuries, one that creates indigenous modes of thought and action, a distinctive visible landscape, and a form of human ecology specific to the locality. Although the usual processes of random cultural mutation, the vagaries of history, and some slight intermixture of peoples, and the diffusion of innovations of all sorts prevents the achievement of total stasis or equilibrium, or complete internal uniformity, it would not be unfair to characterize such a traditional region as one based on blood and soil. In the extreme, it becomes synonymous with a particular tribe or ethnic group.[4]

The interplay of ethnicity and region, of "blood and soil," is implicitly recognized in the Louisiana state legislature's designation of a twenty-two-parish area of southern Louisiana as "Acadiana"—a term derived from the fusion of the words "Acadian" and "Louisiana."

When mainstream America came to Acadiana in the twentieth century in the form of forced English-language education, the mass media, the petrochemical industry, and World War II, the Cajuns found themselves in a position not unlike that of the newly arrived Old World immigrants to the United States. Although this "new world" of the outsider offered many opportunities for a better life, it also threatened to destroy that which was traditional and meaningful in the old life. Local customs were often ridiculed by the more "sophisticated" outsiders, and the use of the French language in advertising, legal documents, and in public schools was forbidden by state law. Many outsiders, and insiders as well, associated Cajun culture with ignorance and poverty.

However, the minority and ethnic revival movements which occurred throughout the United States in the 1960s and 1970s have parallels in southern Louisiana. The Council for the Development of French in Louisiana (CODOFIL) was founded in 1968 and has since sought to strengthen the French component of Cajun identity through language education programs, heritage festivals, publications, and cultural exchanges between Louisiana and France, Quebec, and other French-speaking parts of the world. CODOFIL and related organizations best represent the "Genteel Acadians," the wealthier or more formally educated Cajuns, who have chosen the speaking of standard French as a key rallying symbol for their ethnic revival movement.[5] These Genteel Acadians are opposed by the less organized, but equally verbal, "Proud Coonasses," who often speak a nonstandard Louisiana French dialect or no French at all, and who emphasize the playful and sometimes rowdy side of Cajun life, with its heavy drinking and eating, gambling, cockfighting, and barroom brawls.[6] A popular bumper sticker sums up the Coonass philosophy: "Happiness in Cajun Land is Gumbo, Go-Go, and Do-Do"—food, sex, and sleep. The Proud Coonasses have taken a term once used by outsiders as an ethnic slur and transformed it into a symbol of ethnic regional consciousness. The Genteel Acadians strongly oppose the use of the term Coonass (or its pictorial equivalent) as vulgar and do not identify with the lifestyle that the term represents. On the other hand, the Proud Coon-asses have little interest in learning to speak standard French and some-times see the Genteel Acadians as elitist or hypocritical.

The conflict centering around these two symbolic acts—the use of standard French and the use of the term Coonass—is reminiscent of Barth's observation that ethnic revivalism often brings with it a strug-gle between different segments of the group over the "selection of sig-nals for identity and the assertion of value for these cultural diacritica, and the suppression or denial of relevance of other differentiae."[7] Al-though the struggle between the Genteel Acadians and the Proud Coon-asses continues, neither group is likely to succeed in having its chosen "signal for identity" become *the* Cajun ethnic/regional symbol.[8] That role has been quietly assumed by the crawfish, which is flexible enough to represent both Genteel Acadians and Proud Coonasses, and the majority of Cajuns who fit in between these two extremes. The craw-fish unites Cajuns to each other and to their land, while it also suc-cessfully highlights the boundaries between Cajuns and outsiders.

Each year between December and May the streams, ponds, swamps, and ditches of southern Louisiana produce an abundance of craw-fish. It is estimated that the Atchafalaya Basin Swamp, a half-million-acre area located in central Acadiana, produces almost 6 million kilograms of wild crawfish annually, while manmade crawfish ponds produce another 5.5 million kilograms.[9] There is no way of reliably estimating the amount of additional crawfish obtained by noncom-mercial, Sunday crawfishermen who scour roadside ditches and swampy areas for personal consumption. Yet elderly locals claim that the sup-ply of crawfish has dwindled over the years and look back to a time when crawfish were so numerous that hordes of them crossing the high-ways created traffic hazards, and housewives in low-lying areas could scoop up a bucketful for dinner from their own backyards. Crawfish farming has helped to offset the decline in the natural supply of craw-fish. Both the farms and the major natural crawfish-producing areas are restricted primarily to Cajun-dominated parishes, and almost ninety percent of the crawfish harvest is consumed in Acadiana and New Orleans.[10] Some locals joke that French Louisiana lies "behind the crawfish curtain," separated gastronomically from Anglo-American north Louisiana, where crawfish are often ignored or even scorned as food.

Not only do south Louisianians monopolize the cooking and con-sumption of crawfish, but they also dominate the entire industry, from trapping and processing to distribution. The Cajun is the primary heir to the cultural and technological knowledge pertinent to crawfish foodways in the United States. Thus a strong association between Cajuns and crawfish is understandable. A popularized summary of crawfish legendry, sold locally as a souvenir, states that "when a bayou baby is nine days old, his mother sticks his finger in a crawfish hole, and that makes him a Cajun."[11] A similar acknowledgment of the close association between the two is expressed in the folksong below, *"Cribisse! Cribisse!"* ("Crawfish! Crawfish!"), collected in the 1930s. (The term "Frenchmen" is commonly used in southern Louisiana to refer to Cajuns.)

> Crawfish, crawfish, got no show, baby,
> Crawfish, crawfish, got no show,
> The Frenchman ketch 'im fer to make gumbo, baby.
>
> Get up in the morning you find me gone, baby,
> Get up in the morning you find me gone,
> I'm on my way to the crawfish pond, baby.
>
> Frenchman, Frenchman, only nine days old, baby,
> Frenchman, Frenchman, only nine days old,
> Broke his arm in a crawfish hole, baby.
>
> Crawfish ain't skeered of a six-mule team, baby,
> Crawfish ain't skeered of a six-mule team,
> But run from a Frenchman time he see 'im, baby.
>
> Look all 'round a Frenchman's bed, baby,
> Look all 'round a Frenchman's bed,
> You don' find nothin' but crawfish heads, baby.[12]

The folk song portrays the crawfish as both a living animal with a personality and as a prepared food. In Louisiana, the crawfish exists both as part of nature, in the form of a living animal, and as part of culture, when it is transformed by cooking into food. The dual role of the crawfish-as-animal and the crawfish-as-food in Cajun life is partly responsible for the creature's success as an ethnic emblem. The crawfish can be manipulated symbolically both as animal and as food, and the meaning expressed by the image of crawfish-as-animal is different from the meaning expressed by crawfish-as-food. Thus the crawfish possesses a broad range and flexibility as an ethnic/regional emblem.

The Cajun and the crawfish-as-animal thrive together in the south Louisiana environment. This camaraderie has not gone unnoticed in Cajun popular lore, where the identities of the human and the animal are playfully allowed to blur. A local legend claims that the lobsters which accompanied the Acadian refugees in their trek from Canada to Louisiana shrunk into crawfish during the exhausting journey. These

crawfish remained loyal friends to the Louisiana Cajuns, even model-
ing their chimneyed mud burrows after the mud chimneys on early
Cajun houses.[13] Such personification of the animal is not uncommon
in Louisiana lore. For example, in a joke told by local comedian Jus-
tin Wilson and also found in oral tradition, a mother crawfish, speaking in a Cajun English dialect, calms her offsprings' fears of horses
and cows, but tells them to "run lak de devil" when they see a Cajun,
because "he'll eat anyt'ing."[14] Sometimes the personification process
is reversed, and the Cajun is pictured as taking on the characteristics
of the crawfish. Several informants have remarked, after eating large
quantities of crawfish, "I'll be walking backwards for a week" (referring to the animals' usual form of locomotion).

There is another aspect of the animal's behavior that makes it an
especially appropriate ethnic emblem: its pugnaciousness and tenacity in seemingly hopeless situations. Crawfish with claws outstretched
threaten revenge on their human captors all the way from the trap
to the cooking pot. Local jokes portray a crawfish sitting on a railroad
track, aggressively snapping its claws at an oncoming locomotive.
Cajuns view the crawfish's feistiness with respect as well as humor.
Hallowell suggests that "Cajuns have taken the animal's courage as
a symbol for their own cultural revival."[15] Although it would be more
precise to say that the animal's courage is only one of several factors
that make it an appropriate Cajun symbol, the fighting spirit of the
crawfish nevertheless certainly contributes to the effectiveness of the
symbol. The intrepidity and persistence of the crawfish are paralleled
in the Cajuns' own image of themselves as a people who have man-
aged to fight and survive in the face of deportation, economic hardship, social oppression, and a sometimes hostile environment.

The modern media in Acadiana are constantly finding new applications for the crawfish-as-animal emblem. For example, an outdoor
urban mural in the Cajun city of Lafayette has as its focus a giant
crawfish holding an oil rig in one claw. Bicentennial notecards featured a crawfish fife-and-drum corps, and 1980 presidential campaign
bumper stickers pictured crawfish waving GOP flags. At the 1980
Breaux Bridge Crawfish Festival, where crawfish iconography is carried to the limit, there were T-shirts for sale illustrated with a Cajun-
style band made up of crawfish musicians, and cardboard crawfish
holding Dixie beer cans in their claws advertised a favorite local beverage. A local author has recently published a series of children's books
about Crawfish-Man, a part-human and part-crawfish "superhereaux"
whose goal it is to "keep the peace, justice and the Cajun Way."[16] A
simple Cajun fisherman under ordinary circumstances, Crawfish-Man

is transformed into a powerful, claw-snapping savior of Cajuns who are in trouble. Crawfish-Man is the perfect example of the personified, pugnacious crawfish.

The physical nature of the crawfish-as-animal enhances the power of the crawfish-as-food as an ethnic marker. Like other hard-shelled crustaceans, the crawfish must be boiled or steamed alive, after which the edible parts may be extracted by a rather complicated peeling process. The meat may be eaten immediately after peeling, or it may be used as an ingredient in more complicated dishes. When boiled crawfish are served, each diner is responsible for peeling his or her own crawfish. Thus participation in a crawfish boil requires special cultural knowledge in order to eat the food as served. In addition, a diner's reaction to the sight of the rather "life-like" boiled crawfish may separate the insider from the outsider at a crawfish boil. Therefore this food event is especially efficacious in highlighting ethnic boundaries.

Crawfish boils are common spring social events in southern Louisiana. They are held at private homes or at "camps" (second homes used primarily for parties or for fishing and hunting bases) and are attended by large numbers of relatives and friends. The event requires the presence of a group of people; boiling crawfish for one or two would hardly be worth the trouble. A crawfish boil begins with the acquisition of live crawfish. In the past, the crawfish were obtained directly from the environment, thus requiring that someone in the group know how to catch crawfish. Today, however, many people simply buy live crawfish by the sack at local seafood markets.

Once the crawfish arrive at the site of the boil, the proceedings become a community project. The preparations and cooking take place out of doors; it would be very messy indeed to have a crawfish boil indoors. The job of boiling the crawfish is men's work. (Cajun men are proud of their culinary skills and often do the cooking at large-scale food events.) The men first sort the live crawfish from any dead ones that may be in the sacks. This process requires dexterity if one is to avoid being pinched by the animals' claws, and care must be taken to prevent the escape of any of the animals. The live crawfish are placed in a container of water to "clean themselves out."

Meanwhile, the guests drink beer and comment on the quality of the crawfish, and the men prepare the cooking pot. They may use a large metal container, specially designed for boiling seafood, or perhaps a large metal garbage can that serves the purpose equally well. Today, the source of heat is usually a butane burner connected to a portable butane tank. The pot rests over the fire on a heavy metal tripod. The task of setting up the pot and the butane burner requires a degree of physical strength and is potentially a dangerous job. To make this task easier, Cajuns who can afford it may have complete outdoor crawfish-boil facilities, with a moveable suspended pot, a permanent butane source, and a built-in cooler that holds a keg of beer.

After the water in the pot begins to boil, the seasoning is added. A commercial seasoning mix may be used, or the host may combine the seasonings himself. Red pepper and salt are the predominant seasonings, but other items, such as onions or lemons, may be added as well. New red potatoes or corn on the cob may also be boiled with the crawfish. The water is allowed to boil until the crawfish have been sorted and cleaned, and the seasoned water is frequently tasted, discussed, and added to. When it is agreed that the seasoning is "right," the crawfish are lowered into the pot in a large metal basket. Some people prefer to steam crawfish in a lesser amount of water with a lid, although most people boil them. The "correct" way to cook them may be a topic of considerable conversation. After about ten minutes the crawfish are tested for doneness. This, too, may be a point of slight disagreement, with each man putting in his opinion.

Meanwhile, the people who are not directly involved in the cooking process (often women) have prepared the table by covering it with newspapers and laying out drinks, bread, napkins, and perhaps trays for the discarded shells. Sometimes knives or nutcrackers are provided for cracking the claws of especially large crawfish. The crawfish are served by the men, who lift the heavy basket from the pot and pour the crawfish in a great mound down the center of the table. There are usually no clearly defined "places" at the table — people simply sit down and reach for the nearest crawfish in the pile in front of them. No attempt is made to divide the crawfish into equal amounts for each person; each diner is on his own and may eat as many crawfish as possible until the supply runs out.

Because of the large number of newcomers in Acadiana, it is not unusual for a non-Cajun co-worker or friend to be invited to a crawfish boil. An outsider attending his first crawfish boil potentially faces two problems. First, a non-Cajun may take one look at a boiled crawfish and decide that it is inedible. To a Cajun, of course, crawfish are quite edible; in fact, they are highly desired as food. But to many outsiders, the crawfish, by its very nature, is inedible or even repulsive. Today in the United States, our animal foods usually bear little resemblance to the living animal by the time they reach the kitchen or the table. A hamburger does not look or act like a cow. But crawfish must be alive when first cooked, and, being alive, the main course makes every attempt to escape or pinch the fingers of the cook (or guests). In addition, crawfish, whether alive or boiled, bear a strong resemblance to insects. Live crawfish in a container squirm and crawl over each other and make hissing and bubbling sounds, and boiled crawfish still retain their small, segmented bodies, hard shells, multiple legs, antennas, and protruding eyes. Indeed, crawfish are often called "mudbugs." Since few people in the United States eat insects, it is not uncommon for an outsider to avoid eating what he perceives to be an insect-like creature. Also, some outsiders erroneously believe that crawfish are unsanitary animals, because they live in the mud at the bottom of streams and ditches. One outsider remarked, "I can't believe my eyes when I drive along the interstate and see all those people digging up vermin from the scum in the drainage ditches, and taking them home to eat." Cajuns, of course, are likely to be insulted by such sentiments. A person who is too afraid or too squeamish to eat crawfish is either pitied or resented, and he is certainly not invited back to the next crawfish boil.

If a newcomer decides to eat the boiled crawfish, he faces a second problem: learning *how* to eat the crawfish. The locals, of course, know that the only edible portions of a crawfish are its tail meat, its fat, and, in large crawfish, the claw meat. The tail is broken from the "head" (actually the head and thorax) and the tail meat is quickly removed in one piece from the shell by a twisting and pinching process that is difficult to master. The intestinal vein is separated from the meat and discarded. The fat is extracted from the open end of the head by a finger or by simply sucking the head. The meat is removed from large claws after cracking them with a knife or the teeth; however, the claws of smaller crawfish are discarded.

The speed and dexterity with which a person peels crawfish determines the number of crawfish that a person consumes. Not only does a person who cannot peel crawfish end up with a very light meal, but such a person looks very silly indeed. Cajuns joke about outsiders who try to eat the head of the crawfish, or who tear up the meat in removing it from the shell, or who take a full five minutes to peel and eat a single crawfish, or who eat the intestinal vein by mistake, or who absentmindedly rub an eye with a pepper-covered finger. Of course, if an outsider is a guest at a Cajun crawfish boil, the hosts will be most helpful in teaching the newcomer to eat the crawfish properly. In such a situation, the Cajun is in control and holds the situationally relevant knowledge. Those who know how to eat crawfish seem to enjoy, in a non-malicious way, the ignorance of others, and take pride in being able to teach a novice how to eat properly. Sometimes an insider will peel a number of crawfish and give the meat to the guest.

This is a gesture of high regard; people do not usually take time from their own peeling and eating to peel for others, unless there is a special relationship between the two people. A mother will help her child, for example, or a husband or wife who has finished eating will help the other. A high status 'is attached to the person who eats a great number of crawfish, as indicated by the size of the pile of discarded shells at his place. The ability to consume many crawfish is a reflection of the person's peeling skill and robust appetite, both of which are highly regarded by Cajuns. It is said in Acadiana that a newcomer can become a local only if he can learn to eat crawfish and drink dark roast coffee.

Cajun country has gained international fame in gourmet circles, and many outsiders are eager to become acquainted with the "exotic" local foodways. Although few tourists have the opportunity to attend a local crawfish boil, numerous tourist-oriented restaurants give newcomers a gentle introduction to Cajun cooking in a thoroughly American commercial setting. In such establishments, the pepper content is kept to a minimum (relative to home cooking), and boiled crawfish may be served in relatively small quantities by waitresses who graciously explain the peeling process. Or a customer may order a crawfish dinner that includes several different dishes: gumbo or stew, etoufee with rice, patties, pie, fried crawfish tails, bisque, and the familiar American tossed green salad. In the more expensive restaurants, dishes are available that would rarely if ever grace the table of the average local: avocado stuffed with crawfish dressing, crawfish casserole made with cream sauce, crawfish Newburgh, crawfish cocktail, crawfish and lettuce salad. Non-Cajun ethnic restaurants provide crawfish pizza and Chinese-style crawfish dishes. In all these dishes, the crawfish comes in the form of peeled tail meat. As such, it closely resembles shrimp in appearance, and, of course, does not require the technical knowledge necessary to eat boiled crawfish. Thus, in the heavily advertised Cajun restaurants, where tourists and their dollars are welcome, the loosening of ethnic boundaries is reflected in the setting and the food. To the outsider, these restaurants are "different" enough to be interesting, but not so different as to be threatening or unenjoyable. Smaller, out-of-the-way restaurants also exist in Acadiana, where the clientele is more local, French is more commonly spoken, the food is more highly seasoned, the menu is relatively limited, and the atmosphere is less plush and formal (boiled crawfish are served on newspaper or cardboard, for example). Although such restaurants welcome outsiders who happen by, only the more adventurous are apt to feel comfortable in what is obviously the "insiders'" territory.

People throughout Acadiana display pride in their local foodways. Dozens of major festivals and countless smaller fairs feature Cajun cuisine for the benefit of both tourists and locals. The town of Breaux Bridge sponsors the biennial Crawfish Festival, "the world's biggest crawfish boil," during which tons of crawfish are cooked and consumed. A historical marker in the town reads in part: "Breaux Bridge: Long recognized for its culinary artistry in the preparation of crawfish. The 1958 Louisiana Legislature officially designated Breaux Bridge 'La Capitale Mondiale de l'Ecrivisse' in honor of its centennial year." However, the more elderly residents of Breaux Bridge claim that crawfish-eating was not always something to brag about. Crawfish were "poor people's food," provided freely by the swamps and streams. A story is told in Breaux Bridge about an old crawfisherman who used to take the long way home with his catch from the Atchafalaya Swamp in order to avoid the humiliation of being seen with crawfish by the Lafayette "city folk" picnicking on the levee. Today, he still must take the long way home to avoid the city folk, who now deluge him with offers to buy his crawfish. A local woman in her eighties says, "Now the big shots eat crawfish, and the poor can't afford to. I wish I had eaten more back then; now I can't afford to buy them." An item that was once free for the taking has become an expensive food with "gourmet" overtones.

The development in Louisiana of what might be called "crawfish chic" is widely felt, even in high-level international business circles, as this recent news item illustrates:

> Lafayette's fame as a garden city, a mecca for gourmet food and a "can do" community of decision-makers in the oil industry is well-known in Abu Dhabi, United Arab Emirates.
> One of Acadiana's ambassadors of good will and international trade development is Huey Lambert, vice-president of AMASAR (American Associates of Arabia), and he provides this latest report. The Mansoori Oil Field Division held its second annual "Louisiana Crawfish Dinner Beach Party" in Abu Dhabi on May 24. It was a huge success.
> Huey brought 120 pounds of crawfish for the party; next year he'll have to increase the figure to 300 pounds. Around 200 people attended, 50 from Louisiana, others from France and the Middle East. They loved the food seasoned with south Louisiana pepper sauce.
> Huey met a Texan in London who offered $500 for one of the two containers of live Louisiana crawfish. The AMASAR exec turned him down.[17]

This reversal of status of the crawfish-as-food is undoubtedly related to its effectiveness as an ethnic emblem. Today people are proud to be Cajuns and proud to eat crawfish, and the memory of past humiliations can only serve to strengthen this pride.

The new role of the crawfish as gourmet food partially explains the acceptance of the crawfish as ethnic symbol by the Genteel Acadians. Tail meat may be combined with cream, wine, mushrooms, or other relatively expensive ingredients to produce any number of refined dishes appropriate for posh occasions. Even a crawfish boil may be "dressed up"; a south Louisiana department store sells special napkins, napkin rings, place mats, trays, utensils, and glasses for formal crawfish boils. The store also offers a complete set of crawfish-emblazoned fine Bavarian china for serving all types of crawfish dishes.

On the other hand, Cajuns today are aware of the food's past low status and of the fact that some outsiders still see the crawfish as repulsive. The Proud Coonasses draw on this awareness in their own application of the crawfish as ethnic emblem. A popular bumper sticker in south Louisiana bears a message for those people who still disdain crawfish (and Cajuns): "Coonasses make better lovers because they eat anything." A similar attitude toward criticism of Cajun food habits is reflected by T-shirts that bear the words "I suck heads." In addition, a crawfish boil may be as rowdy as the hosts and guests wish it to be. A crawfish boil can provide an occasion for heavy eating, drinking, and "partying," and as such is a perfect reflection of the self-professed Coonass lifestyle.

Today, live crawfish are available only in southern Louisiana and in a few other nearby market cities. Marketing experts realize that the sales of live crawfish in non-Cajun areas would be low, but attempts are being made to expand the market area for frozen, peeled tail meat.[18] But for now, the consumption of crawfish is limited largely to south Louisiana, where one small-town poet has expressed her gratitude for the animal's presence in "Grace Before a Crawfish Meal":

> Bless us O Lord and bless these
> Crawfish which we are about to enjoy.
> Bless those who caught them, those who prepare them
> And give crawfish to those who have none.
>
> We thank you O God for this wonderful world
> And for all that you have put on it.
> And we give You special thanks O God
> For having put the Cajuns and the crawfish
> Down in the same place. Amen.[19]

NOTES

1. Nicholas Spitzer, "Cajuns and Creoles: The French Gulf Coast," *Southern Exposure* 5, nos. 2–3 (1977):140–55.

2. Jon L. Gibson and Steven Del Sesto, "The Culture of Acadiana: An Anthropological Perspective," in *The Culture of Acadiana: Tradition and Change in South Louisiana,* ed. Jon L. Gibson and Steven Del Sesto (Lafayette: Univ. of Southwestern Louisiana, 1975), 3.

3. Ibid.

4. Wilbur Zelinsky, *The Cultural Geography of the United States* (Englewood Cliffs, N.J.: Prentice-Hall, 1973), 110–11.

5. Patricia K. Rickels, "The Folklore of the Acadians," in *The Cajuns: Essays on Their History and Culture,* ed. Glenn R. Conrad (Lafayette: Univ. of Southwestern Louisiana, 1978), 251.

6. According to CODOFIL research, the word "coonass" was not used in Louisiana prior to World War II. When Cajun soldiers with their "peculiar" French dialect were stationed in France, the French locals referred to them as "conasse"—a word originally used for a bumbling prostitute and later for a stupid person or country bumpkin. The word was apparently brought back to the United States by Cajuns and their Texas neighbors. According to CODOFIL, the unfamiliar French term was heard as "coonass," and has since been interpreted pictorially as the rear view of a raccoon with tail upraised. The term was first used as an ethnic slur against Cajuns, but in the past two decades it has been used in a positive sense by some Cajuns themselves. It has been my observation that the word is now so commonly used by many Cajuns (despite the fact that some Cajuns abhor the term) that the word is quickly losing both its negative and positive connotations and is becoming a simple synonym for the word Cajun.

7. Frederik Barth, "Introduction," in *Ethnic Groups and Boundaries,* ed. Frederik Barth (Boston: Little, Brown, 1969), 35.

8. See the editorial "We Are Not Coonasses!" *Louisiane Française* 32 (March 1980):5.

9. Holland C. Blades, Jr., *The Distribution of South Louisiana Crawfish,* Department of Publications Research Series No. 32 (Lafayette: Univ. of Southwestern Louisiana, 1974), 5.

10. Milton B. Newton, Jr., *Atlas of Louisiana* (Baton Rouge: School of Geoscience, Louisiana State Univ., 1972), 94.

11. Leona Martin Guirard, "Talk About Crawfish," printed souvenir (1973).

12. Irene Therese Whitfield, *Louisiana French Folk Songs* (Baton Rouge: Louisiana State Univ. Press, 1939), 138.

13. Guirard.

14. Howard Jacobs, "The Cajun Palate," *Acadiana Profile: A Magazine for Bi-Lingual Louisiana* 2, no. 3 (Sept./Oct. 1971):21.

15. Christopher Hallowell, *People of the Bayou: Cajun Life in Lost America* (New York: Dutton, 1979), 114.

16. Tim Edler, *The Adventures of Crawfish-Man* (Baton Rouge: Little Cajun Books, 1979), and *Crawfish-Man Rescues Ron Guidry* (Baton Rouge: Little Cajun Books, 1980).

17. Bob Angers, "Anecdotes and Antidotes," *Acadiana Profile: A Magazine for Bi-Lingual Louisiana* 7, no. 4 (July/August, 1979):13.

18. James C. Carroll and Holland C. Blades, "A Quantitative Analysis of the Amounts of South Louisiana Crawfish that Move to Market through Selected Channels of Distribution," Department of Publications Research Series No. 35 (Lafayette: Univ. of Southwestern Louisiana, 1974), 14.

19. Leona Martin Guirard, "Grace Before a Crawfish Meal," printed souvenir (undated).

PART IV

New Group Identities:
Religion and Resocialization

9

Exotic Foods among Italian-Americans in Mormon Utah: Food as Nostalgic Enactment of Identity

Richard Raspa

Exotic foods have characterized Italians in Carbon County, Utah, since their entry into the state at the end of the nineteenth century. In an unpublished social history of Carbon County, Lucille Richens recalls:

I was raised with a whole-hearted contempt for Greeks, Italians, and other southern Europeans who lived there. At one time about 1915 a few of these southern European immigrants lived next door to us. They hollowed out one side of the foundation of their house and installed several hogs. The smell was awful. Complaining neighbors were responsible for their being ordered to get rid of them. They butchered them on the kitchen floor, and when the lady of the house decided to clean the entrails to stuff them with sausage, she tied one end of them securely to the faucet of the only water hydrant in the neighborhood and turned on the water. The odor from this and the entire family nearly drove the Americans out of the neighborhood.[1]

In their migration to the New World, Italian-Americans progressed from a rural society based upon Old World peasant values and a limited food supply to a consumer society based upon contemporary technology and abundant food resources. In the state of Utah, however, they retain certain exotic foods which had formed the dietary repertoire of their Old World village. The dominant Mormon community perceives these foods as exotic, while Italian-Americans treat them as familiar and ceremonial. These foods serve commemorative and celebrative ends more than economic and nutritional ones.[2] Ultimately, the preparation and consumption of exotic food among these Italian-

185

Americans is a nostalgic enactment of ethnic identity and familial solidarity.[3]

The presence of Italians in Utah is surprising, since the state is colored by the history and lore of Mormon culture. Mormons constitute 75 percent of the population in the state, and in some communities 100 percent. However, in Carbon County, located about 120 miles southeast of Salt Lake City, Mormons make up only 40 percent of the population. In the town of Helper, Carbon County, about 30 percent of the population is Italian. The informants for this study are first-, second-, and third-generation Italian-Americans from Helper who trace their ancestry back to the province of Calabria in south Italy.

The first Italian laborers from Calabria began arriving in the 1890s to work in the expanding mining and railroad industries. Infertile Calabria could only produce crops which would not place great demands upon the soil. Life was stark in this, one of the poorest regions in Italy. Arid, rocky terrain and a coarse and indifferent government left the peasant with one certainty: that for him and his family, life would be cut on the teeth of starvation. In this world, immigration to America provided salvation. The intention of many immigrants was to work for a few years, putting away most of what was earned in order to return one day, buy a piece of land, and live on it in the fashion of a *signore* (a term used to refer to the landed gentry of the southern Italian village).[4]

When the first Calabrians arrived on Ellis Island in the 1890s, they were met and recruited by Utah Copper, the Pleasant Valley Coal Company, the Union Pacific, and the Denver and Rio Grande railroads by company agents or by *padrones* (patrons or bosses) — unscrupulous, established immigrants who would extract a percentage of the newcomer's salary for having secured him a job. Upon arrival in Utah, Italians moved into company towns or Rag Towns which sprang up around the mines — towns that were dotted with cheap company houses composed of sheet iron roofs covered by tar paper. Miners were issued scrip instead of currency by the companies so they were constrained to shop in the company store.[5] The lives of the immigrants were circumscribed by their jobs, their families, and the tiny hamlets and mining camps into which they were compressed.

Despite these obstacles, immigrants attempted to replicate some version of the food production and distribution system typical of their agrarian background. One informant recalled that his father sold vegetables and meat in the mining camp.[6] Knowing what each family's food preferences were, he custom-butchered the meat and offered a complete line of fresh breads and vegetables produced on his own farm in Helper, items which he transported manually on a wheelbarrow a distance of several miles to the mining camps. His father worked in the coke ovens in the winter and farmed his own land in the summer. "It was the dream of Italians," said my informant, "to own a home and a piece of ground."

Clearly, Italians preferred food purchased from *paesani* (fellow townsmen) who could prepare the goods to suit individual tastes. The miners could also engage in face-to-face bargaining with the peddlers, a style of negotiation characteristic of village life in Europe, in contrast to the impersonal, fixed economic transactions that occurred in the company stores in the New World.[7] This traditional mode of food acquisition irritated company owners. Early Italian settlers further inflamed company owners as they became embroiled in the United Mine Workers' union activities. They were involved in the 1903, '08, '10, '12, and '23 strikes, protesting such company abuses as the underweighing of coal.[8] During the 1903 coal strike in Carbon County, Italians were locked up in bull pens by the company guards. It is significant that the first thing they did when incarcerated was to cook spaghetti in coffee cans.[9]

Nativist Americans regarded Italians as a violent people — non-whites from southern Europe who practiced Roman Catholicism, displayed socialist tendencies, and enjoyed quaint and often disgusting food. Italians were strangers in the West, different from northern European immigrants with their more recognizable traditions and mores:

By and large the difficulties encountered by a newly-arrived ethnic group vary in direct proportion to its size, the rapidity of its arrival, and its cultural remoteness with respect to other groups in general and to what might be termed the dominant group in particular. On all three counts, the Italian came to the New World almost predestined for serious trouble.[10]

In the course of the last eighty years, however, some changes have taken place. The informants in this study no longer live in Rag Towns; few work as miners; more hold skilled jobs in smelters; some have moved up to become foremen and supervisors on the railroad; and still others have entered the professions. Italian-Americans now are diffused throughout Carbon County.[11]

Like other Americans, the Utah Italians entertain a range of culinary experiences. At one extreme are those, mostly immigrants, who perceive themselves as retaining more or less intact the traditional foodways of the native Calabrian villages; at the other extreme are the children and grandchildren who have expanded their food tastes and preferences to incorporate the cuisine of the dominant American culture. The traditional Calabrian food repertoire achieves its status as exotic against the boundary separating it from Mormon or, more generally, American cookery.[12] For the Latter Day Saints, exotic foods are those items of plant and animal life which are perceived as non-foods, and hence, taboo.[13] Exotic food for Italian-Americans, however, is a paradox. That which is seen by the American community as inferior is apprehended as both familiar and glimmering: familiar in that these foods constitute an historical legacy passed on from generation to generation, organically connected to the pastoral world of the south Italian village; yet glimmering, in that they are seen as heroic foods, conferring upon communicants superior dignity, grace, and style, a cultural *élan vital* which is lacking in other people.[14]

There is a rich spectrum of foods, including breads, vegetables, cheese, and meat prepared by the Calabrians in Utah. All Italian-born informants in Carbon County maintained the tradition of preparing such breads as *taralli* (bread sticks) and *rispelli* (a kind of deep-fried sweetbread). However, while *taralli* and *rispelli* fall into the category of familiar foreign foods, there are other dishes rejected as alien by the Mormon community. Personal narratives surround these folk foods and illuminate them as objects of Old World craftsmanship and sources of ethnic pride and familial history. For example, *frazzini* is a pretzel-shaped bread prepared with the unfamiliar ingredient anise seed. One informant recalled the time when her mother's eager offering of a plate of *frazzini* to a group of visiting Mormon women met only polite refusal.[15] Later, she learned indirectly that the anise seeds reminded the guests of rat leavings. The narrative is recounted in tones of outrage and indignation rather than self-effacement. Coarseness on the part of the guests violating the norm of hospitality rather than inferiority of the food is made the point of the story.[16] Another informant who routinely prepares these traditional grains complains that Mormons believe she does not know how to cook because she is unable to give them exact measurements of the ingredients. As we sat around her kitchen table chatting, she lamented, "Mormons got to have a recipe for everything. When they want a recipe, they want the exact amount."[17] In one swift movement, she suddenly lunged for an empty plate, took hold of the salt shaker, sprinkled some salt in her hand, and thrust it into the dish: "Here, this is how I measure when somebody asks me how much flour or salt you gotta use to make bread or *scalledi*." Her eyes gleamed and her laugh wrinkled her face. Never working from a recipe book, she feels the texture of the food to sense when the preparation is complete, and chuckles at those less talented cooks who fail to appreciate the improvisational aplomb of Italian cookery.

The amount of each ingredient is known not from a recipe book but from the memory of how it is supposed to be. Each food item is produced, whenever possible, in one's own backyard. It is common to see small plots of land behind tiny houses swelling with peppers, tomatoes, onions, endive, eggplant, beets, spinach, potatoes, fava beans, Swiss chard, zucchini, squash, carrots, as well as garlic, parsley, basil, fennel, grapes, fig and walnut trees. A striking thing about such abundance, where every available slice of land is suffused with sprouting green leaves and stalks, is that while giving the casual observer the impression of randomness, the crops are actually organized generically into neat rows. One garden was sloped at the top in order, as one informant said, to water vegetables in a specific order, tomatoes, potatoes, eggplant, and so on, giving more water to some and less to others.

Having immediate access to fresh garden vegetables allows the Italian-Americans to look critically at commercially grown produce sold in supermarkets. "Vegetables and fruit are picked green and lose all their flavor," one informant said. "We only go to the store to buy staple items, like flour, sugar, and salt. That's all. We grow everything else. We don't even eat in restaurants like the young people today. The food has no flavor. We buy sugar, flour, salt, that's all. We conserve everything." [18]

One exotic vegetable dish is called squash patties, made from chunks of squash and chopped-up flowers mixed in an egg batter and deep fried. My informants point out that the flowers give the patties a beautiful red tint. In the past these patties were made almost every Sunday, but today they are reserved for special occasions. One informant remembers taking squash patties aboard a train for the 2200-mile journey from Salt Lake City to Trenton, New Jersey, to visit relatives some twenty years ago. [19] The dish is always praised, the cook treated as a culinary artist who has created a new category of the real in the magnificent transformation of the flower into the fritter.

The most esoteric foods, of course, are the variety of meats: parts of the animal, particularly the internal organs, which are regarded generally as taboo by the wider American community. With a sweep of bravado, another informant queried me whether I had ever eaten chicken feet. When I responded "No," she smiled, arched her back slightly, and reported proudly that chicken feet, simply boiled and seasoned with herbs, are a delicacy she and especially her twenty-year-old granddaughter partake of regularly. She raises her own chickens, saying, "They claim the Texas chicken you get in the supermarket is fed back its own wastes, ground up. We feed our chickens corn and wheat and mush." Another exotic food she prepares is tripe, the walls of the stomach of a cow, first soaked for three or four hours in a pot until tender, then added to a tomato sauce which has simmered with spices and wine for a long time. When her son slaughters a lamb, her granddaughter assists him and then carries the animal's warm brain, holding it bravely in her hands, from the shed to the kitchen where her grandmother mixes it with eggs to prepare a *frittata*, or omelet. It is important that the food be fresh. Another dish my informant stews frequently is *la rouinella*, made from the intestines and gizzard of a chicken wrapped together and cooked slowly in a spaghetti sauce.[20]

Spaghetti, in fact, is the prime source of anecdotes about Mormon attempts to cook food *ala italiana*. Because spaghetti is the most universally recognized Italian food in America, its ubiquitousness has conferred the sobriquet "spaghetti benders" upon Italians in Carbon County. One informant began to dramatize a recurring folk scene in which he casts himself as a traditional folkloric character type—the clever peasant—and the Mormon as the equally traditional, powerful-but-foolish authority, who proceeds to reveal himself as a culinary buffoon:

This guy at work, see, who's a bishop, said to me the other day, "Orlando, today we're gonna make spaghetti for lunch," he says. "OK," I say, "I wanna see how you're gonna do it." So this here foreman gets the pot of cold water and puts spaghetti in it. He puts it on the stove we have at the shop. You know Kennicott [Copper Company] lets us do that, cook and everything right in the machine shop. Anyway, he put them together, the water and spaghetti on the stove at the same time and turns on the heat. You know what happens! Ha. Ha. Ha. Mush. Ha. Ha. Ha. Plain old mush. Ha. Ha. Ha. Those Mormons don't know how to cook the Italian way, *al dente*, where your teeth are supposed to stick in the pasta when you bite into it. "Orlando," he says, "Orrlannndoo, here's how you tell if the spaghetti is done," and he scoops up a noodle and throws it against the wall. Ha. Hahahahahahahahahahahaha-hahahahahahahahahahahahaha. *Porca miseria*, it's supposed to stick to the wall if it's cooked. Hahahahahahahahaha. Hehehehehehehehehehehehehehe. Well then, right after, he turns around and puts catsup on spaghetti. Can you believe that? Catsup on spaghetti!"[21]

By this time Orlando hardly gets the last words out between great squeals of laughter and little explosions of coughing. His body is in convulsions. Then he wipes his eyes and narrates the recipe for preparing spaghetti sauce used by the villagers in his home town in Italy. Goat intestines are wrapped around *finocchio* — fennel stalks — and simmered in a tomato sauce. The tangy sauce acquires a licorice flavor from the fennel and a sweet nip from the intestines, an experience of contrasting tastes and textures in a brilliant culinary synesthesia.

Mormon or American foods are seen as distractions, momentary changes of pace in an otherwise stable cuisine — play food not to be taken seriously. One informant suggested that the main difference between Mormon and Italian cooking is that "theirs is all cream and we use natural gravies, garlic, and olive oil."[22] In Mormon cooking, casseroles and roasts are presented simultaneously on a platter with, say, creamed vegetables and buttered potatoes, followed by an ice cream or pie or other confection for dessert. Italians are accustomed to individual and sequential servings of *pasta* or *minestra* followed by a sauteed veal or beef, an oil-and-vinegar green salad, then fruit to complement the meal. The original flavors of the food are not disguised or sweetened or creamed away. American cuisine is perceived as not offering the dramatic contrasts in texture and taste found in Italian, where it is not unusual to find sweet, salty, and bitter foods presented synchronically, like salty *prosciutto* (cured peppered ham) draped over sweet melon followed by a dry zinfandel wine. While Italian cooking attempts to bring out all the natural flavors of the food, its essence, as one informant said, "is that it's got to tease you."[23]

The Italian food that is perceived as the most exotic by Mormons is goat. Special handling maintains these animals. Petting, brushing, and cleaning precedes milking them every morning at 5 or 6 A.M., then again in the evening around 5 P.M. One informant approaches the grazing of the goats psychologically:

Goats like to browse, like deer. They're fussy and eat sagebrush and acorns. They take the choice. Now in June they're eating flowers and clover and always pick the best. The flower is the tastiest. Cheese, therefore, tastes different according to the season.[24]

The goat produces a piquant cheese called *sciungad* in the Calabrian dialect. "Some people [Mormons] won't eat it in any form, grated on macaroni, or stuffed in ravioli, or even as a substitute for cow's milk," observed one of my informants. She has raised goats and made this traditional cheese by hand for fifty years. She says: "My cheese is pure and in store-bought cheese you don't know what you're eating. You can taste the difference. They put preservatives in the store cheese."[25] It takes four gallons of milk to make three pounds of the *sciungad,* which is the dialect term for *assiugato,* or dried up, referring more properly to a stage in the cheese-making process rather than to the name of the cheese itself. The cheese is officially called *formaggio di pasta filatte,* or the threaded cheese, which refers to the slow process of drawing out the curds into stringy lengths, pulling them like taffy. Hot whey is added to the stringy curds, then the curd is run off and more fresh hot whey is added. The curd rests for thirty minutes, then is stretched into elastic fibers. It is cut into long, thin slices and immersed in hot water and whey, at which point the cheesemaker kneads it by hand like taffy. Then she molds the cheese into balls and places them in hot water, then in cold water and a brine bath, and later hangs them in the cellar to age. Occasionally in the past, worms would appear in the cheese, transforming it into a highly regarded delicacy. Worms could penetrate cheese in storage facilities for any number of reasons. A wooden storage crate, for example, might have had clinging to it a clump of soil containing worms.

The goat is prized by Italian-Americans not only for the cheese it produces, but for the succulent meat it offers as well. In Calabria and Carbon County, goat is served at Easter instead of lamb. The most esteemed part of the flesh is the head, usually stuffed with ground beef and then roasted. For most Americans, eating flesh from the head of an animal lying on a dinner plate would be an unsettling experience. The technology of contemporary food merchandizing invites the separation of food from the vital ecological systems in which animal and vegetative life grow. Industrialized Americans experience food in symbolic transformations, in plastic covered packages, cans, bottles, and other artificial mediums which belie the connectedness of all life systems. Italians, however, do not share the disjunction of human and natural societies. One can tour a butcher shop anywhere in Italy and see complete animals, pelts intact, hanging by feet, or paws, or claws, ready to be sold. There is no mistaking the animals in this context and no way to resist seeing that food is provided by animals which were once alive and an integral part of a natural ecology. Italians and Italian-Americans in Carbon County have not succumbed to the squeamishness of disguising food, masking the complete reality of the animal. To them eating the animal in its natural and unprocessed state is an expression and celebration of man's place in the natural scheme of things.

This perception of food as an immediate, concrete reality raises several questions about the goat. Why are goats eaten for Easter instead of the more customary lambs? And why do Carbon County Italians eat goats' heads with obvious enthusiasm? The answer to the first question may be found in the geography of the region. The mountain ranges and steep terrain of Utah support goats more easily than lamb. An answer to the second question, however, is more complex. The first Italians in Utah were extremely poor, too poor to waste any part of the animal they raised. Furthermore, the goat is revered in Mediterranean mythology as possessing supernatural power. Its horns are made into amulets and occasionally ground into potions to ward off the power of the Evil Eye. The goat figure is the pre-Christian Pan, god of forests and wild life, a symbol of wild energy and ecstasy in nature. Eating the most recognizable part of the goat — its head — allows the communicant to partake of the power of the ingested creature.

Beyond its magical properties, the presence of the goat in the cuisine signifies the contrasting food preferences of Italian-Americans and Mormons. Choosing natural as opposed to disguised food — the graphic head versus more ambiguous cuts of meat from other parts of the animal body — supports Roland Barthes' contention that food is "a system of communication, a body of images, a protocol of usages, situations, and behavior." [26] Preparing and eating exotic food allow the performers to recreate their ethnic identity, maintain traditional boundaries with the dominant culture, and nurture familial closeness. Exotic food functions in a commemorative way to allow participation in Old World customs, evoking a nostalgic yearning for the wholeness of a simpler, pastoral life. Ultimately, these commemorative functions of food express different ways of experiencing the world and different ways of organizing experience. Cooking the Italian way is knowing the world experientially, knowing its textures, its tastes, its shapes and colors, its touch, and its smells. One apprehends the world not as static, sequential, predictable units of experience, but finally as dynamic, holistic, and mysterious.

ACKNOWLEDGMENTS

I wish to thank Rose Ann Waldeck and Philip Notarianni for their careful reading of the text and their keen suggestions.

NOTES

1. Lucille Richens, "A Social History of Sunnyside," Ms. #A 211, WPA Collection, Utah State Historical Society.

2. The relationship among food, ethnicity, and community is discussed by Barre Toelken, *The Dynamics of Folklore* (Boston: Houghton Mifflin, 1979), 72–91, and Mary Douglas, *Natural Symbols* (New York: Vintage, 1970), 11–93. Douglas treats Irish Catholic foodways in England.

3. See "Deciphering a Meal," in Mary Douglas, *Implicit Meanings: Essays in Anthropology* (London: Routledge and Kegan Paul, 1975), 249-75.

4. See Constance Cronin, *The Sting of Change: Sicilians in Sicily and Australia* (Chicago: Univ. of Chicago Press, 1970), 1-119; Carla Bianco, *The Two Rosetos* (Bloomington: Indiana Univ. Press, 1974), 3-158; and Leonard Moss, "The South Italian Family," *Human Organization* (1959):35-41.

5. Philip Notarianni, "The Italian Immigrant in Utah: Nativism (1900-1925)" (M.A. thesis, Univ. of Utah, 1972), 10-13.

6. Interview with Rudy Bruno, 12 Aug. 1978.

7. Oscar Handlin, *The Uprooted*, 2nd ed. (Boston: Little, Brown, 1973). For a view in contrast to Handlin's see Rudolph Vecoli, "*Contadini* in Chicago: A Critique of *The Uprooted*," *Journal of American History* 51, no. 3 (Dec. 1964):407-17.

8. Notarianni, "The Italian Immigrant," 102.

9. Notarianni, "Italianita in Utah: The Immigrant Experience," in *The Peoples of Utah*, ed. Helen Z. Papanikolas (Salt Lake City: Utah State Historical Society, 1976), 303-32.

10. Joseph Lopreato, *Italian Americans* (Austin: Univ. of Texas Press, 1970), 100.

11. See Leonard Moss and Julie Flowerday, "An Italo-American Voluntary Association in Detroit," in *Ethnic Groups in the City*, ed. Otto Feinstein (Lexington, Mass.: Heath Lexington, 1971), 129-34.

12. Frederik Barth discusses ethnic boundaries in the Introduction to *Ethnic Groups and Boundaries: The Social Organization of Cultural Difference* (Boston: Little, Brown, 1969).

13. For a history of familiar and strange foods in America, see Waverley Root and Richard de Rouchemont, *Eating in America* (New York: William Morrow, 1976), 1-68; Dale Brown, *American Cooking: Foods of the World* (New York: Time-Life Books, 1968), 184-202; Reay Tannahill, *Food in History* (New York: Stein and Day, 1973), 320-86.

14. See Mary Douglas, *Natural Symbols*, 11-39, for an analysis of food, ritual, and magical practices.

15. Interview with Jean Caruso, Kearns, Utah, 15 July 1978.

16. Root and Rochemont, 458-82.

17. Interview with Parma Chiodo, Salt Lake City, Utah, 5 June 1978.

18. Interview with John Via, Helper, Utah, 11 Aug. 1978.

19. Interview with Philip Notarianni, Magna, Utah, 3 Aug. 1978.

20. Interview with Mary Bruno, Helper, Utah, 12 Aug. 1978.

21. Interview with Orlando Barber, Magna, Utah, 4 Aug. 1978. Although this incident and several others quoted in the text occurred outside Carbon County, they remain pertinent to the discussion. Italians were used as unskilled laborers in the mines and railroads, and their occupations encouraged a certain fluidity of movement between Carbon County and other parts of Utah where the same attitudes toward foodways are transmitted and maintained.

22. Interview with Mary Bruno, Helper, Utah, 13 Nov. 1978.

23. Interview with Al Veltri, Helper, Utah, 5 Aug. 1978.

24. Interview with Tony Nicoletti, Lark, Utah, 8 June 1978.

25. Interview with Mary Bruno, Helper, Utah, 13 Nov. 1978.

26. Roland Barthes, "Toward a Psychosociology of Contemporary Food Consumption," in *European Diet from Pre-Industrial to Modern Times*, ed. Elborg and Robert Forster (New York: Harper and Row, 1975), 50.

10

Conversion Through Foodways Enculturation: The Meaning of Eating in an American Hindu Sect

Eliot A. Singer

> The Spiritual Master was asked . . .
> how to obtain enlightenment.
> "Like this," he replied, and
> popped a piece of *prasadam*
> into his mouth.
>> *Back to Godhead*

Participation in and identification with a culture—be it ethnic, regional, or sectarian—is not achieved instantaneously through an accident of birth. Enculturation is a process of becoming, a process through which the implicit background of a culture, its set of underlying and motivating assumptions and premises about the way things are and must be, comes to be accepted. Regarded as "too true to warrant discussion," rarely stated explicitly or subjected either to catechizing or to debate, these assumptions and premises seem to the cultural participants to be self-evident or, to use Clifford Geertz's phrase, "uniquely real."[1] But even the self-evident must be apprehended, and it is here that cultural symbols play their essential role of providing convincing yet subtle means for expressing and obviating the self-evident by "creating, revising and obliquely affirming this implicit background, without ever directing explicit attention upon it."[2]

Food is a cultural symbol, and eating is a symbolic act through which people "communicate, perpetuate, and develop their knowledge about and attitudes toward life."[3] Not just an instrumental behavior for obtaining nutrients, eating is a means of expressing beliefs, ideals, and ambitions, a way of saying something about who one is and how one relates to others and to the world.[4] Given its universal importance, food is an exemplary vehicle for enculturation.

Under ordinary circumstances enculturation is a slow, methodical process during which a child learns to accept intuitively all that cultural participation entails. While perhaps not the blank slate once conceptualized by cultural relativists, the child's mind is fairly unformed and malleable. Cultural ideals can be implanted gradually, and although the symbolic texts in which these ideals are embedded must be convincing, they can make up through inundation over time what they lack in immediate intensity. In conversion, however, the circumstances are quite different. Conversion involves what A.F.C. Wallace calls "resynthesis of the mazeway," a total and usually sudden restructuring of a system of beliefs including, often, the most fundamental of assumptions and premises.[5] The neophyte comes to conversion already enculturated and, therefore, must undergo a re-enculturation. Cultural ideals are not newly created; they replace others once firmly fixed. While enculturation still operates through symbols, in conversion the process is telescoped, which means that these symbols must be especially emotionally salient and intellectually potent. Universally able to produce intense responses, food is a symbolic vehicle of special significance in conversion.

Over the last decade conversion has emerged, unprecedentedly, as a paramount process in the cultural development of the United States. "Born-again" Protestantism, evangelical Catholicism, and even zealous Judaism have garnered enormous followings, while Islam, Buddhism, and Hinduism have been imported from the East in a novel devotional rather than, as in the past, contemplative form. Foremost among these new Eastern sects in its impact, duration, and persistence has been the International Society for Krishna Consciousness.

ISKCON is a monastic organization consisting of the American disciples of the late Bengali ascetic, A.C. Bhaktivedanta Swami.[6] Founded in 1966 in order to propagate the *bhakti yoga* principles of the sixteenth-century Hindu-Vaishnava prophet, Chaitanya, to the Western world, ISKCON now has over 3,000 members scattered in temples throughout the United States. Except for a few young children, all of the members are converts who grew up within and were enculturated to mainstream American culture. Most also spent some time participating in the "counterculture."[7] Upon joining ISKCON, however, they are required to abandon all of their prior contacts and beliefs and to follow, almost without questioning, the basic norms and precepts of their new faith. In order to exert this kind of control over its membership, ISKCON must provide very powerful symbols to attest to the veracity of its creed. One of the most powerful of these symbols is *prasadam.*

Prasadam is the name the Krishna devotees give to their foodstuffs; to eat is to take *prasadam.* The word is Sanskrit meaning clearness, brightness, radiance, calmness, kindness, graciousness, and favor. Devotees translate it as "mercy."

Most simply, from the devotees' point of view, *prasadam* is the leftovers of God. It is food first offered to Krishna and only later consumed by the devotees. The offering takes the material substance and sanctifies it. *Prasadam* is spiritual food; to eat it is a holy act. Unoffered food is base, corrupt, degrading; eating it is the most banal of animal behaviors. *Prasadam* is elevated, transcendent, enlightening; eating it is the most glorious of human possibilities. It is so pure that it may be eaten off the floor without contamination. It is so powerfully transformative that even a fly which partakes of it will skip many lives in its next rebirth. In the words of *The Hare Krishna Cookbook,* it is "a spiritual reservoir of bliss."[8]

Devotees may eat only food which has been offered to Krishna. This is the paramount imperative of eating in Krishna Consciousness, and under extraordinary circumstances, such as some depicted in the mythology, it is the only necessary condition for obtaining *prasadam.* Under normal circumstances, however, other rules determine the acceptability of an offering to Krishna.

Devotees are forbidden meat, fish, and eggs in any form. This rule is explicit and emphatic. Along with proscriptions of illicit sex, intoxicants, and gambling, it is one of the four regulative principles of Krishna Consciousness. The devotees accept this prohibition with a deep emotional seriousness. Consumption of any of these foods is grounds for expulsion from the temple. The spiritual sanctions are even more severe since even an undetected lapse is believed to lead to the accrual of bad *karma* which means that, to quote the spiritual master, in the next life "not only will we be bereft of human form, but we will have to take an animal form and somehow or other be killed by the same type of animal we have killed."[9] With spirit souls identical with those of humans, animals have life; eggs are the beginning of life. Flesh eating is equated with the demonic. This equation is animated by the cannibalistic ogres that stalk the pages of the mythology. The ironic juxtaposition of many urban Krishna temples and fast food restaurants provides ample opportunity for depicting outsiders as bloodthirsty debauchers. Devotees who have temporarily retreated to civilian life substantiate the horror of meat eating with testimonials of nausea upon resumption of the practice.

Onions, mushrooms, and garlic are also taboo, although less subject to sanction or emotional intensity. Mushrooms are said to be dirty, in the literal not the pollution sense, and to resemble human flesh in texture. Onions and garlic, unlike other condiments, are claimed to have strong, overpowering smells which offend Krishna. Canned and packaged foods are avoided as well, both because of the possibility of contamination by impure foods and because of Krishna's partiality for fresh foods. There are other readily available foods which the devotees rarely, if ever, eat, not because they are in any way taboo, but because they are not indigenous to Indian cuisine. These include leavened bread, grains such as rye and maize, legumes such as soy and kidney beans, and vegetarian cheeses other than curd.

Those foods which the devotees do eat are categorized according to two independent schemes. The first involves a simple dichotomy between the raw and the cooked. However, these designations do not coincide with ordinary usage.[10] Cooked foods are those fried in *ghee*, or clarified butter. All other foods, whether boiled, treated directly with heat, or unprocessed, are regarded as raw. *Puris*, sauteed vegetables, spicy rices, savories (*samosa, pakora, kachori, poppers*), fried *dahl*, sweet balls, *luglu*, and most chutneys are cooked. Fresh fruit, nectar, sweet milk, sweet rice, sweets, *chapatis*, and most *dahls* are raw.

The second categorical scheme is more complicated and divides food into ten named categories (*dahl*, vegetable, chutney, rice, bread, savory, sweet, fruit, milk-sweet, beverage) and one functional category (yoghurt/sweet rice). These food categories derive from several contrasting features. The dominant opposition is between the hot and the sweet, a dichotomy based simply on taste. Almost everything which the devotees eat is either highly spiced or saturated with sugar. *Dahl*, vegetables, rices, and savories are all hot foods; beverages, sweets, fruits, and milk-sweets are all sweet foods. Chutneys, which contain both spice and sugar, and breads, which contain neither, are both classified as hot.

A second classificatory principle involves what amounts to a fourfold scale in moisture content. The devotees distinguish between foods that are drunk, licked, sucked, and chewed. More descriptively, these can be conceptualized as thin liquids, thick liquids, moist solids, and dry solids. Beverages are drunk; *dahl* and yoghurt/sweet rice are licked; chutneys, vegetables, and milk-sweets are sucked; and rice, breads, savories, sweets, and fruits are chewed.

Further distinctive features are not explicitly recognized by the devotees but can be proposed analytically. Breads and savories are distinguished from rices by the type of grain utilized and further divided by the presence or absence of spice. Chutneys are separated from vegetables and fruits from sweets because they contain fruit. These binary oppositions can be summarized in the following table (with the moisture scale being treated as successive oppositions between liquid and solid, and wet and dry).

	hot	liquid	wet	wheat	spice	fruit
dahl	+	+	−			
chutney	+	−	+			+
vegetable	+	−	+			−
rice	+	−	−	−		
bread	+	−	−	+	−	
savory	+	−	−	+	+	
beverage	−	+	+			
sweet	−	−	−			−
fruit	−	−	−			+
milk-sweet	−	−	+			
yoghurt	−	+	−			

The raw and cooked categories govern the selection of food for the offerings. Krishna is offered food six times each day starting at 4:15 A.M. and ending at 8:45 P.M. The offering, served on silver platters on silver trays, is placed on the altar before representations of Krishna. It is then left for fifteen minutes behind a closed curtain and for another half hour with the curtain open while the devotees sing praises to Krishna. Only a small portion of each preparation is actually placed on the altar, but this serves to sanctify synecdochically the food in its entirety.

The devotees believe that Krishna really consumes some of the food and they attest to this by the "fact" that the offering loses weight. Since it is to be eaten by Krishna, it is imperative that the food be arranged beautifully and cooked to perfection. The chief cook is always an initiated disciple of the spiritual master. The cooking area is always kept clean and pure; leftovers are kept separate and menstruating women are excluded. And since Krishna must be the first to taste the food, the cook must take care neither to taste nor smell that which he is preparing.

Although there are six "feedings" of Krishna every day, the devotees eat only three times. Morning *prasadam*, taken at about 6:30 A.M., and milk *prasadam*, taken at about 7:30 P.M., are simple snacks. Morning *prasadam* typically consists of a cereal such as *halavah*, milk, and fresh fruit; milk *prasadam* usually contains nothing more than a cup of warm sweet milk and, perhaps, a cookie. Both snacks tend to be

4. Food from Krishna's plate is considered especially beneficent.

haphazard affairs in which the devotees come and go, eat silently, and consume only small amounts of food.

Afternoon *prasadam*, taken around 12:00 noon, is an elaborate communal affair attended by all of the devotees who are present at the temple. The meal contains a variety of preparations usually including rice, *dahl*, vegetables, and sweets. Unlike the snacks, for which a brief obeisance to the spiritual master suffices, afternoon *prasadam* is always preceded by the following lengthy prayer:

O Lord, this material body is a lump of ignorance and the senses are networks of paths leading to death. Somehow we have fallen into this ocean of material sense enjoyment, and of all the senses the tongue is the most voracious and uncontrollable; it is very difficult to conquer the tongue in this world. But you, dear Krishna, are very kind to us and have given us such nice *prasadam*, spiritual food to help conquer the tongue. So now we take this *prasadam* to our full satisfaction, and glorify you, Lord Sri Sri Radha and Krishna, and in love call upon the help of Lord Chaitanya, Prabhu Nityananda and Srila Prabhupada.

Afternoon *prasadam* thus contrasts with the other offerings to Krishna in that its primary orientation is towards the indulgence of the devotees' appetites. At other times Krishna is either "fed" exclusively or the devotees' consumption is incidental. In afternoon *prasadam*, Krishna becomes the dispenser of food, instead of being the main recipient; instead of being the eater, He becomes the feeder. It is here that the contrast between the raw and the cooked categories is relevant. In those offerings where Krishna is the focus, only foods classified as raw (e.g. fruit, *chapatis*, sweet milk, nectar, most sweets) are served. But for afternoon *prasadam*, both raw and cooked foods (e.g. *dahl*, spicy rice, fried vegetables) are consumed.

It is in the construction of the afternoon meal that the second, more complex, scheme for categorizing food comes into play. There are two syntactic rules for combining foods to create a grammatical meal of afternoon *prasadam:* 1) there must be at least one preparation that is drunk, licked, sucked, and chewed, and 2) there must be an equal number of hot and of sweet foods. These rules are explicitly stated by experienced devotees and, with the usual room for grammatical mistakes, reflect the reality of the meals served. The most frequent mistake involves the addition of *chapatis*, a relatively unmarked item. Beverages such as milk or nectar are the only foods which are drunk and so one is included at every meal. In theory, all meals should have an even number of preparations, the most simple form containing four items. A standard afternoon *prasadam*, for instance, consists

5. *Prasadam*: spiritual food helps conquer the tongue.

of *dahl,* rice, yoghurt, and nectar. The addition of a hot item to this basic meal requires the addition of a sweet one as well. Elaborations are made so that additional preparations come from categories not already included on the menu. Thus the meal described above would be added to by a vegetable rather than by a second variety of rice.

The everyday meal pattern regularly undergoes two kinds of transformations: feasts and fasts. Feasts are essentially magnifications of afternoon *prasadam* and are substituted for it on certain days. The most common feast is the "love feast" which is served every Sunday to outsiders who are invited to visit the temple for a free dinner and to participate in singing and dancing, listen to a sermon, and be entertained by a film or a play. Between a dozen and several hundred visitors attend these feasts, depending on the location of the temple.

Several regularities can be seen in the feasting transformations. First, there is an increase in the number of preparations. Ideally there should be 108 dishes to represent the 108 *gopis* who were Krishna's lovers in Vrindavana, but in practice eight to twelve is the norm, with feasts at larger temples being somewhat more elaborate. Second, feasts include some items, notably ones that are difficult to prepare, that are rarely or never eaten on everyday occasions, especially such deep fried foods as *puris, samosa, kachoris,* sweetballs, and *luglu.* Third, one of the basic staples, *dahl,* is never served, a fact which the devotees attribute to inconvenience since it would require an additional bowl. Fourth, both syntactic rules are maintained. Sweet rice or yoghurt substitutes for *dahl* as a licked food and a relative balance of sweet and hot items is maintained, although exact equality is not always possible. Fifth, extra items come from categories not already included. Thus a feast is likely to have a vegetable and a chutney or bread, or rice and a savory, rather than two chutneys or two savories. However, with a large number of items and few categories of sweet foods it is sometimes necessary to have two sweet dishes from the same category, but an effort is made to make these dishes as dissimilar as possible.

Besides the weekly "love feast," the yearly devotional calendar includes several special feasts. While there is considerable variation between temples as to the celebration of minor occasions, most devotees attend a major feast about once every two or three months. The most important occasions are Krishna's appearance day (Janmastami), Chaitanya's appearance day, the bathing day of Lord Jagannatha (Shanayatra), and the Jagannatha cart festival (Rathayatra). These feasts are little different from the weekly love feasts although they may be somewhat larger. Occasionally, however, the food is played with in a special way, for instance by building a hill of it to celebrate Krishna's

6. Feasting provides a rare opportunity to socialize.

lifting of Govardhana Hill, or by having a food fight to imitate Krishna's mischief on His bath day.

There are several varieties of the second transformation, the fast. The most common is *ekadasi*, which takes place twice each month on the eleventh day of both the waxing and the waning moon. This fast, which all devotees maintain, requires abstention for an entire day from grains and legumes. Nonetheless, the basic grammatical rules for meal construction remain intact and, indeed, the *ekadasi* meal is very similar to that eaten every day. Special fast foods which utilize roots and nuts substitute for grains and legumes. For example, tapioca replaces sweet rice, potatoes replace rice, and sweet potatoes or peanuts replace flour in sweets. This is true for morning as well as afternoon *prasadam*. Despite the availability of substitutes, however, the devotees do aim for simplicity and lesser consumption on fast days.

There are three fast days on the yearly calendar celebrating the appearance days of Krishna, Chaitanya, and Krishna's brother, Balarama. Each of these requires a total fast, the first two for twenty-four hours and the last for twelve hours; each is followed by a day of feasting. There is also an optional serial fast called *catarmaysa* during which a devotee refrains from spinach for the first month, yoghurt for the second month, milk for the third month, and *urad dahl* for the fourth month. In general there is always the option for a devotee to fast, either totally or partially, as penance or to achieve spiritual advancement. This kind of fasting is infrequent, however, although illness, which is regarded as inauspicious, is often accompanied by a partial fast with curative intent.

Like other Hindus, the devotees accept the notion of an endless cycle of reincarnation from which escape is only possible through the transcendence of spirit over body. The self-realization necessary for this transcendence is considered enormously difficult to achieve due to the myriad distractions and illusions of the material world. Where the devotees differ from most other practitioners of their faith is in the immediacy of the goal. For them the question is how to achieve liberation in this *present* lifetime. The solution, according to ISKCON, is to think of Krishna at the moment of death; anyone whose mind is on Krishna when leaving the body will automatically go "back to Godhead." However, the moment of death is unpredictable and to guarantee success it is necessary to think of Krishna at all times, that is, to become Krishna conscious. Thus enculturation into ISKCON in the fullest sense is isomorphic to becoming Krishna conscious, a process which entails accepting the premise that going "back to Godhead" is indeed the appropriate purpose of existence, accomplishing complete concentration on Krishna, and eliminating all distractions which might interfere with concentration. *Prasadam* is a primary symbolic vehicle for validating and achieving this process.

Devotees can be convinced that it is desirable to escape from the cycle of death and rebirth by revealing, on the one hand, the bitterness and capriciousness of material existence and by giving, on the other, a taste of the divine bliss (*ananda*) that they call "the nectar of devotion." To the devotees the material world is a place of misery; even those who are apparently happy must ultimately succumb to old age and die. Pleasures are fleeting and illusory. *Prasadam* serves to exemplify this truth. Hunger is, of course, one of the major miseries of this world, and the food practices of ISKCON provide ample opportunities to experience hunger. This is done primarily through the three total fasts on the yearly calendar, but *ekadasi* and even the everyday food consumption with its single meal are also situations where hunger, however slight, is the norm. In addition, although this purpose is not manifest, the daily meal with its combination of the very hot and the very sweet serves to demonstrate worldly discomfort by producing an enormous thirst which, at least to the neophyte, is unpleasant.

Nonetheless, taking *prasadam* is, for the devotees, the most sublime of experiences. The meal is anticipated with pleasure and continuously praised. The dishes are tasty, and eating is the only opportunity during the day for self-indulgence. Moreover, the pleasure of eating is enhanced by its association with the divine. Taking *prasadam* is seen as dining with Krishna which is the essence of transcendental life; Krishna's heaven is a place with a luxurious abundance of food where Krishna bathes in an ocean of milk and picnics with his friends on the fruits of the trees. This joy of eating is accentuated in the frequent feasts during which the devotees are encouraged to eat to satiation. Each mouthful is a communion with Krishna, and no one may refuse to eat from the plate on which the food has been placed before the altar. To the devotees, feasting with Krishna is literally heaven on Earth. Thus, *prasadam* gives the devotees a sample of the divine and simultaneously of the bitterness of the material world—and in the comparison, no doubt is left as to which is preferable.

Even for the devotee who wishes to become Krishna conscious, continual concentration is not easy to achieve. Success requires developing an understanding of the nature of Krishna and of man's relationship to Him as well as obtaining a method for focusing attention on Him. Krishna has an inherent duality. He is, the devotees stress, a personality, yet at the same time, He is the embodiment of an omnipotent God. This opposition occurs within the Krishna legend itself, in which Krishna is revealed first as an adorable, spontaneous, mischievous, sensuous, and joyful cowherd boy, and later becomes a stern but wise Lord, an upholder of propriety, and a dispenser of privilege.[11] The child Krishna in the fields of Vrindavana is quintessentially an eater. He sucks milk from His mother's breasts, steals butter and yoghurt, plucks fruits from the trees, drinks from the teats of the cows, picnics with His friends, and appropriates the sacrifices of Brahmins. As a prince, however, He is never seen eating and, on the rare occasions when food is eaten, He is its giver not its recipient, distributing it to Brahmins rather than taking it from them.

Food in the mythology shows Krishna's duality as the supreme enjoyer and the supreme provider, a duality also apparent in the devotees' food offerings. When in the legend Krishna acts as an eater, He consumes only those foods which the devotees classify as raw—milk, butter, fruit, yoghurt, *chapatis,* and boiled rice. However on those occasions when He acts as a provider, He dispenses cooked foods such as sweet balls, spicy rice, and *pakoras.* So when the devotees offer raw foods for those meals where Krishna is the paramount recipient and both raw and cooked foods for those meals where the devotees partake, they are signifying that Krishna is both a consumer of food and its source.

The act of offering and the prayer which precedes the meal serve to acknowledge that all food is rightfully Krishna's and that the devotees may eat it only due to His "causeless mercy." Offering is a means of expressing subservience. Yet it is also the prime method through which Krishna's humanity is revealed. Krishna does eat, although He does not have to do so. In this way He is explicitly contrasted with the Judeo-Christian God, that "stuffy old man who certainly needs nothing like food."[12] This enables the devotees to feel an accessibility to and intimacy with their God which better allows them to develop the love for Him which is conducive to their concentration.

Offering *prasadam* is meant to show that man's relationship to God is one of servitude; the devotees receive His leftovers only out of His kindness. Krishna's willingness to accept offerings which are certainly not of divine opulence is also a kindness. This willingness to accept offerings, no matter how humble, is what enables the devotees to develop their personal relationship with God. A leading devotee explains this phenomenon:

In the *Bhagavad Gita* Krishna says:
"If one offers me with love and
devotion a leaf, a flower, or water,
I will accept it. O son of Kunti,
all that you do, all that you eat,
all that you offer and give away,
as well as all austerities you perform
should be done as an offering unto Me."
Of course He doesn't need food;
He is supreme, absolute. He is never
in need or want of anything. Still,
He asks His devotees to offer Him
these simple fruits of the earth.
The key word is devotion. Whatever
we are offering Him be it a grain or
a fruit, is already His; it is not
and never was, ours. But out of His
causeless mercy, He is so kind to His
devotees that any small offering given
in devotion He accepts and eats. The
Lord is not hungry for our food but
for our hearts; He is not wanting for
our substance, but for our consciousness, our love, our union.[13]

By symbolizing the nature of Krishna and of the devotees' relationship to Him, offering and taking *prasadam* serve to make the act
of eating a reminder of Krishna. By offering Krishna food and by
praying to Him in thanks, the devotees are required to think, "this
is Krishna's food" and therefore to think of Him. But it is not only
the act of eating which is a reminder of Krishna; the very substance
of food is reminiscent of Him. First and foremost, like devotional costume, setting, and accent, *prasadam* is borrowed from India. This is
not to suggest that ISKCON can be explained as an aberration of Indian
culture, but the adoption of Indian customs does remain one of its
significant cultural attributes. It provides a sense of legitimacy and
tradition to what would otherwise be a displaced phenomenon. More
importantly, since Krishna is identified with India and its lifestyle,
an Indian way of life juxtaposed to American surroundings helps to
assert the distinct identity of the Krishna devotees and their unity
with Krishna. For ethnic and regional groups, identity formation is
an end in itself; for ISKCON, identity formation is a means towards
a cultural end—that of achieving Krishna Consciousness—and the

uniqueness of the cuisine is a way of inducing the devotees to think of Krishna. This is why it is crucial that all food products be those traditional to India and not merely vegetarian. For this reason the Indian nature of the food is accentuated; the hot foods are very hot, the sweet foods very sweet, and the rare specialties necessary for authentic Indian cooking—e.g. tamarind, *urad dahl, poppers*—always purchased regardless of expense.

The devotees do not cook Indian food as a matter of their own preference. Food is a reminder of Krishna because it is food cooked for Krishna. Thus, the preparations must be those which are believed to be Krishna's favorites. The dishes must be perfectly cooked with no lumps or burns. The taste and texture must be that desired by Krishna, and the devotees must accept it even if they find it unpalatable. This is especially true of milk, the quintessential food of Krishna in Vrindavana. Milk is drunk warm and sweetened, like, the devotees claim, the milk from the teats of the cows in the pastures. When devotee children complain of this and reject the milk, it is forced on them with the assertion that "this is the way Krishna likes it." So the devotees' sense of taste becomes a means of focusing the mind on Krishna.

Despite such continuous reminders of Krishna, the devotees are greatly concerned about potential distractions and temptations from the material world. No matter how hard they attempt to focus their senses on Krishna by filling their world with Krishna imagery—the paintings on the wall, the sounds of singing and chanting, the smell of incense, the taste of *prasadam*—myriad sensory desires and attachments remain. The devotees believe it is necessary to control the senses to subdue these desires. To the devotees, as stated in their blessing, "of all the senses, the tongue is the most voracious and uncontrollable."

There are two aspects of sensory control: austerity and balance. *Prasadam* is explicitly intended to control the sense of taste through dietary austerity. First and foremost, this is done through the avoidance of meat. This is not so much because the devotees abhor killing—they are ardent destroyers of cockroaches, they keep guns in their temples for self-protection, and their main scripture is an unabashed polemic justifying war—as because Krishna is said not to like meat and because eating it is regarded as self-indulgent. Vegetables as well as animals are believed to possess spirit souls and to be incarnations on the cycle of transmigrations, but it is considered as natural for humans to subsist on vegetables as it is for carnivores to live by the hunt. Since an adequate diet can be obtained from vegetables, to eat meat is to engage in a passion for its taste. Meat is associated with cannibalism and with the demonic. It is thought to be indigestible, leading to alcohol consumption to assist the bowels. It is highly addictive; people develop an insatiable craving for it. Moreover, it is inseparable from sexuality; it is considered to be an aphrodisiac which creates and maintains an insurmountable lust so that a meat-eater can never escape the degradation of the sex act.

The avoidance of meat is not the only austerity involved in taking *prasadam*. Eating is only done in moderation, except for feasts when the devotees are urged to consume as much as possible. The daily fare is monotonous and the total number of calories, while adequate, is low. While hardly bland, the diet has only two fully distinct flavors and these are repeated from day to day. At times budgetary deficiencies at some temples have severely limited dietary variation and quantity. On top of these daily restrictions, the yearly calendar contains numerous personal and group fasts. On these days the devotees must learn to cope with minimal food intake. Through this austerity, they believe that they can develop the sensory control necessary to their liberation.

The austerity is not truly severe, and hunger is not seen as a direct path "back to Godhead." It is just a way of learning to control the senses, and taken to the extreme of starvation it is seen to be just as distracting as is gluttony. A hungry man spends all of his time thinking about food and not about Krishna. As stated in the *Hare Krishna Cookbook:*

Yoga is not for him who eats too much or for him that eats too little. The yoga diet is designed to supply all necessary nutrients without pandering to the whims of our changing senses. The principle of regulation is strictly adhered to and the daily fare is almost unchanging. This is important for if the tongue is agitated for sense enjoyment all the other senses follow.[14]

Senses are also controlled by balancing the properties of food. Each type of food is believed to have an effect on bodily and psychological functioning, and it is necessary not to overdo the consumption of any particular kind of food. Hot foods are associated with bodily passions and awaken the senses. Sweet foods, on the other hand, are filling and lead to lethargy. It is therefore regarded as crucial to maintain a relative balance between foods in the two categories. Similarly, the different kinds of foods are considered to activate different digestive enzymes which means that a person must drink, suck, lick, and chew in order to utilize all bodily mechanisms. The function of *prasadam* is to preserve equanimity in all aspects of eating.

There is a deep irony for the devotees in living in the material world where food is a necessity while seeking the spiritual life where food is irrelevant. To be one must eat; yet they see eating as a degrading act which leads to lust and denies liberation. To escape this paradox they must transcend the banality of sustenance yet still manage to survive. This is the significance of *prasadam*: food which has been transformed and sanctified, food which, for them, can divert temptation and make salvation possible.

Prasadam is a *dominant symbol,* a symbol which sums up and epitomizes the essential and often contradictory concepts in Krishna Consciousness: austerity and indulgence, servitude and intimacy, omnipotence and accessibility, suffering and bliss.[15] *Prasadam* symbolizes simultaneously the austere control of the senses and the celebration of taste in association with the divine. It expresses the duality of Krishna as eater and feeder and of His devotees as givers and receivers. There is the hope of focusing attention on Krishna while eschewing all other desires. In its totality, then, *prasadam* expresses all of the central premises of ISKCON, the premises which the devotees must accept on faith in order to be devotees: that the material world is miserable and the spiritual world is blissful, that God (Krishna) is both a loveable human and an omnipotent divine, that liberation is only possible through sensory control and sublime concentration.

Any aspect of ISKCON culture ultimately refers back to these basic existential premises, but it is clear that taking *prasadam* is a behavior of special significance. Given the devotees' asceticism, eating is a remarkably frequent topic of conversation and there is a special attention brought to it that is found elsewhere only in the most ecstatic rituals.

Prasadam is a powerful symbol that does not merely reflect passively the underlying principles of Krishna Consciousness; it creates them. To be willing to join ISKCON and to undertake a lifestyle that is far from easy, prospective members and neophytes must be firmly convinced that the view of life projected in Krishna Consciousness is plausible, viable, and desirable. Conviction cannot be produced didactically; it must be experienced. This is especially true in ISKCON where "mental speculation" or active inquiry is proscribed, and where Krishna Consciousness is to be attained not by thinking but through doing. Devotees must come to accept what it means to become Krishna conscious by participating in devotional activities, including eating.

When asked what attracted them to ISKCON, many devotees will reply, "the food." The distribution of *prasadam* to the public is one of the major means of proselytizing. It is believed that any contact with *prasadam* will create a magnetic attraction to Krishna which will lead, in this lifetime or another, to salvation. One story tells how "a devotee of Lord Chaitanya once gave a little *prasadam* to a dog; thus the dog later met Lord Chaitanya Himself and attained liberation." [16] When the devotees go out into the streets they take *prasadam* with them to distribute in the hopes of attracting new members. The major open event of the temple week is the Sunday Love Feast. While many people come simply for a free meal, some become regular visitors and ultimately join ISKCON. Indeed, almost all the devotees had their first serious contact with ISKCON at a love feast.

Devotees are not born into Krishna Consciousness; they choose to convert as adults. Joining ISKCON requires a complete break with the past and a restructuring of all behaviors. Taking *prasadam* is not the only enculturative experience for the devotees. The ideas behind Krishna Consciousness are inculcated into them by the interaction of many elements: singing, dancing, chanting, and scrubbing. But of all the behaviors which are of significance in Krishna Consciousness, only one is of parallel importance in secular life — eating. Dancing, singing, and the like are relatively minor aspects of American culture. Eating is not; food plays a dominant role in American life. Taking *prasadam* is not just a change in a minor activity; it is a transformation of one of the most meaningful and emotionally charged of all experiences. Instead of stressing meat, Krishna Consciousness forbids it. Instead of emphasizing personal satisfaction, Krishna Consciousness emphasizes detachment. Instead of eating for the self, the devotees eat for Krishna. Instead of seeing food as an end towards which work is directed, the devotees see food as a means by which liberation is achieved. Thus, as the devotees eat food transformed into *prasadam,* they are themselves transformed into devotees.

Enculturation in the context of conversion undoubtedly differs considerably from enculturation in child rearing. Yet, in some essential way, the process is the same. Cultural participation is not simply a question of identification, of sharing cultural diacritica and heritage, of feeling as if one belongs. Enculturation is a matter of coming to accept as self-evident shared subtle meanings, of coming to take for granted the basic existential criteria of a culture. Everyone learns to eat in a way regarded as appropriate, and indeed as necessary, by a culture. To follow these foodways is a way of reiterating belonging to that culture. But eating is more than this, for food signifies not only cultures as entities, it encodes cultures as systems of meaning.

GLOSSARY

chapatis	unfried, whole wheat flat bread.
chutney	sweet and spicy fruit relish.
dahl	legumes, usually eaten as a spicy soup.
ghee	clarified butter.
halavah	sweet boiled cake, usually made from farina.
kachori	fried pastries filled with potatoes or cauliflower.
luglu	a sweet made from fried chick-pea flour and sugar syrup.
nectar	fruit punch.
pakora	fried vegetables in chick-pea batter.
poppers	fried thin spicy crackers.
puris	fried white flour flat bread.
samosa	fried pastries filled with peas and cauliflower.
spicy rice	fried rice with various spices.
sweet balls	a fried sweet made from powdered milk.
sweet rice	rice pudding boiled in milk.

ACKNOWLEDGMENTS

Many members of the International Society for Krishna Consciousness have helped me with this paper. I would like to single out my friends Dharma Atma and Krishna Mayi for their assistance. Earlier drafts of this paper were read and commented on by Jay Anderson, Janet Theophano, and Don Yoder. Suzanne Sorkin has read and proofread more versions than she would care to remember.

NOTES

1. Mary Douglas, *Implicit Meanings* (London: Routledge and Kegan Paul, 1975), 4; Clifford Geertz, *The Interpretation of Cultures* (New York: Basic Books, 1973), 90.
2. Douglas, 4.
3. Geertz, 89.
4. The perspective on food being used here might be termed "semiotic," as best exemplified in the writings of Mary Douglas and in R.S. Khare, *Hindu Hearth and Home* (Durham, N.C.: Carolina Academic Press, 1976), and R.S. Khare, *Culture and Reality: Essays on the Hindu System of Managing Food* (Simla: Indian Institute of Advanced Study, 1976). For a brief discussion of the "semiotics of food," see Eliot A. Singer, "Thoughts on the New Foodways," *The Digest* 1–2 (Spring 1978):2–4.
5. Anthony F.C. Wallace, "Mazeway Resynthesis: A Bio-cultural Theory of Religious Inspiration," *Transactions of the New York Academy of Sciences* 18 (1956):626–38.
6. For further ethnographic information on ISKCON, see Francine Daner, *The American Children of Krishna* (New York: Holt, Rinehart, and Winston, 1976), and

J. Stillson Judah, *Hare Krishna and the Counterculture* (New York: John Wiley, 1974). My own fieldwork on ISKCON has been conducted since 1971 in Boston, Philadelphia, Pittsburgh, and New Vrindavana (W. Va.).

7. The term "counterculture" was coined by Theodore Roszak in his *The Making of a Counterculture* (New York: Anchor Books, 1969). See also Judah, *Hare Krishna.*

8. Krishna Devi Dasi and Sama Devi Dasi, *The Hare Krishna Cookbook* (Los Angeles: Bhaktivedanta Book Trust, 1973), 8.

9. A.C. Bhaktivedanta Swami, *The Sri Sri Chaitanya Charitamrita of Krishnadas Kaviraja* (Los Angeles: Bhaktivedanta Book Trust, 1974), 222.

10. Nor do they correspond exactly to the standard Hindu categories of raw, *pakka,* and *kacha* in that "raw" as understood in Krishna Consciousness includes what in India are both the highest- and lowest-ranked foods. On the Indian categories, see Khare, *Hindu Hearth and Home.*

11. On the Krishna legend, see W.G. Archer, *The Loves of Krishna* (New York: Evergreen Press, n.d.), and David Kinsley, *The Sword and the Flute* (Berkeley: Univ. of California Press, 1975).

12. Krishna Devi Dasi and Sama Devi Dasi, 8.

13. Kirtanananda Swami, "Introduction," in Krishna Devi Dasi and Sama Devi Dasi, 10.

14. Krishna Devi Dasi and Sama Devi Dasi, 9.

15. The concept of "dominant symbol" is taken from Victor Turner, *The Forest of Symbols* (Ithaca, N.Y.: Cornell Univ. Press, 1967).

16. Krishna Devi Dasi and Sama Devi Dasi, 54.

PART V

*Food Research
and the Implications
for Public Policy*

11

Economic, Social, and Cultural Factors in the Analysis of Disease: Dietary Change and Diabetes Mellitus among the Florida Seminole Indians

Sandra K. Joos

Diabetes is a disorder in which there is a chronic impairment of carbohydrate, fat, and protein metabolism due to a relative or absolute lack of insulin. Ophthalmic, renal, and cardiovascular complications are the eventual result. In the past twenty years, increasing rates of adult-onset diabetes mellitus have been reported in Native American and other populations undergoing acculturation to a modern lifestyle.[1] The disease has only recently become a major health problem of Native Americans, with rates much higher than those found in either U.S. white or Black populations. In the United States population as a whole, the rate of diabetes is between 1 and 3 percent, or 5 and 6 percent for those over age thirty-five; but among Native Americans, the range is from 10 percent among the Navajos to 50 percent among Pimas thirty-five and older.[2]

No single causal factor has been identified in the etiology of adult-onset diabetes, although there are several associated factors: sex; age; number of pregnancies; obesity; physical activity; and diet. Comparison of populations experiencing lifestyle changes indicates that environmental and lifestyle factors interact and contribute to the expression of the disease.[3] Transition from a "traditional" to a "modern" lifestyle inevitably results in new dietary patterns, increasing use of modern technology, and declining energy expenditure. Many researchers have tried to link dietary change in particular with the appearance of certain "diseases of civilization" in these populations.[4]

Some have attempted to identify specific dietary elements which may be responsible for high rates of diabetes and obesity. Others have found that rates of diabetes can be related to the prevalence of obesity, which seems to result from excess caloric intake rather than particular dietary items.[5]

Existing studies of diabetes among Native American groups have neglected to examine the influence of both the historical background and the contemporary social situation on changes in diet and health status in these populations. This essay focuses on one Native American group, the Florida Seminole Indians, and describes the social, economic, and technological changes they have experienced over the past century; it then examines the interaction of the contemporary economic, occupational, and health care environment with learned social behaviors and cultural beliefs about food intake and health. The assumption is that such knowledge of the cultural context of food consumption can be of use to health personnel concerned with altering food habits and improving health status.

The Florida Seminoles are a unique study population because, compared to other Native American groups, they have been relatively isolated from outside influences until recently, and there has been little genetic admixture with whites or Blacks. They are among the most "traditional" or conservative of Native Americans. The native languages (Creek and Mikasuki) are the first languages of many Seminoles. Aspects of their traditional culture, including dress, foods, and medical beliefs and practices, are still evident. Drastic changes in the social, economic, and subsistence spheres of life did not occur until twenty to thirty years ago. Finally, diabetes appeared somewhat later in Florida Seminoles than among most other Native American groups.

The prevalence of abnormal glucose tolerance (the usual screening technique for diabetes) increased from 3 percent in 1952 to about 19 percent in 1969—a six-fold increase.[6] Since 1969, the number of diagnosed, treated diabetics has more than doubled. Almost 85 percent of the diabetics are thirty-five or older (there is no "juvenile-onset" diabetes), and more than two-thirds of the diabetics are women. Obesity, however, seems to be the major risk factor for diabetes in this population. While not all obese individuals are diabetics, all diabetics are obese or were obese at the time of diagnosis. Adult obesity is common; more than 60 percent of those age twenty and older weigh more than 120 percent of their desirable weight for height.[7] Obesity, like diabetes, is a recent phenomenon among the Florida Seminoles. Childhood obesity is also increasing.

Weight loss can reverse or lessen the severity of diabetes and is usually the first line of treatment. However, treatment and control of diabetes through weight loss and/or medication have been largely unsuccessful with Seminoles. As a result, medical complications and hospitalizations are frequent, and an inordinate portion of the resources of the Indian Health Service unit is spent on the care of patients with chronic problems whose treatment includes dietary management. The underlying causes of this situation can best be understood by a consideration of both the historical background and the contemporary socio-cultural context of the Seminoles.

Historical Overview

The Florida Seminoles are descendants of Creeks from Alabama and Georgia who withdrew into north Florida in the early 1700s to avoid the conflicts between the United States, England, France, and Spain. Their numbers were augmented by refugees from the Creek War of 1813–1814 and by Negroes who escaped from plantations to the north. Sturtevant estimates that by the time of the First Seminole War (1817 to 1818) there were about 5,000 Seminoles in Florida.[8]

Between 1817 and 1857, the Florida Indians engaged in three wars with the government of the United States, which sought to retrieve runaway slaves, remove the Indians, and open land for white settlement. Despite continued and bitter fighting, the largest reduction in the Seminole population was due to capture and removal to the Indian Territory in Oklahoma. At the end of the Second Seminole War in 1842, all but about 400 Seminoles had been sent to Oklahoma. An estimated 100 to 200 individuals avoided removal in 1859 by retreating into inaccessible portions of the Everglades and Big Cypress Swamp.[9] From 1859 to 1890, little was seen or heard of the Seminoles, although they conducted some business with outpost traders to obtain guns, ammunition, iron pots, cloth, and some food items in exchange for hides and skins.[10]

When the first whites again made contact with the Seminoles in the early 1880s, the Indians were concentrated in five separate settlements consisting of a number of matrilocal "camps" of one or more extended families. Two of these settlements were primarily Creek-speaking, while the rest were primarily Mikasuki-speaking. Despite the linguistic differences, the groups were united by their religious beliefs and ceremonies, a matrilineal clan system, and ties of marriage.[11]

At this time, Seminoles subsisted by hunting, fishing, gardening, and gathering food. Habitation sites and small crop fields were usually located on well-hidden and inaccessible tropical "hammocks," areas of higher ground in the everglades and swamps. These hammocks were cooler in the summer, protected from frost in the winter, and had very rich soil on which vegetation flourished. [12] Each family within a camp had one or more crop fields totaling one to four acres, often at a distance of several miles from the living site. In their garden plots they grew a variety of vegetables and fruits: maize; "Seminole pumpkin" (*Cucurbita moschata*); pumpkin (*Cucurbita pepo*); sweet potatoes; squash; beans; peas; melons; bananas; sour oranges; and sugar cane. They also raised pigs, chickens, and sometimes cattle. [13]

A number of wild foods were gathered including the heart of the cabbage palm, blueberries, huckleberries, wild plums, guavas, honey, and the roots of the wild cycads *Zamia* and *Smilax*. The roots of *Zamia* and *Smilax* were processed to make flour for bread called "*koonti*" and were used as a starch by both Seminoles and whites in the area. These roots were an important source of food for the Seminoles, and temporary camps were sometimes made at an especially rich *koonti* ground.

They also exploited a wide range of the abundant fauna in their environment. Deer was a primary and favorite source of meat. Dried deer, cut in strips and exposed to the sun, was a staple. In addition, land tortoise, called "gopher" (*Gopherus polyphemus*), aquatic turtle, quail, curlew, duck, bear, alligator, lake bass, trout, and garfish were commonly eaten. Wild turkey was eaten by some of the groups.

There was a clear division of labor based on sex, even though men and women cooperated in garden labor and women did some fishing. Gardening, gathering wild plant food, and food preparation were the primary responsibility of women. Men did all the hunting and most of the fishing. Men and women cooperated in clearing and preparing gardens using only an axe and hoe. [14]

Through the 1930s, the Seminoles were described as physically fit, muscular, and healthy due to their vigorous outdoor life. MacCauley describes them as hard-working and industrious, but not in the manner of "persistent and rapid labor" characteristic of white men. [15] This is in agreement with Nash's description of a high level of physical activity and general pattern of "vigorous exercise," after which a person might "loaf" the rest of the day. [16]

Men and women typically walked many miles to hunt, garden, and trade. Nash says the women of one camp periodically walked forty-five miles to town and back again in several days. [17] Men always left camp early in the morning, on foot or in a dugout canoe, to hunt. [18] Ober reports that men hunted all day and came back at dusk after traversing twenty miles or more "with perhaps fifty pounds of deer meat in addition to rifle and accouterments." [19]

Women also led active lives. The gardens had to be tended; and both cultivated and wild foods had to be gathered, carried back to the hearth, and prepared. The preparation of corn and *koonti* required considerable work. Corn flour was made by pounding the corn to a fine powder in a mortar consisting of a hollowed-out log with a pestle of hard wood. *Koonti* roots had to be dug up, carried back to camp, washed, chopped, grated, strained, and dried. The flour derived from the roots was made into flat bread which was fried or baked on a griddle without grease. Meats and vegetables were usually cooked together in one pot as a stew or soup. *Sofki,* a drink that resembles a thin gruel of cornmeal, grits, or roasted and cracked corn, was always present. Food was plentiful, and even in 1930 Nash found "there was no shortage of food" in the camp he visited. Indeed, it "was feast from morning to night."[20] There were no set meal times and the entire residence group did not necessarily eat together at one time. Rather, the food was left out and people tended to eat whenever they were hungry throughout the day or night.

The Seminoles of the 1880s had made a very satisfactory adjustment to the wet south Florida swamps and glades environment. They had an abundance of food and were described as exceptionally healthy and free of the diseases that ravaged most Native American groups at that time. Their numbers had increased to almost 300 at the time of MacCauley's visit, which indicates they were sustaining high birth and survival rates.

By the 1890s, drainage and development projects were begun which would eventually undermine this way of life. The opening of lands for homesteading and the interest in south Florida as a source of bird plumes and other trade goods led to an influx of white settlers who forced the Seminoles southward and reduced the area of land over which they could move freely. By the turn of the century, they had been consolidated into the Cow Creek, Miami, and Big Cypress bands, groups which formed the population bases for the federal reservations today.

The influx of whites included traders and their families who set up trading posts where Indians brought hides, pelts, and plumes to exchange for gold, silver, and goods. For about forty years, until 1920, the sale of these items formed a major part of the Indian economy. However, drainage, development, white settlement, and conservation laws combined to force Seminoles from their scattered camps, ending the hunting and trapping economy and eroding Seminole economic independence.

Federal and state reservations (Brighton, Big Cypress, and Hollywood) were established in the 1920s and 1930s. Their purpose was to provide sanctuaries where Seminoles could live unmolested; and the land would provide a stable economic base for the tribe after hunting and trapping ceased to be viable economic alternatives. Seminoles began moving onto the reservations in the 1930s.[21]

By this time, the south Florida environment and the lifestyle of the Seminoles had changed considerably from that described by Mac-Cauley and others. The watery environment of the Everglades, described before the 1900s as a "river of grass," had been drained to the extent that it was no longer possible to travel by dugout canoe in many regions. Automobiles and power sewing machines were to be found in some of the camps. Items made for sale to tourists provided a source of revenue. Some families moved for a few months to a few years at a time to commercial camps in Miami and Silver Springs, where tourists could see "authentic" Indians living in their "traditional" ways.[22]

In 1935, a cattle-raising enterprise was initiated at Brighton through an Indian Reorganization Act program. It was met with enthusiasm by the Seminoles at this reservation and has flourished.[23] In 1942, the Big Cypress reservation received some cattle, but the project never thrived as it has at Brighton.[24]

From the 1930s to the 1950s men and women became increasingly involved in wage labor at surrounding truck farms, ranches, and citrus groves. Families sometimes moved for part of a year or for a couple of years to work as field laborers at farms and nurseries. Groups of men and women also migrated throughout the state and beyond as truck farm laborers.

Economic changes since the early 1900s, from a self-sufficient subsistence pattern based on gardening, hunting, and trapping for cash and goods to increasing participation in and dependence on wage labor, resulted in new sources of food and methods of food preparation. Reports made by visitors to the Seminoles reflect a decline in the size of fields cultivated by local bands. MacCauley reported garden sizes of one to four acres for family groups.[25] By 1930, Nash reported that a family of seven cleared at most one-half acre for gardening.[26] Wild plant foods were important in the 1880s, but by 1930 Nash found that Dania (Hollywood) was the only place where much *koonti* was consumed. Although some food items had been purchased from traders since the 1880s, gardens were still an important source of food until twenty-five to thirty years ago. Participation in wage labor allowed less time for gardening and fostered a greater dependence on store-bought goods, mostly non-perishable and inexpensive (e.g. canned meat, rice, grits, dried beans, flour, lard, syrup, and sugar), which were supplemented by fish, turtle, domesticated animals, and occasional game.[27]

Methods of food preparation also underwent modification. Most elderly Seminoles agreed with the descriptions of MacCauley and others and recalled that when they were young, most food was cooked in stews. Frying foods became a common practice only about thirty-five years ago. Before this time, I was told, "about the only fried food was bread." The following description of food preparation was given by a sixty-eight-year-old woman and translated by her daughter:

Meat was boiled until the water was barely gone or made into soup. Even water turtle was used to make soup. There were grits a long time ago and everytime they got meat, even garfish, they made soups out of it. They used to make soup out of fish heads, even birds such as curlews. Her husband used to get up early in the morning to hunt and bring ducks or curlews and they would eat breakfast then and if he was lucky they had a pig. Before her days she heard that they used to hunt bear and get the fat off there and make a deerskin bag to keep the fat in. Later, in her time, they killed a beef and put the fat in the intestine and rolled it up and kept it and when they wanted grease they cut the intestine and used the fat.[28]

Some older Seminoles attributed the increase of fried foods to the introduction of gas stoves by missionaries, who in their proselytizing efforts gave financial and legal aid and gifts to reservation populations in the 1930s and 1940s. U.S. Department of Agriculture commodity foods became available in the 1930s, and included lard and flour which were made into fry bread, a staple today. Some Seminoles claim that the gas stoves made it easier to fry food and that frying food was a faster way to cook than soups or stews because one did not have to keep stirring a pot to keep it from burning. Perhaps more important is the general consensus that fried foods taste better.

Changes in the mode of subsistence also resulted in a decline in physical activity. In the 1930s walking was still the primary mode of transportation, but by the 1940s some substantial changes had occurred. Greenlee observed in 1939 that "modern life" and a decline in game and hunting had left the men with few daily activities.[29] At Brighton, almost every camp owned a car.[30] Thus, by the 1940s there probably was some decline in energy expenditure compared to twenty years earlier. Despite dietary changes and less physical activity, obesity was still not common. Widespread obesity is first mentioned in Garbarino's monograph concerning Big Cypress in the mid-1960s.[31] The consensus of Seminoles today is that they have always been "big," but it has only been in the past ten to twenty years that gross obesity has become common.

A sixty-seven-year-old woman made the following observations through an interpreter, summarizing the effects of the changes in subsistence, activity levels, and diet:

She . . . thinks that even though [Seminoles] used to eat anything, like rice, they used to have a lot of things to do and used to walk around many miles to look for meat. Women at home ground corn and looked for firewood and dragged it back. But now we don't do hardly anything and just ride around in a car and think you can't go anywhere without a car. Women used to boil clothes and dry them but now things are easy and we don't do enough and that is why we are so fat. We used to walk without shoes and many miles. Now there is nothing like that. We used to get *koonti* too. People used to be smaller but now they get too fat, and men too. She cannot remember exactly when people started frying food more but knows that even before if they wanted to fry it they did. She thinks they fry food more often now but she does not know why. But she has seen the change.[32]

The most visible changes have taken place in the Seminoles' lifestyle in the past twenty-five years. With the advent of federally financed housing in the late 1960s, the extended family camp has disappeared. The standard of living has improved and access to medical care has increased. Since 1955, the Indian Health Service has been responsible for providing health care to the Florida Seminoles. Outpatient clinics have been established at each reservation; and as of 1974 allocations have been made to staff them full-time with a physician, nurse, and Seminole health workers (Community Health Representatives and Emergency Medical Technicians).

The availability of jobs has also increased in the past ten years. Many Seminoles who formerly worked as field laborers are employed by various tribal and federal government programs and agencies today. Because of the availability of these jobs, many Seminoles have been motivated to finish high school and attend college. The Comprehensive Education and Training Act (CETA) has also provided many jobs; and at Brighton, catfish farming is an expanding tribal enterprise. Most of these jobs are sedentary office jobs and few people regularly engage in sustained physical activity. Thus, the decline in energy expenditure and the increase in the prevalence of obesity have been the greatest in both children and adults in the last ten to fifteen years.

Contemporary Dietary Patterns, Obesity, and Diabetes

The relation between diet, obesity, and diabetes was explored through use of clinic medical records from all three reservations and in extensive interviews and observation at the Brighton reservation.

7. Rosa Johns, a diabetic Seminole Indian, is pictured with her grandson.

The central question is whether dietary changes are responsible for the increased prevalence of diabetes in Seminoles. It was expected, though, that the relation of dietary change to the development of diabetes is not direct but is mediated by other factors such as caloric intake, energy expenditure, and obesity. The role of specific dietary items in producing obesity and diabetes, as well as economic, educational, social, and cultural factors which influence food consumption, were examined. Knowledge of all these factors is important to understand the etiology of obesity and diabetes in Seminoles and must be considered in attempts to modify dietary behavior.

The Seminoles obtain food from a variety of sources, although most food items in all households are purchased at grocery stores. At Brighton, the closest grocery store is twenty miles away, but there is a small convenience store on the reservation and several in a community six miles distant.

The Seminole tribe participates in and administers several federal nutrition and food supplement programs. Food stamps replaced the Surplus Commodities Program in the early 1970s. The Supplemental Food Program for Women, Infants, and Children (WIC) had about fifty-five to sixty participants at the Brighton reservation in the summer of 1978. The fact that there were no income restrictions accounted for the large number of participants. While the foods are intended for mother and child, they are eaten by everyone in the family and probably make an important contribution to the diet of some families. As of July 1979, families were required to meet low income requirements in addition to demonstrating "nutritional deficiency" to qualify for the program. Those families dropped from the program will have to spend more money on food if they wish to maintain these foods in the diet. A Headstart program operates for nine months of the year and is attended by about thirty children, ages three to five, who receive a breakfast, lunch, and snack. About forty elderly Seminoles receive five noon meals and two evening meals each week through a Congregate Meals program.

A few families have small gardens but the contribution to the food supply is seasonal and minimal. Citrus fruits are obtained free from nearby groves. About twenty households raise cattle for market, and some beef is slaughtered for their own consumption. Some families have chickens for eggs or several hogs. Hunting and fishing provide varying amounts of meat, but in no household is this an important source of food.

In general, the diets tend to be high in calories; the most outstanding feature of the Seminole diet today is the amount of food consumed.

8. The Seminole Reservation at Brighton is twenty miles from the nearest large grocery store. Several convenience stores, such as the one shown here, feature snacks and cigarettes. This Indian girl helps her parents in their store, which has a small luncheonette serving hamburgers and sandwiches.

The prevalence of obesity in this population is a reflection of dietary behavior and excessive caloric consumption.. Analysis of diet recalls obtained from obese individuals revealed that they consumed 250 to 1,600 calories more than are required for persons of their age, sex, height, and activity level.

Carbohydrates in the form of corn and flour products, rice, beans, sugar, and fats (mostly animal in origin) comprise about 85 percent of caloric intake. *Sofki* is still a favorite food. It is made most often from corn, grits, rice, oatmeal, or flour, and less frequently from pumpkin, tomatoes, or guavas. It is consumed with meals and between meals "like coffee." Older people report drinking three to six large (8- to 12-ounce) cups every day, at approximately 75 to 100 calories per serving. Fry bread, made from self-rising flour and water and deep-fried, and rice with gravy are also frequent meal items. The most common and preferred way to cook food is to fry it in lard, vegetable shortening, or, more rarely, oil. If meats are boiled, extra grease may be added "for flavor."

The consumption of refined sugar and carbohydrates in the form of carbonated beverages and snacks has increased tremendously in the past twenty to thirty years, and there has been a corresponding decrease in dietary fiber. The quantities of soft drinks and "junk food" snacks consumed account in part for the prevalence of obesity, especially among young people.

Food lists of weekly grocery purchases, diet recalls, and observation indicate there is adequate, and in most cases more than adequate, protein in the diet, most of it from animal sources. Seminoles have always eaten meat in large amounts. They believe it is necessary for good health and strength and ideally it is served with each meal. It is often cited as a food that is "craved." Today, many of the most frequently consumed meats are high in fat, and this, in addition to the practice of frying foods, results in a diet high in fat. Eggs are consumed regularly in all households, but cheese and small amounts of milk are consumed primarily in households with children.

Vegetables, except for corn, dried peas and beans, potatoes, and tomatoes, are eaten infrequently, particularly by older Seminoles. Nevertheless, there are no vitamin deficiency diseases. Fruits, especially citrus and bananas, are liked and are usually eaten between meals.

The major influence of income on diet seems to be that higher-income families tend to have more expensive meats more often. However, in those lower-income families for whom information was available, the diets were ample in calories and protein.

Eating patterns tend to be "inextricably interwoven with many other

9. The Headstart Program on Brighton Reservation provides two meals a day for preschool children. These children are eating boiled eggs, toast, milk, and canned peaches.

factors in the environment."[33] Food consumption patterns of the Seminoles have changed with the changing environment. Early ethnographers described a pattern of eating when hungry or when food was available, with frequent trips to the hearth for *sofki* and bits of meat throughout the day. Today, most Seminoles follow a three-meal-a-day pattern which is probably structured by the eight-to-five working day and school schedules of children. Between-meal eating is common, though, and for many eating is not stimulated by hunger, but by the presence of food.

No specific dietary items or eating patterns can be related to obesity and diabetes in this population, although intake of sugars and high-calorie foods may be indirectly related to diabetes because they contribute to obesity. The important dietary difference between the obese and non-obese, diabetics and non-diabetics, seems to lie in the total amount of food and calories consumed. The factor common to all diabetics is obesity due to excess caloric intake. A number of factors in the contemporary environment contribute to obesity. Lack of exercise has been mentioned. Several older Seminoles linked the onset of their own extreme obesity to their retirement from outdoor physical labor. Also, calorically dense snack foods are readily available and widely consumed.

In the majority of cases, onset of diabetes is not acute, and a weight-reduction diet and oral hypoglycemics are usually prescribed first. Most diabetics progress to insulin treatment because they do not limit food intake or lose weight, and oral hypoglycemics are not sufficient to control their blood sugar levels. That compliance is not achieved is not due entirely to ignorance; all the people interviewed knew that they must eat less and exercise more to lose weight. Health professionals tend to attribute the failure to follow a weight-loss diet to Seminoles' "inability to take responsibility for themselves." However, they are not behaving in an "irresponsible" manner if one considers that an individual's dietary behavior is in part a response to social and cultural cues. In addition to the factors mentioned above, there are a number of aspects of the social and cultural environment which encourage eating, enhance obesity, and make weight loss and control of diabetes difficult to achieve. These social and cultural aspects of food consumption have not changed as rapidly as economic patterns and total lifestyle.

Exchanges and offering of food as gestures of hospitality are integral to the social fabric. Gathering together to eat is a demonstration of friendship. Food is always present at social gatherings and often at tribal functions. Spoehr observed in 1939 that "the offering of food

is . . . a much-used social mechanism for maintaining friendly relations among the Indians," and this is still true today.[34] People who
do not participate in food exchange may be accused of being unfriendly
or "stingy." This feeling has led to problems in the Congregate Meals
program for senior citizens. Serving size is supposed to be controlled
and leftover food is to be thrown out and not taken home. However,
the Seminole employees who must try to enforce these rules are subject to chastisement from the older Seminoles who find these rules
socially unacceptable.

The success with which an individual follows a weight-loss diet
also may be influenced by other members of the household. Women
who try to diet find it difficult to cook and eat special foods for themselves and prepare something else for the rest of the family. Other family members may protest changes in kinds of foods served or in manner of cooking. One woman periodically tried to implement what she
knew about broiling and roasting foods, but her husband wanted his
food fried.

It became apparent in discussions with Seminoles about weight
loss that there is no established behavior pattern of long-term "self-
control" or self-denial of food to achieve weight loss. This is evidenced
by such statements as "We just can't stop eating," "We Indians just
don't know when to stop," and in one elderly Seminole's declaration
that she was "not going to eat just a little bit" for any reason.

Nevertheless, the idea of dietary restriction is not new to Seminoles. A one-day fast is part of the Green Corn Dance. However, I
was told by young people that they may circumvent this practice and
sneak into town to get something to eat or slip off to where they have
some food stashed. In time past, women were advised to eat less of
everything while pregnant, and were not to gain too much weight
because this would make labor and delivery difficult. Even today, young
women may be admonished along these lines, but little heed is paid.
In addition, food taboos are almost always imposed when one is being
"doctored" with Indian medicine. Several Seminoles remarked on
some of the similarities between what Indian doctors and white doctors tell one not to eat. For instance, salt and pork, two items frequently "tabooed" by white doctors for patients with hypertension or
heart conditions, are also items frequently restricted in Indian medical treatment. Some foods, such as turkey, may be banned for life.
Most Indian food taboos, however, last for a specific period of time,
such as four days or four months, rather than the indefinite period
of doctors' dietary proscriptions. Another problem is that many vegetables and fruits that health personnel ask Seminoles to eat are forbid-

den and avoided during Indian medical treatments. Indian medicine and white medicine are often used concurrently, especially in the older population where Indian medicine is used to cure the "real" cause, which may be due to social infractions or sorcery; and white medicine is used to relieve symptoms. Conflict between the two modes of treatment usually means that the diets recommended by health personnel are not followed.

In the younger population, one finds that most parents make no attempt to limit the amount and kind of food their children eat. Reluctance to tell others what to do and non-interference in the affairs of others is a traditional code of behavior that also is extended to parent-child relationships. Younger mothers who do try to control their children's intake of sweets and junk food are chided by older Seminoles for doing so. The old people, and some young people, tend to think that children should have what they want and that "whatever they want is good for them." The effects of these attitudes are visible in the increasing problems of obesity and rotted teeth in children.

The increase of obesity, both childhood and adult, is not a great cause for concern among the Seminoles. They do not share the American cultural ideal of "slimness." While they agree that some Seminoles are too fat today, the Seminole definition of ideal weight is consistently above the medically prescribed standards of weight for height. A former Seminole health worker told me that when she was thin, people thought she was sick. Another woman told me that her mother complained that her grandchildren were too thin, even though they were of normal weight, and that she (their mother) must not feed them enough. A thirty-four-year-old diabetic was about forty pounds above his ideal weight but felt that he was at the "right weight." He had lost about eighty pounds since the onset of diabetes and described this by saying he had "dried up."

Seminoles also have definite attitudes about the healthfulness of certain foods, and some foods are identified as being uniquely Seminole or non-Seminole. Positive attributes are assigned by Seminoles to some of their traditional foods. For example, meat is to be eaten in quantity because it gives one strength. *Sofki* is also thought to give one strength. Furthermore, it is a good food for babies and a good beverage when one is sick; it is even thought to be more refreshing than water when one is thirsty. *Sofki* is a "cultural superfood" of the Seminoles and is identified as a uniquely Seminole food, one which they should eat to stay healthy. Some Seminoles believe that cancer is caused by failure to drink enough *sofki*. Fry bread is another Seminole food. It is understandable that patients may not be receptive to doctors' and nutritionists' admonitions to eat less of these foods; they identify one as a Seminole and are considered to be healthful.

In diet counseling, patients are encouraged to substitute vegetables for "fattening" traditional foods such as *sofki* and fry bread. In the past, however, green vegetables were not an important part of the diet. Significantly, in the Mikasuki language there is no word for "vegetables." The word they use to translate "green vegetables" is the word for "weeds" in their language, which has a slightly prejudicial connotation. When health personnel tell Seminole patients to eat vegetables, they may be telling them to eat something which is not really considered to be food, or at least is not the kind of food Seminoles believe they need to be healthy.

Knowledge and beliefs held by Seminoles concerning diabetes causation must also be considered, because they influence the patient's perception of the relevance of dietary change to the treatment of diabetes. It is generally known that diabetics have "too much sugar in their blood." Because doctors tell diabetics not to eat sweets, it is assumed that sweet foods cause diabetes. In the Creek language, the word for diabetes is "oshugala," or "sugar." The importance of weight loss to control diabetes has not been made clear, and is secondary to avoidance of sweets in the minds of Seminoles. Also, some of the older people believe the real reason for the increase of diabetes in Seminoles is that women no longer follow the traditional practice of isolation during menstruation and thus expose others to "women's sickness," one manifestation of which is now believed to be diabetes. That many diabetics are not aware of the relations of excess caloric intake and obesity to diabetes, and believe instead that diabetes is due to the abandonment of traditional ways, no doubt also influences compliance with and success of treatment.

It should be mentioned that organizational, administrative, budgetary, and personnel problems within the Florida Service Unit of the Indian Health Service also impinge on the quality and outcome of health care provided to Seminoles. The turnover of doctors and nurses is high (many stay less than one year), and clinics may go for months with no doctor and/or nurse. When there is no clinic doctor, anyone with a problem must use emergency rooms or private physicians with whom the Indian Health Service has contracted for care. Excessive reliance on contract care rapidly depletes the funds allocated to the Service Unit. This creates a situation where emergency and crisis-oriented care have priority, to the neglect of prevention programs.

Implications for Health Care Providers

The situation described here calls for rethinking of the problem and the solutions, particularly in the area of diet counseling. These findings connect social and cultural influences with diet, obesity, and diabetes and suggest more promising approaches to these health problems. While achieving weight control may seem impossible, the potential for success of nutrition education in this area is enhanced by the Seminoles' "felt need" that something should be done about the problem of diabetes.

Perhaps the most important conclusion is that nutrition education programs aimed at preventing or treating diabetes should focus on the prevention or reduction of obesity. It is not clear to the majority of Seminoles that the primary risk factor for diabetes is obesity caused by excessive food intake. This may be due in large part to the fact that explanations of the "four food groups" or the diabetic exchange system during diet counseling do not make clear to Seminole patients the importance of weight reduction.

The Seminole diet is noticeably lacking in vegetables, and because vegetables are less calorically dense the approach has been to encourage the addition of vegetables to the diet. Vegetables are also promoted as necessary for a "balanced" diet. Over the past fifteen years, Seminoles seem to have learned from health personnel that to solve the problem of diabetes, "balanced" diets with more vegetables and milk are needed. While these changes might be desirable, they tend to deflect attention from the real issue of weight loss. A diabetic father in his mid-thirties felt that the best way to prevent diabetes in his children was to see that they had "three square meals a day." His oldest child, however, is obese, and the others very probably will become obese as they grow older.

The approach of health personnel has also worked against cultural beliefs and assumptions and therefore has not been successful in promoting dietary changes. Diet counseling should be tailored to the audience. It is doubtful that the older generation will ever view vegetables as an acceptable food. A more realistic attitude may be to encourage them to eat smaller portions of their traditional foods rather than to emphasize the addition of vegetables. The primary emphasis in the older population, where weight loss and better control of diabetes and other chronic conditions is the goal, should be on decreased intake as opposed to substitution. Furthermore, with most older Seminoles an emphasis on reduction of sweets and addition of vegetables is not appropriate, since sweets do not constitute a significant portion of caloric intake. Since some milk products and vegetables are eaten by younger Seminoles, there might be more success with the "balanced" diet or "four food groups" approach in this age group. Nevertheless, it should be clear that, in addition to improving the quality of the diet, the goals of weight reduction and the prevention of obesity require that amounts of food be controlled.

It is also evident that diet counseling should include the entire family where possible. Indian medical practices, especially for serious disease, involve other family members in the treatment process. Moreover, there are usually other family members who are obese or have a disease which would benefit from dietary management. The fact that women find it difficult to prepare separate meals for themselves and their families, and soon abandon a diet, suggests that the one-to-one interaction of health personnel and patient cannot be translated adequately into the family setting.

Even though parents express concern about the health of children and dietary habits that degrade health, their reluctance to enforce good habits or restrict items of low nutritional quality has a negative effect on the potential for change. Even when a parent is willing to limit certain foods to his or her children, this may be counteracted by the disapproval of other household members. This situation illustrates forcefully that education of mothers can have only limited success when other household members and caretakers who have an impact on availability of food and diet behavior are ignored or not included. New modes of treatment and education must focus on the family in order to overcome the impediments to dietary management which arise from the social setting and cultural beliefs.

The findings concerning the relationship between obesity and diabetes among American Indians indicate that priorities, goals, and strategies in diet therapy must be adjusted to the kind of diabetes being treated. Day-to-day consistency of intake of calories, carbohydrates, protein, and fat at each feeding, while important in the management of insulin-dependent diabetes, is not necessary in obese patients who do not require insulin. To treat non-insulin-dependent diabetes and prevent or slow the development of complications, weight loss through caloric restriction is of utmost importance.[35] The rationale behind weight reduction should be carefully explained, and the exchange system abandoned or modified to increase success. West found that with Oklahoma Indian diabetics "fairly good results" with weight loss were achieved when the risk of not doing so was carefully explained and understood by the patient.[36] This has yet to be attempted with Seminole diabetics.

It can be concluded that adult-onset diabetes among Seminoles may be preventable through the prevention of obesity. The evidence from the Seminoles and other Native American populations suggests that the epidemic of diabetes can be reversed through modifications of the environment and behaviors which predispose to and precipitate diabetes. Treatment and control could be enhanced through modification of these same factors. Strategies suggested here could be employed by health practitioners to help Seminoles improve their health status.

NOTES

1. Russell A. Judkins and Leslie Sue Lieberman, "Biomedicine and Nutrition," *Society for Medical Anthropology Newsletter* 6 (1974): 14–17; Kelly M. West, "Diabetes in American Indians and Other Native Populations in the New World," *Diabetes* 23 (1974):841–55.

2. Peter H. Bennett, Norman Rushforth, Max Miller, and Philip Lecompte, "Epidemiologic Studies of Diabetes in Pima Indians," in *Recent Progress in Hormone Research,* ed. Roy O. Greep (New York: Academic Press, 1977); James V. Neel, "Diabetes Mellitus — A Geneticist's Nightmare," in *The Genetics of Diabetes Mellitus,* ed. Werner Creutzfeld, Johannes Kobberling, and James V. Neel (Heidelberg: Springer-Verlag, 1976); Cheryl Ritenbaugh, "A Re-examination of Diabetes Among Navajos" (unpublished manuscript, 1972).

3. Cynthia Eaton, "Diabetes, Culture Change and Acculturation: A Biocultural Analysis," *Medical Anthropology* 2 (1977):41–63; H. Keen and R.J. Jarrett, "Environmental Factors and Genetic Interactions," in *The Genetics of Diabetes Mellitus.*

4. Denis P. Burkitt, "Some Diseases Characteristic of Modern Western Civilization," *British Medical Journal* 1 (1973):274–78.

5. Kelly M. West, *Epidemiology of Diabetes Mellitus and its Vascular Lesions* (New York: Elsevier-North Holland, 1978).

6. William C. Sturtevant, "The Mikasuki Seminole: Medical Beliefs and Practices" (Ph.D. diss., Yale Univ., 1955); David Westfall and Arlan L. Rosenbloom, "Diabetes Mellitus Among the Florida Seminole," *AMHSA Health Reports* 86 (1971): 1037–41.

7. Sandra K. Joos, "Social, Cultural and Nutritional Aspects of Diabetes Among the Florida Seminole" (Master's thesis, Univ. of Florida, 1979).

8. Sturtevant, "Mikasuki Seminole," 68.

9. Ibid., 70.

10. Harry A. Kersey, Jr., *Pelts, Plumes and Hides: White Traders Among the Seminole Indians, 1870–1930* (Gainesville: Univ. Presses of Florida, 1975); Clay MacCauley, "The Seminole Indians of Florida," *Bureau of American Ethnology* 5 (1887):469–531; Frederick A. Ober, "Ten Days with the Seminoles," *Appleton's Journal of Literature, Science and Art* 14 (1875): 31 July, 142–44; 7 August, 171–73.

11. MacCauley, 495–96.

12. Joseph R. Henderson, "The Soils of Florida," *University of Florida Agricultural Experimental Station Bulletin* 334 (Gainesville, Fl., 1939).

13. MacCauley, 504–5, 510; Ober, 172; William C. Sturtevant, "R.H. Pratt's Report on the Seminole in 1879," *Florida Anthropologist* 9 (1956):1–24.

14. MacCauley, 503; Sturtevant, "Pratt's Report," 7.

15. MacCauley, 503.

16. Roy Nash, "Survey of the Seminole Indians of Florida," 71st Congress, 3d Session Senate Document 314, Serial 9347 (1931), 6.

17. Ibid., 7–8.

18. MacCauley, 512; Ober, 172.

19. Ober, 172.

20. Nash, 9.

21. Kersey, 18–21.

22. Ibid., 36.

23. Robert T. King, "The Florida Seminole Polity" (Ph.D. diss., Univ. of Florida, 1978).

24. Merwyn S. Garbarino, *Big Cypress: A Changing Seminole Community* (New York: Holt, Rinehart, and Winston, 1972).

25. MacCauley, 510.

26. Nash, 6.

27. Robert F. Greenlee, "Aspects of Social Organization and Material Culture of the Seminole of Big Cypress Swamp," *Florida Anthropologist* 5 (1952):25–32.

28. Joos, 27–28.

29. Greenlee, 30.

30. Alexander Spoehr, "The Florida Seminole Camp," *Field Museum of Natural History, Anthropological Series* 33(1944):114–50.

31. Garbarino, 54.

32. Joos, 28–29.

33. Corrine S. Wood, *Human Sickness and Health: A Biocultural View* (Palo Alto: Mayfield Publishing Co., 1979), 98.

34. Spoehr, 145.

35. Kelly M. West, "Diet Therapy of Diabetes: An Analysis of Failure," *Annals of Internal Medicine* 79(1973):425–34.

36. Kelly M. West, "The Diabetes Problem in American Indians with Special Reference to Oklahoma Indians" (mimeographed report submitted to the Indian Health Service, 1978).

12

Food for Ethnic Americans: Is the Government Trying to Turn the Melting Pot into a One-Dish Dinner?

Judy Perkin and Stephanie F. McCann

Scene: A public service announcement on national television. Viewers are urged to eat right for healthy lives. Every day, choose foods from the Basic Four: (1) meat or meat alternates; (2) fruits and vegetables; (3) breads and cereals; and (4) milk and dairy products.

Millions of Americans have heard this advice, and few question this information or even pause to consider the source of these recommendations. The advocacy of a pattern of food choices to a mass audience reflects the role of the government in determining what Americans eat, a role that has expanded steadily as Americans have moved away from food self-sufficiency to obtaining food from outside the home. But the national population to whom this advice is directed is composed of many groups with strong ethnic identifications. In what ways does the government address the subject of the food choices of ethnic Americans and the implications of these choices for health?

Historically, one could argue that the government to a certain extent reflected the needs of the agricultural industry in nutrition advice given to the American public. The major source of government advice about diet has been, and continues to be, the United States Department of Agriculture. This Department first recommended the Basic Four Food Groups more than twenty-five years ago (in 1956), and the Basic Four concept has served as the major cornerstone of government advice with regard to the consumption of a nutritionally adequate diet.[1]

Since the choice and manner of food presentation in the Basic Four seem to reflect an orientation toward the marketing of agricultural products, one could view this advice as being politically and culturally biased. Although the concept of the Basic Four Food Groups is based upon the provision of key nutrients, and from that an adequate diet, it does not fully utilize knowledge of food composition and of prevalent alternative food sources among ethnic groups.[2] For example, inclusion of the milk and dairy product group as a must for good eating ignores the fact that among some U.S. ethnic groups (Black Americans, Chinese Americans, and Mexican Americans) there is a large percentage of the population which is unable to digest lactose, the sugar found in milk.[3] Adherence to the Basic Four Food Groups diet plan could actually make these Americans sick. The major nutrient provided by the milk and dairy product group is calcium. Among ethnic groups with a high prevalence of lactose intolerance, alternative sources of dietary calcium are turnip greens (Black Americans), soybeans, soy sauce, and green vegetables (Chinese Americans), and tortillas prepared with lime (Mexican Americans).[4] The Basic Four ignores these alternative calcium sources which have evolved as culturally acceptable foods for these ethnic groups. The Basic Four also ignores the fact that adaptation to various levels of calcium intake is possible and has, in fact, occurred in some ethnic groups.[5]

Another limitation of the Basic Four is that it fails to guide ethnic Americans in the choice of foods as they are actually prepared and consumed.[6] Individual ethnic Americans frequently need to make decisions about combination dishes (foods with multiple ingredients). The nutrition education approach of the Basic Four is not an effective aid in decision-making about the nutritional adequacy of such foods as hopping john, enchiladas, or lasagna. Guidance would be more useful if it were based upon what people *eat* rather than appearing to make nutrition and health concerns secondary to what people *buy* from the agricultural industry.

In recent years, government groups have begun to address themselves to the relationship of nutrition to health and disease prevention. This emphasis is part of the government's efforts to decrease spiraling health care costs by stressing health promotion and preventive medicine. In January 1977, as the beginning of a change in the government's approach to dietary advice, the Select Committee on Nutrition and Human Needs of the United States Senate announced the release of a document entitled *Dietary Goals for the United States.*[7] These goals were put forward to provide guidelines for consumption of a diet which, unlike the average American diet in the Committee's view, did not have "too much fat, too much sugar or salt." The Senate

Committee expressed the view at this time that the current, and in their view excessive, diet has led to many health problems prevalent within the United States today—specifically the problems of "heart disease, cancer, obesity, and stroke." The picture drawn by the Committee of the current diet is based upon the nutritive value of the U.S. food supply expressed on a per capita basis. All of this food may not be eaten, and certainly it is not equally consumed by each person within the country.

The Dietary Goals were presented in two ways in the Senate Committee report: first, as goals which stated percentages of nutrients or absolute amounts of nutrients which should appear in the diet; and second, as suggestions for food selection and preparation. The goal statements were modified in December of 1977 and are as follows:

1. To avoid being overweight, consume only as much energy (calories) as is expended; if overweight, decrease energy intake and increase energy expenditure.

2. Increase the consumption of complex carbohydrates and "naturally occurring" sugars from about 28 percent of energy intake to about 48 percent of energy intake.

3. Reduce the consumption of refined and processed sugars by about 45 percent to account for about 10 percent of total energy intake.

4. Reduce overall fat consumption from approximately 40 percent to about 30 percent of energy intake.

5. Reduce saturated fat consumption to account for about 10 percent of total energy intake; and balance that with polyunsaturated and monounsaturated fats, which should account for about 10 percent of energy intake each.

6. Reduce cholesterol consumption to about 300 mg. a day.

7. Limit the intake of sodium by reducing the intake of salt to about 5 gm. a day.[8]

The changes in food selection and preparation advanced by *Dietary Goals* were:

1. Increase consumption of fruits and vegetables and whole grains.

2. Decrease consumption of refined and other processed sugars and foods high in such sugars.

3. Decrease consumption of foods high in total fat and partially replace saturated fats, whether obtained from animal or vegetable sources, with polyunsaturated fats.

4. Decrease consumption of animal fat, and choose meats, poultry and fish which will reduce saturated fat intake.

5. Except for young children, substitute low-fat and non-fat milk for whole milk, and low-fat dairy products for high fat dairy products.

6. Decrease consumption of butterfat, eggs and other high cholesterol sources. Some consideration should be given to easing the cholesterol goal for pre-menopausal women, young children and the elderly in order to obtain the nutritional benefits of eggs in the diet.

7. Decrease consumption of salt and foods high in salt content.[9]

The Dietary Goals advocated by the Select Committee are controversial; the content of the Dietary Goals as well as the manner of presentation have been received with both disapprobation and acclaim. Many health professionals do not regard the link between diet and disease with the certainty suggested by the rationale behind the promulgation of the goals. Other health professionals feel that the link exists, and that following the dietary advice of this publication could decrease the prevalence of certain diseases (cancer, cardiovascular disease, and obesity) within the U.S. population.[10]

When confronted with a copy of the goals as stated in the Senate publication, most Americans would have had a difficult time in deciphering them. For example, what does the phrase "an increase in total carbohydrates" mean? What does "decreasing saturated fat content" signify in terms of an individual's choice of breakfast, lunch, or dinner? What is a "saturated fat"? Is it identified on food packages? In some ethnic groups, customary food choices may not be adequately related to the committee's advice to eat more fruits, vegetables, and whole grain products and to eat less meat, eggs, butterfat, refined sugar, and salt.

The latest nutrition message of the U.S. government is embodied in a 1980 publication entitled *Nutrition and Your Health: Dietary Guidelines for Americans,* released jointly by the U.S. Department of Agriculture and the Department of Health, Education, and Welfare.[11] This publication is based upon the relationship of nutrition to health as outlined previously in *Dietary Goals for the United States* and represents a simplification of the statements about changes in food selection and preparation which accompanied the earlier Dietary Goals. A statement about alcohol use also was added. The new Dietary Guidelines state:

1. Eat a variety of foods.
2. Maintain ideal body weight.
3. Avoid too much fat, saturated fat, and cholesterol.
4. Eat foods with adequate starch and fiber.
5. Avoid too much sugar.
6. Avoid too much sodium.
7. If you drink alcohol, do so in moderation.[12]

These Dietary Guidelines are recommended in a general way for all Americans, despite the fact that the government does not know if the diseases supposedly prevented by following this advice are equally prevalent among U.S. ethnic groups. Disease statistics in government publications are most frequently reported under the categories of "white," "black," and "all others." A few reports, however, break down the category of "all others" into more meaningful ethnic categories.[13] It appears that the government is attempting to convey the message of good nutrition in one way to all people. The government dietary advice tends to assume that the majority of Americans are middle-aged men with potbellies who are susceptible to heart disease. The new Dietary Guidelines may indeed be relevant to many Americans, but they should be evaluated to determine their relevance to specific ethnic populations. The National Health Planning and Resources Act of 1974 (Public Law 93–641) recognizes the ethnic heterogeneity of the U.S. population and mandates that health programs for ethnic minorities be designed to meet the needs and customs of the people they serve.[14] Unfortunately, nutrition advice from governmental sources has not yet been adequate to allow nutrition and health educators to comply with this mandate.

The assumption of dietary and cultural homogeneity that underlies the government's directives with regard to American food choices is inappropriate. The United States has a rich cultural heritage of foodways. Traditional ethnic food choices have persisted, although sometimes in modified forms. Foods of ethnic groups are also now shared. Sharing has occurred not only in the home; ethnic food is increasing in popularity as food which is eaten outside the home — in restaurants, fast-food shops, hospitals, and other institutionalized food services. The nutrition message delivered by the government does not address this cultural diversity.

The intent of the remainder of this discussion is to demonstrate how the government's dietary advice could be translated into acceptable diets for various American cultural groups. Can the government advice as stated be made relevant for the individual, the family, the ethnic group, and the community? More broadly, this discussion raises issues for nutrition and health educators who are attempting to find an effective means of communicating the message of good nutrition. What are culturally relevant strategies of nutrition education? One of the greatest challenges of our time is the translation of the science of food and nutrition into everyday dietary behavior.

This discussion relates ethnic food patterns to *Dietary Guidelines for Americans* and focuses on health problems potentially related to diet which have been identified in four of America's largest ethnic populations: Mexican, Black, Chinese, and Italian. Menus for each ethnic group, based upon proposed changes in food selection and preparation, are included. It should be noted that concepts regarding what constitutes a "traditional" ethnic dietary pattern may be unclear. Subcultural differences do exist, as do individual preferences, so any one individual of a particular ethnic group may not necessarily consume a diet similar to that described for the ethnic group as a whole. The extent to which individuals have incorporated new products into their previous dietary pattern also may vary widely.

The advancement of dietary advice by the government does represent a move in the direction of health promotion and indicates a recognition of the importance of people's dietary patterns for their health and total well-being. As detailed below, these general guidelines can be made feasible within the dietary behavior of an ethnic group and responsive to health problems prevalent in that group.

If an ethnic American incorporated into his diet the changes in food selection and preparation suggested here, what would a typical day's menu include? The table of ethnic menus details sample day menus for Mexican Americans, Black Americans, Chinese Americans, and Italian Americans that have been included in the following detailed discussion. These menus are based on recommendations made in the publication *Dietary Guidelines for Americans*. Amounts of food items consumed would have to be determined on an individual basis depending upon caloric needs.

The Mexican-American Diet

According to the U.S. Bureau of the Census, nearly eight million Mexican Americans were living in the United States in 1980. Foods which have been introduced from Mexico are eaten not only by these individuals; but as this culture has been assimilated into the United States, other individuals of different cultural backgrounds have come to enjoy traditional Mexican foods. Americanized versions of Mexican foods have also begun to appear, and Mexican-type foods are even

ETHNIC MENUS BASED ON U.S. DIETARY GUIDELINES

	Mexican American	Black American	Chinese American	Italian American
BREAKFAST	Hard white rolls Vegetable oil margarine Guava jelly Orange juice *Atole de Arroz* (with low-fat milk and artificial sweetener) *Café con leche* (evaporated skim milk)	Grits Skim milk Biscuits Jelly Vegetable oil margarine Orange juice Coffee	Cream of rice or wheat (mixed with ginger and brown sugar) Skim milk Steamed bread Steamed egg with skim milk Orange juice or tomato juice, tea	Oatmeal or farina (cooked with skim milk and sugar) Toasted Italian bread Vegetable oil margarine Orange juice Coffee with skim milk
LUNCH	Fish (broiled) Spanish rice Refried beans (fried in small amount of vegetable oil) *Picante* sauce Tortillas Lettuce and tomato Salad topped with shredded goat cheese (vinegar and oil dressing) Sugar-free beverage	Macaroni and cheese (made with low-fat pasteurized cheese) Greens Bread Margarine Chopped banana and watermelon balls Skim milk	Rice (enriched) Poultry (stir-fried in soybean oil) Chinese vegetables (broccoli, spinach, cabbage, carrots, mushrooms) Bread Yogurt (low fat) with fruit, tea	Chicken stew (made with Italian noodles, eggplant, mushrooms, broccoli, peppers, tomatoes) Tossed salad (vinegar dressing) Italian bread Coffee with skim milk
DINNER	Chicken (baked) *Calabazita* (Mexican squash) and *Fidello* (vermicelli) *Picante* sauce Tortillas Vegetable oil margarine Flan (made with skim or low-fat milk) Fresh cold prickly-pears Sugar-free beverage	Catfish (broiled) Black-eyed peas Sweet potatoes Green beans Vegetable oil margarine Bread Gingerbread Iced tea	Rice (enriched) Lean meat (stir-fried in soybean oil) Chinese vegetables Tofu (soybean curd) Bread or rolls Rice cakes Tea	Lasagna (noodles, lean meat and low-fat cheeses) Tossed salad (vinegar dressing) Italian bread Vegetable oil margarine Italian pastry Grapes Coffee with skim milk

Ethnic menus developed by the authors and based upon changes in food selection and preparation suggested by *Dietary Guidelines for Americans*.

marketed by the fast-food industry. Mexican food is one of the most popular ethnic foods sold in the U.S.[15]

In December 1980, the government released a Spanish version of *Dietary Guidelines.*[16] This translation represents an initial effort to communicate governmental dietary advice to Mexican Americans; however, the publication is merely a translation of the English version and does not discuss the guidelines in terms of either Mexican-American food habits or health problems.

The traditional Mexican-American diet can easily provide adequate starch as suggested in *Dietary Guidelines.* Common sources of starch frequently consumed as part of the Mexican-American diet include tortillas, rice, vermicelli (*fidello*), and beans.[17] The high fiber intake resulting from tortilla consumption has been studied and cited as a potential contributor to health.[18]

Sugar, not only in the traditional form of *dulces,* but also in the form of soft drinks, is a notable part of the Mexican-American diet.[19] Reduced consumption of refined carbohydrates may be difficult to achieve for some individuals who practice Mexican-American foodways. To promote a diet which is in line with the government directives, advice should be given to limit intakes of sweets and soft drinks. Individuals could be counseled to replace regular soft drinks with diet beverages if they desire to reduce sugar intake without interrupting the habit of soft drink consumption. Alternatively, since fruit juice drinks are popular among Mexican Americans, use of these could be encouraged rather than soft drinks.

Government guidelines counsel against excessive fat intake as one means of heart disease prevention. Evidence with regard to appropriateness of this guideline for heart disease prevention in the Mexican-American population is unclear. A study of heart disease in New Mexico indicated that Hispanic males had lower death rates than did their Anglo counterparts.[20] A similar pattern of heart disease mortality has been noted when Mexican Americans in Texas were compared to the Anglo population.[21] These findings would suggest that the admonition to avoid fat as a health measure may be more relevant to the Anglo than the Mexican-American population. However, suggestions for some reduction of fat intake in the Mexican-American diet could be made, since at least one study has noted that fat may contribute more than the recommended 30 percent of total dietary calories.[22] More will be known about the relationship between fat intake and the health of Mexican Americans when data from the recent government Health and Nutrition Examination Survey focusing on the U.S. Hispanic population are released.[23]

Fat is consumed in the Mexican-American diet in the form of bacon (*tocino*), sausage (*chorizo*), lard (*manteca*), margarine (*margarina*), butter (*mantequilla*), and oils (*aceites*).[24] Bacon, sausage, lard, and butter contain large amounts of saturated fat, and therefore the use of these items would be limited in a diet which is in line with advice of the government. The use of margarine with liquid vegetable oil as the major ingredient should be encouraged for cooking purposes and for use at the table.

Hidden sources of fat in the Mexican-American diet include milk, cheese, and meat.[25] The use of low-fat or skim milk as opposed to fresh, whole cow milk could be promoted for milk-drinking individuals. Many Mexican Americans, however, are lactose-intolerant and do not consume milk in large quantities. Reduction of fat intake via modification of the type of milk consumed may not be particularly effective for this group. Evaporated milk, used in *cafe con leche,* can be purchased in the skim milk variety and its use could be advocated to lower dietary fat intake. Goat-milk cheese is approximately 54 percent fat, while cheddar cheese is approximately 72 percent fat.[26] The use of goat-milk cheese, which is very popular, could be encouraged, and low-fat pasteurized processed cheese also can be used to make very palatable enchiladas, *chili con queso,* or other Mexican foods.

Fish and poultry are relatively low in fat and have a prominent place in Mexican cuisine.[27] Frequent use of these as protein sources in menu planning could be encouraged. High-fat meats in the Mexican-American diet include: pork cracklings (*chicharrones*), beef intestine (*intestino de res*), beef tongue (*lengua de res*), and squab (*paloma*). These meats should be consumed in limited quantities to reduce fat intake. Beef (*carne de res*) and goat meat (*cabra* or *cabrito*) are medium-fat meats and should be used in moderation.[28]

While the relative magnitude of heart disease as a Mexican-American health problem remains unclear, obesity has been noted as a health problem in the Mexican-American population by the Ten State Nutrition Survey.[29] Reduction of caloric intake to a level commensurate with energy expenditure may be an even more crucial point to stress in health promotion for this population group than reduction of fat intake per se. The relative obesity of many individuals in the Mexican-American population may be related to a culturally desirable body image (the concept that a body should be "well-fleshed").[30] Health education would have to attempt to alter this concept of an ideal body type to be more in line with concepts of body weights conducive to health maintenance.

Recent evidence also suggests that hypertension may be a serious health problem for Mexican Americans. In a Texas study, Fonner examined cause-specific death rates for Mexican Americans and standardized these rates to those of Anglos. Mexican-American males and females both had higher rates for hypertension than did their counterpart groups in the Anglo population.[31] Nutrition educators working with this population should emphasize the need to "avoid too much sodium" since some Americanized Mexican foods—for example, canned tamales and *enchiritos*—are relatively high in sodium content.[32]

The government's admonition to consume alcohol in moderation may be particularly relevant to certain segments of the Mexican-American population. There is insufficient data to characterize alcohol consumption of this U.S. ethnic group as a whole, but a California study found that the alcohol-related death rate for males with a Spanish surname was 10 percent higher than the rate for the general population. The alcohol-related death rate for the total Spanish surname population was, in contrast, lower than for the general population.[33] This finding suggests that Mexican-American males might do well to follow the guideline related to moderating alcohol consumption. One study has also identified the *agringado,* or Mexican American who enters Anglo society, as being a candidate for potential alcohol abuse.[34] *Agringados* may be another Mexican-American group for which government advice to moderate alcohol consumption may be applicable.

The Black-American Diet

The most commonly described foodways for Black Americans derive from the southern rural heritage. Foods associated with farm settings, such as fresh vegetables, fish, and game are prominent in most descriptions of foods consumed by Black Americans.[35] According to the 1980 census, most American Blacks (approximately 18 million) lived in urban areas.[36] The foodways brought from past rural experiences need to be examined in light of new eating patterns which have been established in the urban setting. One investigation of urban blacks who migrated northward to a large metropolitan area has basically concluded that the "core diet" (or most commonly consumed foods) was not substantially different from the diet consumed in the southern rural setting, although the time of food consumption was changed to meet the demands of new occupational schedules followed in the urban environment.[37] The traditional diet of Black Americans is becoming popular with other Americans as well. "Soul food" is now served in restaurants, and cookbooks are spreading the message of how to prepare these foods.

Obesity was found to be very prevalent among Black women in both the Ten State Nutrition Survey and the U.S. Health and Nutrition Examination Survey.[38] Both *Dietary Goals* and *Dietary Guidelines* encourage the maintenance of ideal body weight for height. Counseling with regard to caloric intake and activity will obviously be important when dealing with individuals from this ethnic background.

Examination of 1977 mortality rates indicated that the age-adjusted death rate for heart disease was 24 percent higher for Blacks than for whites, and that the age-adjusted death rate for cerebrovascular disease was 75 percent higher for the Black population.[39] Black Americans would appear to be an appropriate target group for dietary strategies aimed at prevention of heart disease. Data from the Health and Nutrition Examination Survey, however, have not shown a relationship between increased fat intake and increased cardiovascular disease in the Black-American population.[40]

Dietary Guidelines counsels avoidance of "too much fat, saturated fat, and cholesterol" to decrease the risk of heart disease. Fat sources in the Black American diet include butter, margarine, oils, and lard. Pork fat, especially in the form of salt pork or ham hock, is commonly used in cooking vegetables. Cooks should be encouraged to use lean fresh pork cuts for flavoring since this would contribute to a reduction of both fat and salt intake. Milk and meat are other sources of fat. Buttermilk is a beverage commonly enjoyed by Black Americans.[41] The use of buttermilk made from skim milk could help to reduce fat intake. Only 2 percent of the calories in skim buttermilk are contributed by fat, compared to 23 percent of calories in buttermilk made from whole milk.[42] Information with regard to the fat content of meat dishes can also allow a family to use with moderation those items providing the greatest amount of fat. High-fat meat dishes eaten as a part of the Black American diet are pig's feet, spareribs, beef tongue, sweetbreads, ham, and frankfurters.[43] *Dietary Guidelines* suggests choosing poultry and fish as protein sources as a means of lowering fat intake. Chicken is already a well-accepted food in the diets of most Black Americans, as is fish. Butter, cheddar cheese, eggs, kidney, brains, liver, and sweetbreads should be limited to reduce the amount of cholesterol in the Black American diet.[44]

An adequate intake of starch and fiber among members of the Black American population may be achieved using food types already consumed in the diet. Examples of starch and fiber sources in the Black American diet are grits, cornbread, biscuits, fresh corn, bread, and rice.[45] Simple sugar sources include white table sugar, cane syrup, molasses, jams, jellies, cookies, soft drinks and other sweetened beverages, pies, and cakes.[46] The use of these foods should be moderated, not only to limit simple sugar intake, but also to maintain a level of caloric intake conducive to maintenance of ideal body weight.

Americanization of the diet (consumption of less fiber and more saturated fat) has been cited as a potential contributor to the high prevalence of colon cancer within the total population.[47] The government dietary advice addresses this problem with advice to consume more fiber and less saturated fat. It is interesting to note that the incidence of colon cancer is much higher among American Blacks than among Nigerian Blacks.[48] This difference may in part be due to Americanization of the diets of these peoples of African origin and adds credibility to the government dietary advice for the Black American.

Black Americans would be wise to follow the advice to avoid too much sodium since hypertension, which may be exacerbated by large quantities of dietary sodium, is a well-recognized health problem prevalent in this ethnic group.[49] Racial differences in salt preference may exist. An article appearing in *Science* reported a significant difference in preference for salty taste between Black and white youngsters, aged nine to fifteen years. More Black youngsters indicated a taste preference for salt.[50] An awareness should be developed to encourage limited use of salt and salt pork in cooking, as well as limited use of salt at the table.

The moderation of alcohol consumption may also be a legitimate goal for some Black Americans. Reported rates of alcoholism in the U.S. are higher for Black females than for white.[51] Alcoholism among Blacks is an appropriate area for further research. In 1974 Frederick Harper published a 30-year review of 16,000 alcohol-related studies and only 77 (or .4 percent) of these studies reflected findings or discussion of Blacks.[52] Any problems of alcoholism will probably not be addressed most effectively as a dietary change, since alcoholism needs to be seen within a broad social context.

The Chinese-American Diet

Many of the food preparation techniques employed by Chinese cooks already follow government dietary advice. Because most foods are steamed, boiled, or stir-fried in small amounts of fat, problems with over-consumption of fats are unlikely to occur. Continued use of soybean and peanut oils (composed primarily of unsaturated fat) should be encouraged.[53] This avoidance of over-indulgence in visible fat products, coupled with widespread usage of plant foods, seems to indicate that concern about cholesterol, saturated fats, and hence dietarily related heart disease, would be unfounded for the Chinese-American population. Unfortunately, there are no recent epidemiological data to support this premise. Information published in 1973 and 1975 indicates that the atherosclerotic heart disease mortality rate for Chinese Americans is lower than that for the non-Chinese-American population.[54] Available data also indicate that first- and second-generation Chinese Americans have a higher prevalence of coronary heart disease than do their Asian counterparts.[55]

In addition, intakes of foods high in sugar content are unlikely to present a problem with this ethnic group since dessert items are still not widely accepted by the Chinese.[56] Starches, in the form of cereal and highly diverse vegetable sources, have remained significant in the diet. There is evidence to suggest, however, that the consumption of rice by the immigrant population is decreasing, while the consumption of American cereals is increasing.[57]

Suggestions to increase reliance on fruits to raise the carbohydrate content, as well as to increase the variety of the diet, may or may not be well received. According to one source, cultural attitudes in some regions of China dictate that fruit is a delicacy and that certain fruits should be ingested by men only. Unfortunately, no further information was given by this source as to the specific fruits designated for male consumption or the cultural assumptions surrounding these beliefs.[58] A study of Chinese Americans in California has reported that usage of apples and peaches has increased, while traditional fruits like persimmon, lychee, and pineapple are being consumed less frequently.[59]

As lactose intolerance is also a problem exhibited by a large percentage of the Chinese population, low consumption of dairy products has been the rule, with cheese and milk rarely being used beyond weaning. Therefore, the introduction of saturated fat from this dietary source probably is not potentially hazardous, even though increased intake of these products after migration has been noted.[60] One possible detrimental consequence of a low intake of cheese and milk is the development of calcium or vitamin D deficiency. Yogurt consumption has increased as the Chinese have come in contact with the foodways of other American groups, and the calcium obtained from yogurt may be such that an insufficient intake of this nutrient would not occur.[61] Other potential calcium sources in the Chinese-American diet are soybeans and soy sauce. Exposure to sunlight or consumption of vitamin D-fortified food products could allow for sufficiency with regard to vitamin D. If milk is not consumed, these alternative sources of calcium and vitamin D should be considered.

Other modifications in the traditional menu have included a decline in the diversity of animal products consumed, with such seafood items as crab, prawns, sharksfin, squid, and duck most affected. In addition, studies highlighting food habit changes in migrating groups of Chinese people from various regions have indicated that significant Americanization of the native diet has occurred. Dietary questionnaires and intake records reveal that formerly breakfast menus consisted of Chinese cereals, soybean products, and eggs, compared to current consumption practices which incorporate American-style breakfasts to a great degree.[62]

Because lunch is a meal likely to be eaten away from home and is thereby open to outside influence, it is not surprising that studies indicate a greater substitution of Western foods for traditional items in the luncheon. Formerly, lunch intake consisted of meat and vegetable dishes with rice. The evening meal has proved to be the least affected by American influences. Although it is now likely to be less structured than it once was, the dinner menu still consists mainly of rice with accompanying Chinese meat and vegetable dishes (in larger quantities than at lunch).[63]

The admonition found in the Dietary Guidelines to consume alcohol in moderation also seems to be currently practiced by Chinese Americans. Alcoholism is not a major health problem for this ethnic group. Abstention from alcohol consumption, in fact, seems to be a predominant behavioral pattern.[64]

Some Chinese Americans may need to moderate soy sauce intake in order to follow advice about limiting sodium intake. One source has also indicated that diets of poor, elderly Chinese may be high in salt content due to the use of seasonings and food preserved with salt. Nutrition educators should suggest alternative seasonings and food preservation methods. Enrollment of the Chinese-American elderly in feeding programs has also been suggested to aid in improvement of a diet that is high in carbohydrate and salt and low in protein and vitamins.[65]

The Italian-American Diet

A major emphasis of *Dietary Guidelines for Americans* concerns the avoidance of too much fat, particularly saturated fat. It might seem that the traditional Italian diet would be high in fat. High-fat cheeses are well liked and are eaten alone, as well as incorporated in the preparation of many dishes. Also, popular meats like veal, beef, pork, and chicken are often fried, adding even more fat to the diet. Italians also enjoy fatty, highly seasoned meats, such as sausage and salami; organ meats are frequently used. Fish products, canned in oil or fried, are utilized in soups and stews. The cholesterol content of the diet is another area worthy of consideration, as eggs are often incorporated into omelets and main dishes.[66]

Although data on the prevalence of heart disease in the Italian-American population are not available through U.S. government sources at this time, existing information would indicate that perhaps the fat and cholesterol content of the Italian-American diet is not as much of a problem as one might anticipate. A study comparing the age-adjusted frequency of heart disease in New York Jewish and Italian-American populations found that the frequency of heart disease was notably lower in Italian-American males. After eliminating a variety of physiological factors, this study concluded that the difference in disease frequency might be due to the higher unsaturated fat content of the Italian diet.[67] A study from Italy also suggests that Italian-American diets may not be particularly conducive to the development of heart disease. A study of the incidence of heart disease among Olivetti factory workers in southern Italy indicated a lower rate than in the U.S. population. Dr. Mario Mancini, the principal investigator of the study, stated, "My advice to southern Italians is to continue on that diet and not to change it as they become more affluent or emigrate to America. Otherwise, they will increase their risk for coronary heart disease."[68] A study conducted in Philadelphia found that acculturation of Italians in the United States is indeed associated with an increase in mortality from cardiovascular disease.[69]

Italians in their native country rank much lower than both U.S. whites and non-whites in terms of age-adjusted death rates for cancer of the colon.[70] Statistics for age-adjusted death rates are not available for Italian-Americans, but the Italian statistics may indicate that traditional dietary patterns are not particularly associated with the colon cancer mortality rates which prompted the U.S. dietary advice to cut down on fat consumption and increase fiber intake.

One suggestion to bring the Italian-American diet more into line with the U.S. government dietary advice would be to encourage greater usage of low-fat dried beans and peas which are currently being used to flavor dishes like soup, stews, pasta, and salads. Also, continued use of a wide group of vegetables and fruits is warranted. Both raw and prepared green vegetables are popular, and salads are consumed with great frequency. Additionally, raw fruits including grapes, oranges, tangerines, and figs are enjoyed and used as dessert items.[71] The consumption of these fruits along with the vegetables would help to ensure adequate starch intake as suggested by the Dietary Guidelines.

The staple item present in the Italian diet is pasta; ingestion of these types of foodstuffs also has a positive effect on the starch content of the diet. Cornmeal and rice are used often, and bread is usually eaten at every meal. Olive oil, a rich source of unsaturated fat, is already popular, and its use could be encouraged.[72] Fidanza, in an examination of food consumption patterns in Italy, states that ". . . the *Dietary Goals for the United States,* proposed by the Select Committee on Nutrition and Human Needs of the United States Senate, find strong support in the several positive characteristics of the contemporary Italian diet; with minor modifications, it is quite similar in nutrient composition to recommendations."[73] The Italian-American diet could potentially also be easily modified to be in line with government advice.

The suggestion to drink alcohol in moderation, however, may run counter to cultural drinking behaviors. First-generation Italian Americans have been reported to drink frequently but have also been reported to have low rates of alcoholism. Italian-Americans beyond the first generation have been reported to drink even more heavily than their first-generation counterparts.[74] The adoption of government advice with regard to alcohol consumption may not readily occur unless an individual Italian American has a drinking problem and seeks help.

The Politics of Dietary Advice for Ethnic Americans

The preceding discussion demonstrates that the typical diets of various ethnic groups could be modified to incorporate the guidelines for food intake put forward by the U.S. government. Suggestions and information addressing the needs and preferences of our various subcultures are not included in government publications on this topic. Is this an oversight, or is there a conscious or unconscious effort toward lessening ethnic identities by the promotion of one diet for the American people?

Part of the answer may be discerned by viewing government directives on diet and health as the result of a complex interaction of various pressure groups which may have multifarious vested interests in what the government will say about what people eat. For instance, pressure-group influence is evident in the government's message with regard to cholesterol and health. The public has been encouraged to limit egg consumption.[75] Pressure groups that have tended to promote this government directive are 1) members of the scientific community who believe cholesterol to be a health menace and 2) companies that sell vegetable oil products. On the other hand, the government has also responded to pressure from egg farmers and is promoting the sale of eggs. In this instance, the contradictory government response to pressure has left the American consumer in a quandary.[76] How can one take seriously the suggestion to limit egg consumption while the government encourages egg purchases?

Government food programs such as the Food Stamp Program claim to promote social equality by providing the poor with the means to buy a nutritionally adequate diet.[77] The government does not prescribe which foods are to be purchased, and this may be viewed as maintenance of freedom of choice.[78] If the education given to food program participants does not begin with a recognition of ethnic food habits and beliefs, is this not also a denial of the concept of freedom of choice? People should be helped to choose an adequate diet within the context of foods and practices that are familiar to them. If freedom of choice is truly to exist, education must address itself to many choices and messages, not just one. One reason for failure to do this may be lack of representation of ethnic groups in the decision-making process. Predominant pressure groups seem to have promoted education about monolithic food choices either in the interest of economic gain or out of ignorance with regard to the importance of food in the lives of persons of other subcultures.

The Black-American and Spanish-American communities have received some government attention. In fighting for their political rights, these two groups have also achieved some government recognition of their health rights and eating habits. These ethnic communities are increasingly viewed as important pressure groups influencing government decision-making. Recognition of their distinct eating patterns and health status is also occurring.[79] Political pressure has also resulted in a recognition of the role of ethnic differences and culture in nutrition and food aid given to other countries.

This essay shows how eating patterns of four American ethnic groups could be modified to coincide with current government nutrition and health advice. Pressure from ethnic groups within this country may convince the government to investigate whether current eating patterns are consistent with standards of health. It would behoove the government to sponsor more research in the area of ethnic foods and in the area of documenting the dietary changes of various ethnic groups as Americanization occurs. Findings of such studies could provide a stronger base for a health education approach to the food behavior of ethnic groups.

The government's focus on the Hispanic population in a recent Health and Nutrition survey, and the delineation of special health and nutrition problems in the Black population, are worthy of commendation. A few ethnic recipes using *Dietary Guidelines* principles are included in the United States Department of Agriculture American Dietetic Association *Food* series.[80] Efforts such as these need to continue. Ethnic groups, as political pressure groups, can influence governmental decisions about food, nutrition, and health. Governmental dietary advice should reflect the cultural diversity of America and not, by design or default, attempt to turn the melting pot into a one-dish dinner.

NOTES

1. Helen Guthrie, *Introductory Nutrition,* 4th ed. (St. Louis: C.V. Mosby, 1979), 353.

2. Eleanor N. Whitney and Eva May N. Hamilton, *Understanding Nutrition,* 2nd ed. (St. Paul: West Publishing, 1981), A101.

3. Guthrie, *Introductory Nutrition,* 39; Janet Schrieber and John Homiak, "Mexican Americans" in *Ethnicity and Medical Care,* ed. Alan Harwood (Cambridge: Harvard Univ. Press, 1981), 284.

4. Guthrie, 145–47.

5. Food and Agriculture Organization of the United Nations, *Calcium Requirements: Report of an FAO/WHO Expert Group* (Rome, Italy: Food and Agriculture Organization/World Health Organization, 1962), 29–30; Guthrie, 139–40.

6. Whitney and Hamilton, A100–101.

7. U.S. Senate, Select Committee on Nutrition and Human Needs, *Dietary Goals For The United States,* 2nd ed. (Washington, D.C.: U.S. Government Printing Office, 1977).

8. Ibid., 4.

9. Ibid.

10. Michael C. Latham, Lani S. Stephenson, and Alfred E. Harper, "Perspective: U.S. Dietary Goals," *Journal of Nutrition Education* 9 (Oct.–Dec. 1977): 152–57.

11. U.S. Department of Agriculture and U.S. Department of Health, Education and Welfare, *Nutrition and Your Health: Dietary Guidelines for Americans* (Washington, D.C.: U.S. Government Printing Office, 1980).

12. Ibid., 3.

13. U.S. Department of Health, Education and Welfare, Public Health Service, Office of the Assistant Secretary for Health, *Health: United States 1979,* DHEW publication no. (PHS) 80–1232 (Hyattsville, Md.: Dec. 1979); Claudia Moy and Charles Wilder, "Health Characteristics of Minority Groups, United States, 1976," *Advance Data From Vital and Health Statistics,* number 27 (Washington, D.C.: U.S. Department of Health, Education and Welfare, Public Health Service, 14 April 1978).

14. Schrieber and Homiak, 264.

15. "Food Trends In The '80s," *Institutions* 85 (15 Dec. 1979):91.

16. Departamento de Agricultura de los Estados Unidos y Departamento de Salud y Servicias Sociales de los Estados Unidos, *Nutricion y Su Salud: Una Guia Para Su Dieta* (Washington, D.C.: U.S. Government Printing Office, 1980).

17. American Dietetic Association, *Cultural Food Patterns in the U.S.A* (Chicago: American Dietetic Assoc., 1976):14–15; Valley Baptist Medical Center Food Service Department, *Descriptions of Mexican-American Foods* (Modesto, Calif.: NASCO, 1980), 3.

18. John G. Reinhold and J. Salvador Garcia, "Fiber Of The Maize Tortilla," *American Journal of Clinical Nutrition* 32 (June 1979):1326–29.

19. *Cultural Food Patterns,* 15.

20. Robert W. Buechley, et al., "Altitude And Ischemic Heart Disease in Tricultural New Mexico: An Example of Confounding," *American Journal of Epidemiology* 109 (June 1979):663–66.

21. Schrieber and Homiak, 279–80.

22. Phyllis Acosta, "Nutritional Status of Mexican-American Preschool Children In A Border Town," *American Journal of Clinical Nutrition* 29 (Dec. 1974):1359.

23. U.S. Department of Health and Human Services, Public Health Service, National Center for Health Statistics, *News of the Hispanic Health and Nutrition Examination Survey* No. 2, Jan. 1983.

24. Woot-Tsuen W. Leung and Marina Flores, *Tabla De Composicion De Alimentos Para Uso En American Latina* (Bethesda, Md., and Guatemala City: Interdepartmental Committee of Nutrition for National Defense and the Institute of Nutrition for Central America and Panama, 1961), 590, 78–80.

25. *Cultural Food Patterns,* 14.

26. Leung and Flores, 79.

27. *Sunset Mexican Cookbook* (Menlo Park, Calif.: Lane Books, 1969); Mary-Lou Day, Marvin Lentner and Shirley Jaquez, "Food Acceptance Patterns of Spanish-Speaking New Mexicans," *Journal of Nutrition Education* 10 (July–Sept. 1979):122.

28. Leung and Flores, 65–69.

29. U.S. Department of Health, Education and Welfare, Health Services and Mental Health Administration, *Ten State Nutrition Survey, 1968–1970,* DHEW publication no. (HSM) 72–8133, 1970.

30. Sam Schulman and Anne Smith, "The Concept of 'Health' Among Spanish-Speaking Villagers of New Mexico and Colorado," *Journal of Health and Human Behavior* 4 (Winter 1963):230–31.

31. Schrieber and Homiak, 280.

32. Jean A. T. Pennington and Helen Nichols Church, *Bowes and Church's Food Values of Portions Commonly Used,* 13th ed. (Philadelphia: Lippincott, 1980):16, 21.

33. Engmann and Associates, "Alcoholism and Alcohol Abuse Among The Spanish-Speaking Population In California: A Needs And Services Assessment," Report for Office of Alcoholism, State of California (San Francisco, July 1976).

34. William Madsen, "The Alcoholic Agringado," *American Anthropologist* 66 (April 1964):355–61.

35. Robin Sanders, et al., *Soul Food: Origins And Preparations* (New York: Butterick, 1977), 7–8.

36. U.S. Department of Commerce, Bureau of the Census, *Statistical Abstract of the U.S.: 1980* (Washington, D.C.: U.S. Government Printing Office, 1980).

37. Norge Jerome, "Northern Urbanization and Food Consumption Patterns of Southern Negroes," *American Journal of Clinical Nutrition* 22 (Dec. 1969):1667–69.

38. *Ten State Nutrition Survey;* U.S. Department of Health, Education and Welfare, Public Health Services, *Dietary Intake Findings: United States, 1971–1974* (Washington, D.C.: U.S. Government Printing Office, 1977).

39. U.S. Department of Health and Human Services, Public Health Service, Office of Health Research, Statistics, and Technology, National Center for Health Statistics, *Health Data On Blacks in America* (19 Nov. 1979).

40. John A. Morrison, et al., "Black-White Differences In Plasma Lipids And

Lipoproteins In Adults, The Cincinnati Lipid Research Population Study," *Preventive Medicine* 8 (Jan. 1979):34.

41. *Cultural Food Patterns,* 14–15.

42. Pennington and Church, 103.

43. *Cultural Food Patterns,* 13.

44. Ibid., 12–14.

45. Ibid., 13; Judy Perkin, "An Analysis of the Relative Influence of Race, Income, Education, and Food Stamp Program Participation/Nonparticipation on the Food and Nutrient Consumption of a North Florida Urban Clinic Population in Conjunction with a Survey of Nutrition Related Habits and Attitudes" (Dr.P.H. thesis, Univ. Texas School of Public Health, 1981):188–89.

46. *Cultural Food Patterns,* 14.

47. Denis Burkitt, "Epidemiology of Cancer Of The Colon and Rectum," *Cancer* 28 (July 1971):3–13.

48. Ernst Wynder and Bandoru Reddy, "Epidemiology Of Cancer Of The Colon: Incidence, Diet and Metabolic Factors" in *Carcinoma of the Colon and Rectum,* ed. Warren Enker (Chicago: Year Book Medical Publishers, 1978), 312.

49. Friedrich Luft, et al., "Differences in response to sodium administration in normotensive white and black subjects," *The Journal of Laboratory and Clinical Medicine* 90 (Sept. 1977):555.

50. J.A. Desor, Lawrence S. Greene, and Owen Maller, "Preferences for Sweet and Salty in 9 to 15 Year Olds and Adult Humans," *Science* 190 (Nov. 1975):686–87.

51. John Coney, *Exploring the Known and Unknown Factors in the Rates of Alcoholism Among Black and White Females* (San Francisco: R and E Research Associates, 1978).

52. Frederick Harper, "Alcohol and Blacks: State of the Periodical Literature" (Manuscript, National Center for Alcohol Education, Arlington, Va., Oct. 1974).

53. *Cultural Food Patterns,* 5.

54. Katherine Gould-Martin and Nin Chorswang, "Chinese Americans" in *Ethnicity and Medical Care,* ed. Alan Harwood (Cambridge: Harvard Univ. Press, 1981): 140.

55. Haitung King and William Haenszel, "Cancer Mortality Among Foreign And Native-Born Chinese In The United States," *Journal of Chronic Diseases* 26, no. 10 (1973):623–46.

56. Louis Grivetti and Marie Paquette, "Nontraditional Ethnic Food Choices Among First-Generation Chinese in California," *Journal of Nutrition Education* 10 (July–Sept. 1978):111.

57. Grace Yang and Hazel Fox, "Changes in Food Habits of Chinese Living in Lincoln, Nebraska," *Journal of the American Dietetic Association* 75 (Oct. 1979):423.

58. *Cultural Food Patterns,* 4.

59. Grivetti and Paquette, 110.

60. Ibid.

61. Ibid.

62. Yang and Fox, 423.

63. Ibid.

64. Gould-Martin and Nin, 143.

65. Ibid.

66. *Cultural Food Patterns,* 5.

67. Frederick Epstein, E.P. Boas, and Rita Simpson, "The Epidemiology of

Atherosclerosis Among A Random Sample of Clothing Workers Of Different Ethnic Origins In New York City," *Journal of Chronic Diseases* 5 (March 1957):300-28.

68. Mario Mancini, Donald Frederickson, and Sami Hashim, "If You Had 60 Seconds . . ." in *Atherosclerosis,* ed. F.J. Stare (New York: Medcom Learning Systems, 1974):73.

69. John Bruhn, Billy Phillips, and Stewart Wolf, "Social Readjustment And Illness Patterns: Comparisons Between First, Second and Third Generation Italian-Americans Living In The Same Community," *Journal of Psychosomatic Research* 16, no. 6 (1972):387-94.

70. Wynder and Reddy, 310.

71. American Dietetic Association, 6.

72. Ibid.

73. Flaminio Fidanza, "Changing Patterns of Food Consumption In Italy," *Journal of the American Dietetic Association* 77 (Aug. 1980):136-37.

74. Don Cahalan, Ira Clain and Helen Crossley, *American Drinking Practices: A National Study of Drinking Behavior and Attitudes,* Monographs of the Rutgers Center of Alcohol Studies, no. 6 (New Brunswick, N.J.: Rutgers Center of Alcohol Studies, 1969):49.

75. "Toward A National Nutrition Policy," *Science News* III, (8 Jan. 1977):22.

76. Ibid.

77. U.S. Congress, Congressional Budget Office, *The Food Stamp Program: Income or Supplementation?* (Washington, D.C.: Congress of the United States, 1977):5.

78. Don Parlberg, "Food and Economics," *Journal of the American Dietetic Association* 71 (Aug. 1977):108-109.

79. National Center for Health Statistics, Vital and Health Statistics Series II, *Data from the Health Examination Survey and the Health and Nutrition Examination Survey* (Washington, D.C.: U.S. Government Printing Office, 1979); *Ten State Nutrition Survey.*

80. United States Department of Agriculture, Science and Education Administration, Human Nutrition Center, Consumer and Food Economics Institute, *Food* (Washington, D.C.: U.S. Government Printing Office, 1979); United States Department of Agriculture, Science and Education Administration, Human Nutrition Center, Consumer and Food Economics Institute and the American Dietetic Association, *Food 2* and *Food 3* (Chicago: American Dietetic Association, 1982).

Selected Bibliography

American Dietetic Association. *Cultural Food Patterns in the U.S.A.* Chicago: American Dietetic Association, 1976.

Anderson, E., and Anderson, M. "Cantonese Ethnohoptology." *Ethnos* 37 (1972):134–47.

Anderson, Jay Allen. "Scholarship on Contemporary American Folk Foodways." *Ethnologia Europaea* 5 (1971):56–63.

Arnott, Margaret L., ed. *Gastronomy: The Anthropology of Food and Food Habits.* The Hague: Mouton, 1974.

Barth, Frederik. *Ethnic Groups and Boundaries.* Boston: Little, Brown, 1969.

Barthes, Roland. "Toward a Psychosociology of Contemporary Food Consumption." In *European Diet from Pre-Industrial to Modern Times,* edited by Elborg Forster and Robert Forster, 47–59. New York: Harper and Row, 1975.

Benet, S.M., and Joffe, Natalie F. *Some Central European Food Patterns and Their Relationship to Wartime Problems of Food and Nutrition.* Washington, D.C.: National Research Council Committee on Food Habits, 1943.

Bennett, John. "An Interpretation of the Scope and Implications of Social Scientific Research in Human Subsistence." *American Anthropologist* 41 (1946):553–73.

Bennett, John. "Food and Social Status in a Rural Society." *American Sociological Review* 8 (1943):561–69.

Bennett, John; Smith, Harvey; and Passin, Howard. "Food and Culture in Southern Illinois." *American Sociological Review* 7 (1942):645–60.

Bossard, James H.S. "Family Table-Talk: An Area for Sociological Study." *American Sociological Review* 8 (1943):295–301.

Brown, Linda Keller, and Mussell, Kay, eds. "American Food and Foodways." *Journal of American Culture* 2 (1979):392–570.

Bruhn, C.M., and Pangborn, R.M. "Food Habits of Migrant Workers in California." *Journal of the American Dietetic Association* 59 (1971):247–355.

Camp, Charles. "Federal Foodways Research, 1935–1943." *The Digest* 2 (Summer 1979):4–17.

Camp, Charles. "Food in American Culture: A Bibliographic Essay." In "American Food and Foodways," edited by Linda Keller Brown and Kay Mussell. *Journal of American Culture* 2 (1979):559–70.

Camp, Charles. "Foodways." In *Handbook of American Popular Culture,* v. 2. Edited by M. Thomas Inge, 141–61. Westport, Conn.: Greenwood Press, 1980.

Camp, Charles. "Foodways in Everyday Life." *American Quarterly* 34 (1982): 278–89.

Cantoni, M. "Adapting Therapeutic Diets to the Eating Patterns of Italian Americans." *American Journal of Clinical Nutrition* 6 (1958):548–55.

Committee on Food Habits. *The Problem of Changing Food Habits.* Washington, D.C.: National Research Council Bulletin, no. 108, Oct. 1943.

Committee on Food Habits. *Manual for the Study of Food Habits.* Washington, D.C.: National Research Council Bulletin, no. 111, 1945.

Conlin, Joseph. "Did You Get Enough of Pie? A Social History of Food in Logging Camps." *Journal of Forest History* 23 (1979):165–85.

Cummings, Richard Osborn. *The American and His Food: A History of Food Habits in the United States.* Chicago: Univ. of Chicago Press, 1940.

Cussler, Margaret, and de Give, Mary L. *Twixt the Cup and the Lip: Psychological and Sociocultural Factors Affecting Food Habits.* New York: Twayne, 1952.

de Give, Mary L., and Cussler, Margaret T. *Bibliography and Notes on German Food Patterns.* Washington, D.C.: National Research Council Committee on Food Habits, 1944.

de Give, Mary L., and Cussler, Margaret. "Interrelations Between the Cultural Pattern and Nutrition." Washington, D.C.: United States Department of Agriculture, Extension Service Circular, no. 266, Aug. 1941.

The Digest: A Newsletter for the Interdisciplinary Study of Food. Philadelphia: American Folklore Society, Foodways Section, 1977– . (c/o Dept. of Folklore and Folklife, 415 Logan Hall/CN, Univ. of Pennsylvania, Philadelphia, PA 19104).

Douglas, Mary. "Deciphering a Meal." In *Myth, Symbol, and Culture,* edited by Clifford Geertz. New York: Norton, 1971.

Douglas, Mary. *Implicit Meanings.* London: Routledge, Kegan Paul, 1975.

Douglas, Mary. *Purity and Danger: An Analysis of the Concepts of Pollution and Taboo.* London: Routledge, Kegan Paul, 1966.

Douglas, Mary, and Nicod, Michael. "Taking the Biscuit: The Structure of British Meals." *New Society* 39 (1974):744–47.

Fleigel, Frederick C. *Food Habits and National Background.* University Park: Pennsylvania State Univ. Agricultural Experimental Station Bulletin, no. 684, Oct. 1961.

Fratto, Toni F. "Cooking in Red and White." *Pennsylvania Folklife* 19 (1970): 2–15.

Garreau, Joel. *The Nine Nations of North America.* Boston: Houghton Mifflin, 1981.

Gillespie, Angus K. "Toward a Method for the Study of Food in American Culture." In "American Food and Foodways," edited by Linda Keller Brown and Kay Mussell. *Journal of American Culture* 2 (1979):393–406.

Gizelis, Gregory. "Foodways Acculturation in the Greek Community of Philadelphia." *Pennsylvania Folklife* 19 (1970–71):9–15.

Gizzardini, G., and Joffe, Natalie F. *Italian Food Patterns and Their Relation-*

ship to Wartime Problems of Food and Nutrition. Washington, D.C.: National Research Council Committee on Food Habits, Aug. 1942.

Gonzalez, Alicia. "'Guess How Doughnuts Are Made': Verbal and Non-Verbal Aspects of the *Panadero* and His Stereotype." In *"And Other Neighborly Games": Social Process and Cultural Image in Texas Folklore,* edited by Richard Bauman and Roger D. Abrahams. Austin: Univ. of Texas Press, 1981.

Gottlieb, David. *A Bibliography and Bibliographic Review of Food and Food Habits Research.* Washington, D.C.: Quartermaster Food and Container Institute for the Armed Forces, 1958.

Guthe, Carl E. "History of the Committee on Food Habits." In *The Problem of Changing Food Habits.* Washington, D.C.: National Research Council Bulletin, no. 108, Oct. 1943.

Halverson, John. "Animal Categories and Terms of Abuse." *Man* 11 (1977): 278–300.

Hilliard, Sam. "Hog-Meat and Cornpone: Food Habits in the Ante-Bellum South." *Proceedings of the American Philosophical Society* 113 (1969):1–13.

Hilliard, Sam. *Hog-Meat and Hoe Cake: Food Supply in the Old South.* Carbondale: Southern Illinois Univ. Press, 1972.

Hilliard, Sam. "Pork in the Ante-Bellum South: The Geography of Self-Sufficiency." *Annals of the Association of American Geographers* 59 (1969): 461–80.

Jerome, Norge. "Diet and Acculturation: The Case of Black-American In-Migrants." In *Nutritional Anthropology,* edited by Norge Jerome, Randi Kandel, and Gretel Pelto. New York: Redgrave, 1979.

Jerome, Norge. "Northern Urbanization and Food Consumption Patterns of Southern Negroes." *American Journal of Clinical Nutrition* 22 (1969): 1667–69.

Jerome, Norge. "On Determining Food Patterns of Urban Dwellers in Contemporary United States Society." In *Gastronomy: The Anthropology of Food and Food Habits,* edited by Margaret Arnott. The Hague: Mouton, 1974.

Joffe, Natalie F. "Food Habits of Selected Subcultures in the United States." In *The Problem of Changing Food Habits.* Washington, D.C.: National Research Council Bulletin, no. 108, Oct. 1943.

Joffe, Natalie F., and Walker, T.T. *Some Food Patterns of Negroes in the United States of America and Their Relationship to Wartime Problems of Food and Nutrition.* Washington, D.C.: National Research Council Committee on Food Habits, 1944.

Jones, Michael Owen; Giuliano, Bruce; and Krell, Roberta. "Foodways and Eating Habits: Directions for Research." *Western Folklore* 40 (1981).

Jones, Suzi. "Regionalization: A Rhetorical Strategy." *Journal of the Folklore Institute* 13 (1976):105–18.

Joyner, Charles. "Soul Food and the Sambo Stereotype: Foodlore from the Slave Narrative Collection." *Keystone Folklore Quarterly* 16 (1971):171–77.

Kraut, Alan M. "Ethnic Foodways: The Significance of Food in the Designation of Cultural Boundaries Between Immigrant Groups in the U.S.,

1840–1921." In "American Food and Foodways," edited by Linda Keller Brown and Kay Mussell. *Journal of American Culture* 2 (1979):409–20.

Leach, E.R. "Animal Categories and Verbal Abuse." In *New Directions in the Study of Language,* edited by E.H. Lenneberg. Cambridge, Mass.: MIT Press, 1964.

Lee, Dorothy. "Cultural Factors in Dietary Choice." *American Journal of Clinical Nutrition* 5 (1957):55–61.

Levi-Strauss, Claude. "The Culinary Triangle." *Partisan Review* 33 (1966): 586–95.

Levi-Strauss, Claude. *The Origin of Table Manners.* New York: Harper and Row, 1968.

Levi-Strauss, Claude. *The Savage Mind.* Chicago: Univ. of Chicago Press, 1966.

Lewin, Kurt. "Forces Behind Food Habits and Methods of Change." In *The Problem of Changing Food Habits.* Washington, D.C.: National Research Council Bulletin, no. 108, Oct. 1943.

Lloyd, Timothy Charles. "The Cincinnati Chili Culinary Complex." *Western Folklore* 40 (1981):28–40.

Marshall, Howard Wight. "Meat Preservation on the Farm in Missouri's 'Little Dixie.'" *Journal of American Folklore* 92 (1979):400–17.

McKenzie, J.C. "Social and Economic Implications of Minority Food Habits." *Proceedings of the Nutrition Society* 26 (1967):197–205.

Mead, Margaret. "The Changing Significance of Food." *American Science* 58 (1970):176–81.

Mead, Margaret. *Food Habits Research: Problems of the 1960s.* Washington, D.C.: National Research Council Publication, no. 1225, 1964.

Mead, Margaret. "The Problem of Changing Food Habits." In *The Problem of Changing Food Habits.* Washington, D.C.: National Research Council Bulletin, no. 108, Oct. 1943.

Moore, Harriet Bruce. "The Meaning of Food." *American Journal of Clinical Nutrition* 5 (1957):8–11.

Pangborn, Rose Marie, and Bruhn, C.M. "Concepts of Food Habits of Other Ethnic Groups." *Journal of Nutrition Education* 2 (1971):106–110.

Pangborn, Rose Marie, and Bruhn, Christine M. "Social Process and Dietary Change." In *The Problem of Changing Food Habits.* Washington, D.C.: National Research Council Bulletin, no. 108, Oct. 1943.

Passin, Herbert, and Bennett, John W. "Social Process and Dietary Change." In *The Problem of Changing Food Habits.* Washington, D.C.: National Research Council Bulletin, no. 108, Oct. 1943.

Pirkova-Jakobson, Svatava, and Joffe, Natalie F. *Some Central European Food Patterns and Their Relationship to Wartime Problems of Food and Nutrition.* Washington, D.C.: National Research Council Committee on Food Habits, 1943.

Pyke, Magnus. *Man and Food.* New York: McGraw-Hill, 1970.

Regelson, Stanley. "The Bagel, Symbol and Ritual at the Breakfast Table."

In *The American Dimension: Cultural Myths and Social Realities,* edited by W. Arens and Susan P. Montague. Port Washington: Alfred Publishing, 1976.

Root, Waverly, and de Rochemont, Richard. *Eating in America: A History.* New York: Morrow, 1976.

Sackett, Marjorie. "Folk Recipes as a Measure of Intercultural Penetration." *Journal of American Folklore* 85 (1972):77–81.

Simoons, Frederick J. *Eat Not This Flesh: Food Avoidance in the Old World.* Madison: Univ. of Wisconsin Press, 1963.

Society for Nutrition Education. *Food Habits: A Selected and Annotated Bibliography.* Washington, D.C.: Society for Nutrition Education, 1973.

Soler, Jean. "The Dietary Prohibitons of the Hebrews." *New York Review of Books,* 14 June 1979.

Sorre, Max. "The Geography of Diet." In *Readings in Cultural Geography,* edited by Phillip I. Wagner and Marvin W. Mikesell, 445–56. Chicago: Univ. of Chicago Press, 1962.

Soulsby, T. "Russian-American Food Patterns." *Journal of Nutrition Education* 4 (1972):170–72.

Theophano, Janet. "Feast, Fast, and Time." *Pennsylvania Folklife* (Spring 1978):25–32.

Toelken, Barre. *The Dynamics of Folklore.* Boston: Houghton Mifflin, 1979.

Tuan, Yi-Fu. *Topophilia: A Study of Environmental Perception, Attitudes, and Values.* Englewood Cliffs, N.J.: Prentice-Hall, 1974.

Tull, Marc. "Kosher Brownies for Passover." *New York Folklore* 4 (1978):81–88.

Weaver, William Woys. "Food Acculturation and the First Pennsylvania-German Cookbook." In "American Food and Foodways," edited by Linda Keller Brown and Kay Mussell. *Journal of American Culture* 2 (1979): 421–32.

Welsch, Roger. "'Sorry Chuck'—Pioneer Foodways." *Nebraska History* 53 (1972):99–113.

Welsch, Roger. "'We Are What We Eat': Omaha Food as Symbol." *Keystone Folklore Quarterly* 16 (1971):165–70.

Wilson, Christine S. "Food Habits: A Selected Annotated Bibliography." *Journal of Nutrition Education* 5 (1973):39–72.

Yoder, Don. "Folk Cookery." In *Folklore and Folklife,* edited by Richard M. Dorson, 325–50. Chicago: Univ. of Chicago Press, 1972.

Yoder, Don. "Pennsylvanians Call It Mush." *Pennsylvania Folklife* 13 (1962): 27–49.

Yoder, Don. "Sauerkraut in the Pennsylvania Folk Culture." *Pennsylvania Folklife* 12 (Summer 1961):56–59.

Yoder, Don. "Schnitz in the Pennsylvania Folk Culture." *Pennsylvania Folklife* 12 (Fall 1961):56–59.

Contributors

ROGER ABRAHAMS is Kenan Professor of Humanities and Anthropology at Scripps and Pitzer Colleges. Previously, he was in the departments of English and anthropology of the University of Texas for nineteen years, the last five as chairman of English. He has published on Afro-American folklore and culture, Anglo-American song, children's lore, and is presently at work on a study of key words in American cultural practice.

LINDA KELLER BROWN is Council Associate, American Council on Education in Washington, D.C. She was formerly at the Center for Social Sciences, Columbia University, where she directed the Cross-National Project on Women as Corporate Managers. She has served as Resident Scholar for the International Communication Agency. She holds a Ph.D. from the Department of American Civilization at the University of Pennsylvania and has taught at Rutgers University and the City University of New York. With Kay Mussell, she co-edited a special section on American food and food-ways for the *Journal of American Culture.*

KAREN CURTIS has an M.A. in urban studies and is completing her doctorate in anthropology at Temple University. Her interest in Italian Americans developed after a period of study in Italy. She has done extensive fieldwork in one Italian-American community and has held research positions emphasizing ethnography in educational and urban policy agencies. Her papers and publications include works on ethnicity and food as well as the development of ethnic communities.

ANGUS K. GILLESPIE received his Ph.D. in American civilization from the University of Pennsylvania. He is currently teaching American studies and folklore at Rugters—The State University of New Jersey. He has done fieldwork in the Pine Barrens of New Jersey; he is also the founder and director of the New Jersey Folk Festival. In 1980, he was given a recognition award by the New Jersey Historical Commission for his "leadership in developing public interest in the collection, preservation, and appreciation of New Jersey folklore, as founder and editor of *New Jersey Folklore: A Statewide Journal.*"

JUDITH GOODE received her Ph.D. from Cornell University. She is director of urban studies and an associate professor of anthropology at Temple

University. She has done fieldwork in urban Latin America. After several studies and two books on urban anthropology, her interest in ethnicity led her to her current research and publication in the anthropology of food. She is active in the developing fields of nutritional anthropology and urban anthropology.

C. PAIGE GUTIERREZ, a Danforth Fellow, received an M.A. in folklore and a Ph.D. in cultural anthropology from the University of North Carolina at Chapel Hill. Her dissertation research on south Louisiana foodways was carried out in St. Martin Parish, Louisiana. Her research interests include an interdisciplinary approach to the study of the Gulf Coast as a culture region. She has been appointed as scholar-in-residence for Biloxi, Mississippi, by the Mississippi Committee for the Humanities.

SANDRA K. JOOS received an M.A. in anthropology from the University of Florida and a Master of Public Health from the University of Texas School of Public Health at Houston. She is now a Ph.D. candidate in Community Health Sciences. Her particular interests lie in the social and behavioral aspects of health and disease.

SUSAN KALČIK did graduate work in folklore at the University of Texas. She has worked for the Smithsonian Institution since 1975. Her research and publications are in the areas of American ethnicity, women's culture, and folkloristics.

STEPHANIE F. McCANN received her M.S. in nutrition from the University of Florida. She is currently a dietitian with the U.S. Air Force Program in San Antonio, Texas.

WILLARD B. MOORE developed an interest in foodways during childhood visits to his neighbors' kitchens in an ethnic neighborhood in Poughkeepsie, New York. Since then, he has earned a Ph.D. in folklore at Indiana University and enjoyed ethnic and regional culinary delights during research in southern Indiana, eastern Kentucky, Georgia, Minnesota, and California. His publications include *Molokan Oral Traditions* (1973) and "Folklife Museums: Resource Sites for Teaching," *Indiana English Journal* (1978). Moore currently lives in Minneapolis.

KAY MUSSELL holds a Ph.D. from the Program in American Civilization at the University of Iowa. She is an associate professor of literature and American studies at The American University in Washington, D.C., where she directs the American Studies Program. Her book, *Women's Gothic and Romantic Fiction: A Reference Guide,* was published by Greenwood Press (1981). With Linda Keller Brown, she co-edited a special section on American food and foodways in the *Journal of American Culture.*

JUDY PERKIN received her B.A. degree in anthropology and M.A. in nutrition from the University of Texas at Austin. She completed her Dr.P.H. in community health at the University of Texas School of Public Health. She is currently teaching in the Allied Health Services Program at the University of North Florida.

LESLIE PROSTERMAN earned her M.A. and Ph.D. in folklore and folklife from the University of Pennsylvania. Her dissertation was on the aesthetic systems in the judging and exhibition sections of county fairs in Illinois and Wisconsin. With Janet Theophano, she co-founded and edited *The Digest: A Newsletter for the Interdisciplinary Study of Food.* She teaches in the Department of Family and Community Development at the University of Maryland, College Park.

RICHARD RASPA received his Ph.D. in English from Notre Dame and has taught at the University of Utah and Wayne State University, where he is currently an associate professor. His publications include *Keys to American English, Discovery in Literature,* articles on folklore and drama, and a co-authored study of an Italian-American folk artist.

ELIOT A. SINGER is a Ph.D. candidate in folklore at the University of Pennsylvania and has taught folklore and anthropology at The Pennsylvania State University, Fayette. He has written on the ritual, drama, preaching, and medicine of the "Hare Krishna People" with whom he has done fieldwork. He is currently doing research into the semiotics of food in narrative discourse.

AMY STROMSTEN is an assistant professor of art at Rutgers University in New Brunswick, New Jersey. She has photographed American subcultures since 1970, including a recent publication, *Homes on Wheels,* which documents van, recreational vehicle, and mobile home inhabitants. Her photographs are represented by Neikrug Gallery in New York City, and she has had numerous exhibitions in museums and universities.

JANET THEOPHANO is completing her doctorate in folklore at the University of Pennsylvania. She has had fieldwork experience among ethnic groups, particularly Italian Americans, in Philadelphia, leading to a variety of papers and publications. She has been central in the development of *The Digest,* an interdisciplinary newsletter on food studies. Her interests include ethnicity, foodways, and the field of ethnography and education.

BRETT WILLIAMS received her Ph.D. in anthropology from the University of Illinois. She has done research among Chicanos in Illinois and Texas as well as Black and white migrants from the South to cities in the North. She is an associate professor of anthropology and American studies at The American University in Washington, D.C. Her study of the American hero John Henry has been published by Greenwood Press.

Index

Acadian, *see* Cajun
Acculturation, 38–39; and American food system, 68; and foodways, 41, 55; generational differences in, 40–41, 56–57, 69; of Chinese Americans, 251; of ethnic groups, 61; of Vietnamese Americans, 59
Advertising of food, 25
Affinity groups, as units of measure, 69, 84
African foodways, 33–34
Allport, Gordon, 47
American Dietetic Association, 255
Americanization of ethnic foods, 60
Anderson, E., 72
Anderson, M., 72
Animals, and stereotypes, 33; as food, 28–29; food categories of, 31–32, 34
Arnott, Margaret, 38–39

Barth, Frederik, 46, 172; and ethnic group definition, 44–45
Barthes, Roland, 12, 193
Basic Four Food Groups: and diet counseling, 234–35; and government policy, 238–39
Bennett, John, 38, 40–41, 68, 71
Berger, Arthur, 53
Black Americans, 41, 239, 243, 254–55; and food stereotypes, 54; and meal formats, 75; diet of, 244, 247–49; stereotypes of, 29, 51–52
Boundaries, ethnic: among Cajuns, 171, 175; among Italian Americans (Utah), 188, 191, 193; and religion (Molokan), 92; food-sharing in maintenance of, 177; markers of, 185; foodways as communication across group, 50–51, 54; foodways in definition of, 49; of ethnic groups, Russian Molokan, 104, Tejano, 122;

Boundaries, ethnic (*cont.*)
of groups, 5, 27, 45–46; and food-sharing, 47; in foodways research, 66
Boundaries, regional: among Cajuns, 171; in Pine Barrens, 149–150, 152, 154
Braudel, Fernand, 26–27
Bruhn, C.M., 43, 52
Byrne, Brendan, 162, 164

Cajun, definition of, 170
Cajuns, 13; ethnic symbols of, 9; in Louisiana, 169–80
Capitalism and Material Life: 1400–1800 (Braudel), 26
Categories: animal, 21, 31–34; food, in ISKCON, 198–99, 209
Caterer, Kosher, 131; function of, 128–29, 132, 134, 139–40
Chang, K.C., 72
Change: in ethnic foodways, 7, 40, 68, 70, 73, 86, 254; in ethnic groups, 11; in food choice, among Jewish Americans, 133–34, 138, 140; resistance to, of ethnic groups, 41; role of status in, 40
Chase, Benjamin, 38
Chesapeake Bay, 9
Chicano, *see* Mexican Americans
Chinese Americans, 239, 243; and the wok, 9; diet of, 244, 249–51; restaurants, 4
Cohen, Abner, 45–46
Committee on Food Habits, 11, 52
Common Council for American Unity, 42–43, 51
Conversion, and enculturation, 196, 212; in ISKCON, 211–12
Cookbooks: ethnic, 4; in ISKCON, 197; of Pine Barrens, 147, 164

Saussure, Ferdinand de, 12
Schuchat, Molly, 54, 56
Select Committee on Nutrition and Human Needs (U.S. Senate), 239–41, 253
Seminoles, in Florida, 14, 218–24, 226, 228, 230–36
Semiotics, 46
Simoons, Frederick, 50
Sinton, John W., 148
Smithsonian Institution, 38
Status: communities and, 69; foodways and changes in, 50
Stereotypes, 35; and language, 22; animal, 32–33; ethnic, 37, 52; ethnic and regional, 13; of nationality groups, 54; of Tejano women, 114, 118
Stern, Gerald, 147
Structural linguistics, 12
Structuralism and foodways, 12–13
Swedish Americans, 56
Symbol: and enculturation, 206; and ethnic identity, 45; and exclusion from groups, 49; and food stereotypes, 21; and foodways, 44; and group identity, 47, 53, 55; food as, 30, 100, among Cajuns, 179; among Italian Americans (Utah), 193; in ISKCON, 211; regional, 169–70, 173–74; food as cultural, 195–96; food as ideological, 93; foodways and ritual, among Tejanos, 120; foodways as, 55, among Russian Molokans, 110; manipulation of, 45–46; tamale as, 113, 119
Symbolic manipulation of foodways, 13

Taboo: among Jewish Americans, 130, 138; among Russian Molokans, 94–95, 105; among Seminoles, 231–32; foods and, 30, 32; foodways and, 51; in ISKCON, 197–98, 209–10; Italian-American (Utah) foods, 189
Tejanos, in Illinois, 6, 113–24; kinship among, 116; *see also* Mexican Americans

Ten State Nutrition Survey, 246, 248
Theophano, Janet, 59
Time-Life *Foods of the World,* 4
Tuan, Yi-Fu, 146, 166
Tull, Marc, 60

U.S. Department of Agriculture, 241, 255
U.S. Department of Health Education and Welfare, 241
U.S. Health and Nutrition Examination Survey, 248, 254
Units of measure, 86; affinity groups as, 69, 84; ethnic groups as, 67–68; households as, 69–70; in foodways research, 66; meal cycle as, 72, 84–85; meal format as, 72; recipes as, 72; region as, 68

Variation: intra-group, 10–11, 243, among Jewish Americans, 132; among Russian Molokans, 92, 109; regional, 122
Vietnamese: acculturation of, 38; foodways and death, 48
Vietnamese Americans: and ethnic identity, 58; in Georgia, 59; stereotypes of, 37

Wallace, Anthony F.C., 12, 196
Weinstock, S.A., 39
Welsch, Roger, 150
Williams, Phyllis, 42, 49
Women: among Cajuns, 176; among Russian Molokans, 96–98; among Seminoles, 220–21, 235; among Tejanos, 113–15, 117–23; costume of, among Russian Molokans, 103–105; influence in food choice, 68; resistance to change by, 40; transmission of foodways by, 80

Yoder, Don, 5, 39

Zelinsky, Wilbur, 170

Ethnic and Regional Foodways in the United States has been composed into type in Baskerville on a Compugraphic digital phototypesetter by Metricomp, Inc.

The book was designed by Gary Gore, printed offset by Thomson-Shore, Inc., and bound by John H. Dekker & Sons. The paper on which the book is printed has acid-free characteristics for a projected shelf life of at least three hundred years.

THE UNIVERSITY OF TENNESSEE PRESS : KNOXVILLE